I Had A Wheelbarrow

A Fan's Story of a Notts County Adventure

by Luke Williamson

www.ihadawheelbarrow.co.uk

PURE PHASE PUBLISHING

First Published by Pure Phase Publishing
88 Manor Road, Derby, DE72 3LN
www.purephase-publishing.co.uk

Part of The People's History of Football series
www.peopleshistoryoffootball.com

ISBN 978-0-9561144-4-0

About the Author

Luke Williamson was born in 1982 and first visited Notts County Football Club in 1987. By 1988 he and his dad were regulars and for the 1989/90 campaign they became season ticket holders. Luke was born in the Meadows, just a few hundred yards from Meadow Lane, and spent his youth living both there and on the other side of the river in West Bridgford. He started writing at the age of eighteen doing small pieces on football and sixties pop culture. *I Had A Wheelbarrow* is his debut book after he spent the early part of his twenties fronting a sixties beat-combo band in Leicestershire called The Carnabys. He currently lives and works in Loughborough (17.1miles from Meadow Lane) and is player-manager for a Sunday League team in Leicestershire.

ltwilliamson@hotmail.co.uk
www.luke-williamson.co.uk

Acknowledgments

First of all, thanks to those who helped me get as far as the finished article you have before you. My proof readers, Matt (you don't have to always say *"It's up to you"* when making comments), Paul (please try to save any notes you make – simply saying *"Yeah, it's good"* makes it hard to develop), Vanessa (try and learn some football terminologies such as *"glancing header"* amongst others) and my Dad (for taking the book away on holiday with a highlighter and coming back with a 'never been used' highlighter three weeks later).

Thanks to those who were company at Notts games along the rollercoaster ride that was 2009/10. Seany Ward for being addicted for the first half of the season and going on the road with me, Mark Beeby for the regular meet-ups, drinks in The Navi, games in the lower part of The Kop and for introducing me to the legendary Colin Slater, and Danny Willoughby whom I joined for a fair few games during the final few months of the season and have since got myself a season ticket with in The Derek Pavis Stand.

I'd like to thank some more high profile people also. Ray Trew for inviting me to the board room to discuss the book, Daphne and John Mounteney for making me feel so at ease in the board room when I felt a little out-of-my-depth, Jim Rodwell for the odd funny story and for allowing me the chance to tell him how The Wheelbarrow song was born, John Thompson and Steve Cotterill for taking the time to speak to me on a busy press day prior to Rotherham at home and to Tommy Johnson for being my hero.

Thanks also to press-officer Ralph Shepherd who gave me a fascinating insight behind the scenes, to the various fans, including Dave Peck who opened my eyes to pre-Munto happenings and of course to Colin Slater for what I feel was one of the most exclusive interviews anyone has ever had the pleasure to have carried out with the great man over dinner and a drink.

Thanks to Michael Lutwyche who gave me the initial confidence to try and write and release this book and Stewart Smith, Derby fan, author and publisher for helping me across the finishing line in recent months.

To finish, extended thanks to those that have been close to me and have supported me in this 'idea' since I initially decided I was going to write a book. To my Mum who listened to things she maybe did not understand, my little sister for bringing me cups of tea and biscuits during the painful editing days and my Dad for always being a voice on my shoulder who ensured I asked the questions of myself that needed asking during the development.

My Dad receives a further additional mention because ultimately, it is because of him that I have this addiction/obsession with Notts County and the beautiful game. All young lads (or girls) should be introduced to the game by their father. I hope this tradition does not fade in an ever-changing footballing world.

Without the support of the aforementioned people, this book would not have been possible and I'd have undoubtedly needed motivation from other sources to push me across the finishing line.

Thanks also to Jade for being a massive part of my life and a huge inspiration at the start of my writing. I hope you can read this one day and enjoy it for what it is. And finally to anyone else who played a big part in this time in my life. Thanks to Emma for nearly being everything I'd imagined and to Sarah for keeping my feet on the and I had to acknowledge to make my life worth living. There are more of you too but the production of this book is based on the number of pages and frankly, I am pushing the limits as it is.

In memory of:
Mama & Rara – grandparents
Who I miss visiting before each game

and
Andrew Day – fan
Keith Alexander – manager
Richard Butcher – player
All of who lost their lives at tragically young ages during the writing of the book

"I had a wheelbarrow, and the wheel fell off,
I had a wheelbarrow, and the wheel fell off,
I had a wheelbarrow, and the wheel fell off,
I had a wheelbarrow, and the wheel fell off,
County, County, County, County..."

To the tune of 'On Top Of Old Smokey'
Originally sung by Notts fans 17.04.1990
Shrewsbury Town v Notts County

There are a few views of where the above song originated amongst Notts fans. This is the version I choose to believe:

On 17th April 1990, as Notts trailed 2-0 away at Shrewsbury, the home fans started singing 'On Top of Old Smokey' in their strong, West Country accents. Mocking these fans for the way they spoke (or sang) the Notts following began to mimic the song singing the above words.

Despite only being ten minutes remaining in the game, Notts fought back to draw 2-2 with goals from Tommy Johnson and Kevin Bartlett. It was an important evening for Notts County and following the draw, they would not lose again during the 1989/90 season which ended in a trip to Wembley Stadium for the first time in the clubs history.

The song played a part in Notts' promotion push and when Craig Short and his team mates came off the returning coach in Nottingham with victory achieved, he was seen with a plastic wheelbarrow given to him by a fan on that famous day.

Supporting Notts was magical back then. Nearly twenty years later, the magic appears to be back.

Falling In & Out Of Love

Ok, I admit, I am addicted to football. Although over the past few years I overcame my addiction to a certain extent, I am still very much addicted. In recent seasons I have attended fewer games, pretended that I was not thinking of the scores at 4.45pm on a Saturday afternoon when out for the day and I've told myself I did not need to buy the latest shirts.

Unfortunately, for many, it is what is known as growing up. Or settling down. Or whatever terminology you give it in your neck of the woods. Either way, my addiction had changed of late. I was consigned more to watching from the comfort of my sofa (I utter the words armchair supporter) rather than travelling the country but, never-the-less, it was still football. My partner has not accepted my footballing ways since we got together. Far from it. However, we appear to have met on some sort of middle ground in recent seasons which means I don't spend the whole weekend dedicating myself to the game I love and I spread myself and my attention into other areas of everyday life.

However, as the 2009/2010 football season begins, I cannot help but feel like all her hard work is going to be tested to the limits. After all, it is in my old home town that former England, Lazio and Benfica Manager (and supposed ladies man) Sven-Goran Eriksson has arrived on the scene as a Director of Football. And it is for the very club I grew up following, Notts County. The Oldest Football League Club in the world no less.

Bizarrely, his arrival at my club would go on to eclipse most of the stories during the summer months from the rest of the footballing world. For once, it was not the almighty, super-successful, global institutions dictating our back pages. This time it was one of the smaller fish. So what if Real Madrid were embarking on the biggest ever spending spree the globe had ever witnessed bringing in Kaka and Cristiano Ronaldo to name but two. The Notts saga was something much bigger. Outrageous even. As I realised the full implications of the news, I started to think back to better days. For I am one of those who had, for reasons I stand by 100%, began to lose faith in the beautiful game even if I had not detached myself entirely.

I lost faith in football, and therefore to some extent Notts County and what the club stood for some time ago. Teetering on the edge of mere existence for prolonged periods, Notts County have not treated their loyal fans to much in recent years. The issue, as many Notts fan would confirm, is the fact that by recent I mean the better part of a decade or two. In fact, ever since relegation from the elite division in England, Notts County have gradually faded, whimpered and struggled to the point that simply still being in existence is perhaps an achievement. Sometimes, phases of hope and success can keep fans going through the more turbulent and harsh campaigns. For Notts though, it is some years since the likes of Don Mason, John Chiedozie and Pedro Richards strutted their stuff for Notts.

If you were to look at the history of English football, I doubt you could find a season that was worse than 1991/92 for dropping out of the top flight. Along with my beloved Magpies two other clubs, namely Luton Town and West Ham United, were relegated in the May of '92 after a long, gruelling season that offered the dangling carrot of Sky Sports television money and worldwide media exposure for the following campaign.

When Sky Sports signed up to broadcast live football featuring England's finest, no one could have predicted the impact it would have on the game as a whole. The timely arrival of Satellite television coincided with The Taylor Report in 1989 (published in 1990) which sought to recommend improvements that clubs could, or rather should, make to their stadia and the match day experience following the tragic events of Hillsborough on 15th April 1989, when 96 Liverpool fans lost their lives. But as the report outlined the need to make football grounds a safer place to watch the game, Sky offered an alternative for those who still did not wish to risk it amongst the hooligans that had reportedly blighted our game since the seventies.

If it was a change that the people had wanted, it was indeed what they were set to get. There would be an impact of an unprecedented nature with everything from ticket prices, merchandising, player's contracts and transfer fees spiralling out of control. But as the rich became richer, the poor became broke and for every club that benefited from the BSkyB boom, there were four or five that didn't and Notts County certainly were one of them.

Ok, so West Ham were also relegated in 1991/92 but have since had success and on closer inspection, a whole host of clubs survived to see the new era begin but have since fell from great heights. Champions of that campaign were Leeds United whilst just two places below them finished Sheffield Wednesday. Meanwhile, in eighth, ninth and tenth respectively were Notts' rivals from over the river along with Sheffield

United and Crystal Palace. Further down in the table, Queens Park Rangers, Wimbledon, Southampton, Oldham, Norwich City and Coventry City all contributed to the top flight season, later proving that the Sky Sports era was not a sure fire route to success whatsoever.

Just by looking at this list of clubs that went on to fall out of the elite division in England, you can see that there were no guarantees when the Sky Sports money men rolled into town. Wimbledon ceased to exist, later becoming MK Dons, relocating, rebranding and losing all identity with the club it once was whilst the likes of Leeds United and Southampton struggled so badly on and off the field that administration, and further more point deductions, meant they were consigned to more years in the lower realms than their fans would care to remember. Elsewhere, Sheffield Wednesday, Oldham, Norwich and the red lot from over the river all went on to not only become relegated from the top flight, but fall further down the league structure without the administration suffered by Leeds and the Saints. Meanwhile QPR, Palace, Sheffield United and Coventry have had little more than average seasons since their relegation with Sheffield United under the guidance of Neil Warnock being one of the rarities (a top flight return).

So being one of the elite group on the dawn of the new era may not have brought Notts any guarantees had they survived that season. But it might, just might, have helped.

As Notts County tumbled, this party began on our television screens that alleviated the English game into the most watched leagues in the world. Overtaking Serie A in Italy, both England and Spain became the new dominant league to watch and with BSkyB, England seemingly took number one spot in the years that followed.

Has the revolution been good for football? On face value, of course it has. Football was in something of a sad state prior to the radical changes that took place thanks to Sky owner Rupert Murdoch and his media empire. Rather like the state of the country at the time, the game was in need of change and repair. England had spent the back end of the 1980's without European football following the Heysel Disaster in '85 which saw a stand collapse at a game involving Juventus and Liverpool. Weeks prior to this, a decaying stand at Bradford's Valley Parade caught fire killing over 50 fans whilst the hooligan culture had seemingly swept up and down the country and had found itself to be as common place in the stands as it is now for clubs to be owned by foreigners.

With Sky, new impetus and idea's were on offer and without them, perhaps the English game would not be seeing its own clubs reach European Cup Semi's and Finals with the frequency that they are now doing. As with any change, there has to be some luck along the way and in Bobby Robson's England side, the national game found itself on the perfect stage. The England side of Italia '90 arguably over-achieved but in doing so, there was new found pride in the nation and her players. Although defeated in the Semi-Final, the likes of Gary Lineker and Paul Gascoigne came back as heroes as opposed to the damning verdicts that would ultimately follow the national teams in the years that followed.

The new era became something of a promised land and everyone began to want in on the whole thing. The money that top clubs saw coming through their books increased considerably in the years that were to follow. Star players suddenly began to earn tens of thousands per week. Those tens of thousands eventually moved on to hundreds of thousands until, in the summer of 2009, the Daily Mirror told of how Chelsea skipper John Terry was offered a reported £250,000 per week by Manchester City...to play football.

Millionaires and billionaires have come across to our shores from Russia, the United States, the Middle East and across Europe to buy in to what is ultimately regarded as the greatest league on the planet. Players have become the all-powerful, all-demanding, business models with image rights, signing on fees, release clauses and extravagant bonuses, mostly down to the revolutionary ruling in favour of Jean-Marc Bosman in 1995 which saw greater rights for players. Meanwhile, you and I on the terrace have seen the cost of supporting our clubs rise far quicker than the normal rate of inflation and as such, some fans have simply been priced out of the game.

In the ever changing, business minded-world, we suddenly had clubs, players and fans finding themselves in the centre of a rebranded footballing era. As the First Division initially became the Premiership, and later the Premier League, the rest of the English football would eventually follow suit. Following the launch of the new top flight in the nineties, 2004/05 would see the Football League rebranded accordingly, with what was the old Second Division now known as the Championship, Third Division now known as League One and the old Fourth Division now known as League Two.

In League Two, England's lowest Division in the professional league don't forget, we can pay £20+ for a ticket, £3 for a programme, £2.50 for a hot dog and £6 for two average pints of beer in plastic cups. From League Two upwards, these prices can only go the same way.

We buy into ideas that we're not *proper* fans unless we have the home, away and third shirt. Clever marketing and peer pressure ensures we take the necessary steps to have all our club colours (even the ones that are temporary colours) but by the time we spot the first bobble in the fabric it matters not one jot as the next shirt is due for release with the only change from last season's shirt spottable under a microscope.

Meanwhile, numerous clubs have upped from their old grounds that were steeped in tradition and character, moving to pastures new that are all too familiar as Derby County's Pride Park looks just like The Stadium of Light in Sunderland and The Emirates of Arsenal resembles a bigger version of The Walkers Bowl in Leicester. The only difference from new ground to new ground is the colour of the seating and the quality of the football on offer.

No longer are sides filled with six or seven local lads, born and bred in the ground's surrounding streets with the same accent as the fans and the same memories of the past. No players speak of it being *"a dream come true"* to represent the side you support without you questioning how this is the case what with him being as good as a foreigner in your own city.

So whilst we have lapped up the glamour and 24/7 football culture (Sky viewers just flick to channel 405 or whatever new number it is by the time you are reading this), what have we lost? For me, it is simple: Identity.

Back in the day, when my old man and his old man before him began watching football, the game was played by people you knew. People who, despite the pride of being a professional footballer, were just like you and me. Every day, normal folks making their way in life by doing the job they were good at.

Players from yesteryear were not multi-millionaires living in the most expensive houses in your area. Yes, there were exceptions to the rule like the George Best's of this world but on the whole they were the guys stood next to you at the bar on a Saturday night (Best neatly fitted this category too but you get my point).

They were the guys you saw down the corner shop on a Monday evening or the guys that financially, were not to dissimilar from us fans. But how, in this modern world we live in, can you identify with someone who earns more in a month than you may earn in a decade or even your whole career? You simply can't.

Whilst it only became really evident at the top of the game, the effects it had on the rest of football were there if you looked close enough. The lower leagues lost potential young fans who suddenly all wanted to support Manchester United, Arsenal and Liverpool. The stars of the Premier League were catapulted to a celebrity status that we all wanted to know about and within a matter of weeks, the rest of the

Football League seemed to become detached, as though they were running as a totally separate entity. The culture we saw footballers living in became something we expected from them all, regardless of whether they played for Aston Villa or York City. Footballers were pigeon holed. It suddenly felt like us and them.

Perhaps this was not just football that was becoming detached from the real world. The emergence and growth of the English game appeared to run in tandem with a new found hunger for celebrity culture. Other than the occasional Miss World that George Best seemed to pick-up, no one ever really showed much interest for the player's wives. Fast forward to the new era and everyone knows who's-dating-who, couples would often be dubbed *'the new Posh & Becks'* and the term WAG is commonly known throughout the game. And if you are unsure what it means, I think it is better you remain ignorant to it. Trust me, you are not missing out.

Interest in those lower leagues was just not as common as the interest in the top flight. For one year, Saint & Greavsie (for those that can remember) attempted to continue with their Saturday lunch time show on the Football League (but minus all the big teams who were now covered by Sky). They had to talk, discuss and act as though the Premiership did not exist. It was an ignorance that was forced upon them in order to try and see their Football League show survive.

And as the rich got richer (albeit on bank loans and living beyond their means in some cases), the poor clubs were forgotten about and the recession hit those who were hard-up the worst. But with the money, the foreign stars, the media coverage and the global focus firmly heading towards the English game, there was no better time to be in on the act.

For Notts County it was not to be however and relegation in 1992 to what would become initially Division One after the Premiership's launch meant an immediate return would be vital. However, in the first season in new surroundings it was not to be and the Magpies struggled to adapt to life outside the top flight as the media focus remained on the elite division. Manager Neil Warnock, a guy who had led the club to two successive Wembley promotions, was sacked in the January after a turn in the clubs fortunes saw results slip and after that, Notts stuttered into a 17th place finish.

The following year, a Mark Draper inspired Notts' side would rise to the heights of seventh with the midfielder himself netting fourteen goals in the league alone. But Notts would narrowly miss out on the Play-Off places meaning not only their hopes of promotion were dashed but they were left in the shadow of local rivals from The City Ground as well as Leicester City and Derby County of whom all finished above them.

It would later prove to be Notts County's last chance however and the following year, relegation loomed with Draper sold to Leicester City, for a then staggering fee of £1,250,000, and fans favourite Charlie Palmer leaving for Walsall. Notts finished rock bottom and made their way through three managers during the campaign with Mick Walker, Russell Slade and Howard Kendall all being shown the door before Wayne Jones and former Liverpool man Steve Nicol were put in temporary charge for the final few games.

Two years later and with more doom and gloom witnessed by the dwindling support at Meadow Lane, Notts County would hit their lowest ebb yet when in 1996/97, the club finished rock bottom once again, this time in Division Two, consigning the side to the lowest of the professional divisions in English football. It was the first time since 1971 that the Magpies would have to turn out week after week, both home and away against clubs from the lowest echelon of the professional structure. It was agony to watch something go from the dizzy heights of the top flight, drawing at home to clubs such as Manchester United and beating the likes of Chelsea and Sheffield Wednesday to the pain of playing Exeter and Torquay just six years later.

In 1997/98 however, the Notts faithful would get some respite. Under the guidance of Big Sam Allardyce, who'd previously enjoyed success with Blackpool, Notts County went on to win Division Three with what was a hefty 99 points by anyone's standards. Moving into top spot on December 13th 1997, Notts never looked back, staying top for the rest of the campaign as goals from Sean Farrell and Gary Jones gave optimism to the 6,000 or so regular match-goers and pride was given back to the city's family club.

Despite two steady eighth place finishes either side of the millennium, Notts County were no longer viewed as one of the bigger clubs in a small pond. Seemingly selling anyone that showed potential, Notts would also lose Manager Allardyce who resigned in October 1999 when the lure of his former club Bolton Wanderers became too strong. From 2001 onwards, Notts would scrape the bottom of the barrel of what was then Division Two before relegation struck again in 2004 and demotion to the newly dubbed League Two meant Notts were back amongst the bottom 24 clubs of the professional league.

Renamed divisions and new sponsors did nothing to hide the fact that Notts were again battling for little more than pride and as the club failed to acclimatise to the lowest division, two seasons running Notts would do what would be regarded as *'just enough'* to fight off the threat of a further relegation which would see them fall out of the Football League entirely.

In 2007/08, Notts would finish 21st in League Two (or rather more bluntly third from bottom), confirming the club had major reasons for concern. It would be their lowest ever Football League finish since the league's formation back in 1888 and with little sign for a bright future, attendances continued to fall with the average for the following season in 2008/09 hitting a near-to-all-time low of 4,445. On the pitch the club was in a poor state of affairs whilst off it, the fans were voicing their disapproval by staying away from Meadow Lane in their numbers.

As 2008/09 drew to a close under manager Ian McParland, no one would argue that the club had changed for the worse. McParland himself described the club as *"lacking soul and atmosphere"* in comparison to his playing days with Notts.

For me? Well I look at the club in recent years and then think back to what I'd consider the good old days. I'd look back fondly to when goalkeeper Steve Cherry gave me his gloves after an impressive clean sheet. Or the chat I had with Phil Turner on the day I watched Notts County take on Nottinghamshire County Cricket Club in a charity cricket match. Or more surreal was perhaps the night I sat at the top of my stairs when I should have been tucked up in bed, and listened to my auntie being dropped off home by a charming young Geordie lad by the name of Tommy Johnson after a night out.

Notts County was a way of life back then. On a Saturday it would be over to my grandparents for Football Focus. Buy a programme, go to the local pub with my dad and my uncle Danny, sing my heart away to The Wheelbarrow song, leave after 89 minutes to beat the mad rush, go jungle training (more to follow on that much later) and back in time for Final Score with Tony Gubba, Des Lynam, the league table and a packet of Jaffa Cakes.

These are fond memories I retain from my childhood. On the weeks we were not down at Notts, we'd be in the car travelling to Coventry or Sheffield, or if money was tight, sat in the back yard listening to BBC Radio Nottingham with Colin Slater. It was a simple way of life and it took up the majority, if not all, of our Saturdays. But I was happy with it.

At the age of twelve however, I began to get more serious with my own playing career. No longer was I playing at Under 10's or Under 11's with 10am kick-offs on a Saturday morning. We now had afternoon games and it became a choice between playing and watching.

For anyone who is passionate about the game, and believe me I always have been, it is easy to understand both sides of the argument. Turning down playing to watch your beloved clubs is a tough call but no hardship. Likewise, missing your club in the hope you might grab a winner yourself that afternoon is a worthwhile sacrifice. I, with my dad as my manager, made the choice and we embarked on six hugely enjoyable years playing and managing respectively in the local Nottinghamshire leagues for West Bridgford Colts.

Perhaps this was a turning point however as in the years that followed, my relationship with Notts County Football Club suffered and suffered badly. This was a time when there was no broadband internet access in every household. In fact back then, to me the net was the thing Tommy Johnson used to hit with such venom and the electronic version meant nothing to me. There was also minimal coverage of the teams outside of the top flight on the box. The only highlights you saw would be one or two goals on Central News Update from an encounter that maybe involved three or four goals and a sending off. The dedication to deliver any sort of highlights package was lacking.

So for the years that followed, our visits to Meadow Lane became less frequent. Fortunately, playing in Nottingham's Young Elizabethan League meant that we did not have games every week. On our free Saturday's we'd venture to Notts if the fixtures list had been kind enough to throw up a home game and for the seasons that followed, we felt we had the best of both worlds. I played with hunger and ambition, hoping that one day I could wear the black and white of Notts in front of thousands of fans. But it also meant I did not see Notts every week. It was a sacrifice I was willing to make however and in turn, I could carry the hope that one day, I'd be able to join my hero's and have my name sung from the terraces.

But that was the way it was and as I grew up, I had to compromise and realise that I would probably never have that relationship with the club, or any club, ever again. Then again who knows? Life has this way of throwing a surprise or two.

Here We Go Again

It was Tuesday 21st July and as I sat to my desk at work readying myself for a soul-destroying day typing in numbers and addresses in my normal, nine to five, run-of-the-mill, office job, a text popped up on my phone from a mate and ardent football fan Irish Chris.

"Heard about Sven? He's going to Notts..."

Initially, I assumed this to be some sort of joke. A mild, little wind-up, produced by the media or some ambitious journalist hoping to create a stir or get his name spotted. After all, it is not too long since the Swede left (or was ousted) from Manchester City and moved abroad for a post with the Mexican FA. Whilst neither of those spells would be deemed as a major success, this is still a man with a pedigree within the game. So from the head coach of England to Notts County via Manchester City and Mexico appeared to be something of a made-up tabloid story to try and sell a few copies and get folks talking.

As I trawled the internet and sent a few e-mails and texts to try and find out more, the audacious coup began to carry more substance with each passing minute of the day. From Sky Sports to the BBC, all and sundry were revealing the latest as Notts County were set to announce the amazing news that Sven was coming to Meadow Lane.

You see, for those not entirely in the know, the summer months had seen Notts County become the centre of some unbelievable takeover bid often saved for the top twenty or so clubs who ply their trade in the English Premier League. Foreign investors, billionaire owners and filthy rich business tycoons have become the *'in'* thing of recent years to the extent that a takeover from abroad is not as exciting as it was on the day Roman Abramovich took Chelsea off the hands of Ken Bates, the bloke that reminds us all of Santa Claus.

Ahead of the 2009/10 season, no fewer than half of the clubs that competed in our top flight had foreign investment in one form or another whilst owners were no longer local families but more likely to be money men from Russia, the United States or the Middle East.

Whether they be viewed as the latest accessory or merely a toy for which they can enjoy and occupy their minds with, the one thing that owning a football club guarantees is that you will not make your money back.

So here we sit, with Sven on board, as new owners Munto Finance look to move our club onwards and upwards. They have a vision and a dream. They call it 'the project' and the aim is the top flight and beyond. It all started off somewhat quietly. They came, saw what they wanted and made their offer. The previous shareholders paved the way and negotiated the deal with the supporters trust who owned part of the club and quicker than you or I could work out why, it was all happening and the club was sold.

Munto Finance is a company that was set-up as a subsidiary of Qadbak Investments. In simple terms, Munto Finance was used to purchase Notts County on behalf of the Swiss-based investment company Qadbak with Qadbak the parent company of the more publicly named Munto.

Outgoing Chairman John Armstrong-Holmes, speaking at a fans forum stated in the summer stated *"Don't ask me how much money is involved because we won't tell you. We do have proof of funds. They are substantial proof of funds. More substantial than this Football Club has seen in its history. It is the most historic opportunity this Football Club has ever had."*

In the weeks that followed, the Supporters Trust gifted their shares, following a vote after the fans forum, and no sooner had the news become public knowledge, the deal appeared to have been done.

No longer did it appear foreign investors wanted a big name club from which to play their games. Now, a small, traditional League Two club was just as glamorous an attraction according to Armstrong-Holmes:

> *What's in it for Munto? Not much actually. You have to understand the psyche of the sort of people we are dealing with here. We are the world's oldest club and have no debts of any significance. They see the opportunity to build something from here to the top.*

> *Munto are doing it for the Kudos. If we get to the Premiership, or rather when, they will get the benefits. They expect to lose money at first. But they'll put it in. We've got the bankers draft to prove it. You can't beat it.*

Following the takeover, fans were captured on the news telling the camera's how they cannot remember, in their 50 years of following the club, a more surprising turn of events than that of recent weeks. Camera crews, reporters and neutrals were all honing in on the latest revelations down at Meadow Lane and they appeared to be camped outside the big, black iron gates of the Derek Pavis Stand waiting for the next instalment.

Like a full speed rollercoaster with no desire for brakes or caution, the accelerator was firmly pressed down to the floor and we fans had no choice but to sit tight, try to understand it all and enjoy the ride.

Now though, the season is finally upon us and we can finally put behind us all the roving reporters and exaggerated storylines. We can ignore the suggestions of famous veterans expected to be turning out in black and white for the coming season as now, it has arrived. The 2009/10 season is here.

It has been a hell of a long week and stressful in more ways than one. I've just found out that I may be being made redundant (I say redundant but it is more to do with the fact I have not passed the necessary training requirements with my trial period due to expire) and pre-season is well underway for the side I manage, CSKA Carnabys. The squad is taking shape and I've one or two new signings which will hopefully mean I won't have the added pressure of playing as much as I did last season. The old legs feel far more tired than they did at my last club and I get a buzz out of picking the side and making the decisions. So why not take more of a back seat if possible? Or perhaps I should stop contemplating retirement at 26 and just get on with it?

I've also had a tough week trying to persuade someone to take the short trip to Meadow Lane for Notts' opening league game of the season with former big-boys Bradford City. Since 2005, I have lived in Loughborough and although it is only a short train ride from Nottingham, it'd be nice to share the trip with someone else. It was a tough task from the first thought though. Leicester City are also at home today immediately ruling out two or three of my most likely candidates to come down to a game. Kieran, my brother, is working all hours at East Midlands airport as the majority of his staff have the dreaded swine flu and my partner Jade is working or would have otherwise humoured me and gone to her first game.

As I ride over on the train, I can't help but try and work out when last I saw Notts' play on the opening day. I remember I used to make a promise to myself, even through the tough times, that I'd visit the ground as often as possible and see them in action. I think the last time I was here for the first home game of a new season was back in 2006 however.

What I do know though is that there is a real atmosphere as I arrive at Nottingham train station. I am not saying it reminds me of Wembley on Cup Final day because it doesn't. But it is very much like it used to be back in the days of Steve Cherry, Craig Short, Mark Draper and Tommy Johnson. There is a real buzz about the place as I step out of the station and I am passed by four or five lads no older than fourteen all wearing Notts shirts. It suddenly hits home that it has been a very long time since I've been here properly. By properly I mean a regular, fortnightly visitor so to speak. These lads would not have even been born when Draper was sold to Leicester City, never mind remember who he was. It makes me, at just 26 years of age, already feel well beyond my years.

I cross the zebra crossing and walk into the Bentinck Hotel, a rundown little pub just across from the station in the Nottingham City Centre. It's the sort of simple, no frills type of pub you can pop in before a match. The beer is average, the temperature in the room is like a sauna and to be honest, I've never ventured in here in the past 26 years of my life and I've not really been worse off for the lack of the experience. I stand at the bar, check my phone and continue to read the paper as I sip my pint. The pub is generally quite busy. I think steady would be the landlords view but none-the-less they're selling some beer. It is not the greatest pint a punter will ever have I am sure but then it does not claim to be either.

There is a group of Bradford fans, easily recognisable as a family with the three generations, mixed genders and official club merchandise on show, sat tucked away over in the corner. They keep themselves to themselves as the steady influx of Notts fans venture off the main drag and into the bar. Behind me there are several of what I'd consider to be the archetypal, middle-aged, Notts fans sat alone, bitter in hand and Racing Post spread out on the table. They have minimal interest in the world around them and what is happening but to give them their due, they appear happy enough in what they are doing. For them, this Saturday is no different to the numerous opening days of the last three or four decades. If Munto Finance and Sven had not come to town, they'd still be sat in the same place, in the same bar, with their same thoughts knocking around in their heads. If anything we, and I include myself in this, have gate crashed their world as they know it and the one route of escapism they had in their life.

I am not suggesting that the money and exposure and the new players are not to their liking. They, after all, are the fans that have kept the club in existence for the past God knows how many years. But they are the constant by which we can all measure ourselves. Loyal supporting or fair-weather fans, we're all in this together now however and we all hope for the same outcome. I cannot help but feel for some of them though. They'll still be here if it all goes the proverbial tits up. Will the rest of the match goers?

Finally my old man walks past the window to which I am gazing out of and I am no longer alone as he and his wife Julie, enter the bar. We exchange the pleasantries, get a round of beers in and skirt around the reason why we're all here. It's not that we don't talk about football much but on today of all days, perhaps he feels as much an imposter as anyone? My old man has also become disenchanted with football in recent years and if it is true that I had began to lose faith in the game, then he must now be the biggest sceptic going.

At the tail end of last season, the thought of either of us coming down to Meadow Lane with hope and expectation this season would have been preposterous. We'd have laughed half heartedly at our own misfortune that expectation was even on the agenda as we knew disappointment would follow. After all, this was the club that had taken everything we had, the blood, the sweat, the tears and the hope. And they gradually diluted it into a non-existence that both we as fans and the club as a whole had become.

Eventually, after mentioning the topic of the Great British weather and explaining why my job is on the line, we get onto the subject of football.

"That Lee Hughes should be handy at this level" I hasten to point out.

"We boo that fucker don't we?" he adds.

My old man jokes but his cynical views on the world cannot be blamed. This is the same Lee Hughes who was convicted of causing death by dangerous driving let's remember. I point out however, that the lad has done his time and will, regardless of morale standings, be a top player in League Two as the pub begins to fill even more with a rush of last minute drinkers before they make their way to the ground.

As it fills, my dad admits that he is a bit excited and can't remember it being like this for some time. As the years have tallied up, his views on the games and those within the game have dwindled into little more than contempt. He still loves the game as a sport but he just possesses a much more damning, cynical view on the world as it is now compared to when he was younger. Perhaps that is just a development for all of us as we grow older.

Both my dad and I cite 1991 as a memorable time in football though and specifically an FA Cup clash with Manchester City when we were at a packed Meadow Lane and missed Gary Lund scoring a last minute winner as we'd exited to avoid the rush leaving the ground. Now that was a day to remember. We left after 89 minutes in the knowledge we'd have to go to Maine Road for a replay that we'd not be able to win. City were a bigger side than us and therefore we had to do them on our own turf. It is strange however that a game in which we missed a last minute winner is such a fond memory. Looking back now, it epitomises the era and the times.

After we finish our drinks we make our way to the ground and the closer we get, the busier the streets become. I'm not being over ambitious and hoping for a sell-out as I know this will not be the case. Just seeing a crowd of any sorts down Notts is a nice image these days. Traffic on the surrounding roads has come to a standstill and this has not been seen around these parts since the early nineties. As we make our way through the crowds, both my Dad and Julie spot faces that they know from in and around the city. This is traditionally a local, family club and there will be concerns that the new happenings may change all that. A leopard cannot change its spots however and as we get within spitting distance of the stands, we grind to a slow walk rather than the brisk pace of which we had kept up en route. Bradford fans are queuing all the way behind the Jimmy Sirrel Stand where the away fans will gather today, fresh in anticipation for the new campaign and hoping to be the first side to thwart Notts, the new big boys of the division.

Rich Yorkshire accents dressed in claret and gold pave the streets as we pass by without a glimmer of acknowledgement. Carbone, McCall, Wetherall and Beagrie are just a few names spotted on the back of shirts that show a glimpse to a time most have forgotten. Well most outside Bradford for sure but this is a club who feel they are bigger than what they are. They consider themselves a big club and the Premier League patches on the shoulders suggest this may have once been the case.

We care little for these considerations and the sentiment is lost on any Notts fan who thinks that Bradford deserve the three points before a ball is even kicked though. How much bigger can you get than the history of being the oldest league club in the world after all? It beats a European Cup or two in my book. I'll tell you that along with half of this city.

We arrive at the old tree at the Meadow Lane corner of the ground and the sea of black and white is more potent and glorious than in any year this side of 1993. Fans ranging from six to well past sixty mill around the entrance. Some are still waiting for tickets from the ticket office. Some try to blag cash on the turnstiles and they soon learn that this has all changed.

As with any other season down at Notts, there are still stewards on the big main gates seemingly letting in familiar faces without a fuss or a care in the world. Back in the late nineties we'd be let in these very same gates by my aunt or my granddad (both from my mum's side of the family) who worked their Saturdays at Meadow Lane and The City Ground respectively.

As we approach the turnstile with our tickets in hand, we learn we are very much in the minority. Forward planning is a must down here as it appears that the organisation is still very much amateur even if the club has moved upwards in ambition and interest. As we walk behind a busy Derek Pavis Stand, the stairwells are as heaving as they have been for over a decade. Meanwhile, the young girls working the refreshment bars are being ran off their feet like they didn't know was possible and a rather muffled speaker system attempts to give us an impression of the starting line-ups.

We walk up the gangway and some stewards attempt to direct the crowds of late-comers to their seats. Again, the clarity (or lack of it) is partly down to the lack of experience. In previous years, anyone could sit anywhere and no one really cared. Being a steward at Notts was about as stressful and demanding as having to play out on the park itself. Granted one is a better role than the other but neither would be overly stressful shall we say?

One chap tells us we have to sit in the seat stated on the ticket. He is adamant and demanding whilst the next guy we come to at the bottom of the stairs advises us to sit anywhere. It's a joke and we are laughing but we are not overly worried. Fortunately our allocation is a good one and we worry very little about moving the present occupiers on their way as we take our seats just moments before the teams ready themselves for their entrance.

Opposite us, 2,000 Bradford City fans are in full voice. Singing their hearts away, standing in unison and showing their true colours. In fact, the colours are something to behold on this warm, August afternoon. The claret and gold shines across as the sun glares into the visiting fans eyes but they appear to show no concern. They are here to spoil the party and knock the Magpies off their perch and firmly back down to earth after the exciting takeover and stories of recent weeks.

The sides walk out and it is one massive standing ovation. This is it. 2.58pm on the opening weekend of the season:

The blood, the sweat, the tears, the pain, the early mornings on the train
Your thoughts, your dreams, the hope and fear, the busy streets and pricey beer
The vendor man, the programme seller, at 10-1 they're worth a tenner
The hustle and bustle, first sight of the ground, the unknown player your manager found

That lush green grass on a sunny August day, and looking forward to Lincoln away
The new front man and clapping hands, we'll follow our side all over this land
The new home shirt cost fifty quid, whilst summer exits lift the lid
Music blares as sides walk out and fans all rise, they sing and shout

4-4-2 or 4-5-1, let's keep it simple, don't play it long
Good one-two's and big three points, goals so good fans rock the joints
Finally the summer is all but gone and football is here so break out in song
For the next nine months may shape our life and keep us free from trouble and strife

After all we've waited long enough, wandering B&Q and all that stuff
For now it's here, we'll watch our team, it's our god-given right to moan and scream
But with just one strike dreams can be dashed, I just hope that this season the feeling lasts
So here we go, let's hold on tight, and we'll re-do it again on Tuesday night

Every single club all over the country has their hopes and dreams intact at this very moment. No damage is yet done. Title challenges, play-off aspirations or a nice cup run. Every way you look at it there is something to play for and Notts and Bradford are no different. Both well within their rights to take three points today and mount a serious challenge for promotion.

Notts County boss Ian 'Charlie' McParland is some 50-yards below us, slightly to the left. He's berating and moaning, shouting and screaming as hoards of press men saturate what is his technical area. There are no two ways about it. These guys should not be there. Tripods set-up and cameras so big that the lens' are almost touching his face, Charlie begins to bang on at security to get these clowns out of his way. If we were not already aware of it, we are now. The circus has firmly arrived in town. As the last camera man is pushed away by Charlie, the two dugouts retire to their seats. McParland's opposing number Stuart McCall steps forward and attempts one last shout of encouragement to his Bradford team.

I guide my eyes around the park, picking out names on shirts and faces I may recognise but ashamedly, I know very few. Russell Hoult is the shot-stopper for today and in our number one, I am fully aware that this is a guy well regarded within the game as a fine keeper. He should be considered as more than adequate for a League Two club.

Elsewhere on the park, Notts County feature the well-known, and fairly disliked, Lee Hughes up top. He was, to all intents and purposes, a handful for Oldham and Blackpool in recent seasons and prior to his short term period inside for causing death by dangerous driving, he was a handful for other clubs too including West Brom where he was something of a cult hero. He partners a very similar looking figure in attack of who I am aware of but know very little about. Luke Rodgers is a diminutive but physical striker signed from Yeovil who likes to put his foot in and earns plaudits for his effort and work rate. Elsewhere, Ricky Ravenhill stands tall in the middle of the park after his arrival from Championship side Doncaster whilst Craig Westcarr looks likely to start wide right.

The remainder of the side is made up of players of who I admit I know somewhat less about. Brendan Moloney, on loan from across the river, starts at right back whilst Stephen Hunt is left back. In the centre of defence, Graeme Lee, signed from none other than today's opponents Bradford during the summer whilst his partner in the middle is John Thompson, another one who used to ply his trade across the river as did Westcarr. Ravenhill and Westcarr are joined by Ben Davies (wide left) and Neale Bishop (central) in the midfield four.

I am fairly quick to familiarise myself however and, having decided to research the squad in more depth prior to today, I advise my old man accordingly over who is who, what's what and who came from where.

Last time we were both sat together at this ground on a weekly basis, players like Mark Stallard, now at non-league Corby Town, and veteran club favourite Ian Richardson were regulars in the side. They are long gone and it all seems some time ago now. Since then we have admittedly grabbed games as and when.

There is no time to stand, or sit, on ceremony however and as Bradford kick-off, I have that feeling that can only be associated with the opening day. Optimism, belief, desperation and fear are all rolled into one. As I look across to my left, a packed Kop Stand is in full voice, singing of their beloved Wheelbarrow and asking Sven, Charlie and anyone else that is interested to give them a wave.

On six minutes new boy Luke Rodgers, both energetic in appearance and pace, is sent clear through on the Bradford goal. It's a heavy ball however and despite his best efforts, the on-rushing Eastwood in the Bantams goal blocks with his chest. It's a good start though and my already high spirits have been raised. Moments later however it is the

24

visitors turn to raise expectations when Colbeck is found with a neat cross only to see his diving header well saved by the experienced Hoult. It is a lively start and with this, the whole stadium seems to raise the volume a notch in the hope that each set of fans can lift their boys to that much needed level.

Lee Hughes looks strong on the ball and clever off of it. He instantly knows where his team mates are and it appears he is one step ahead at all times. A class above, he is central to all that has happened so far and he's already looking a worthwhile punt for top scorer in the division. On seventeen minutes Craig Westcarr, looking somewhat clumsy, beats his man wide on the right. He delivers a powerful, whipped in cross which is met by the head of Rodgers, flicked on and....yes it's there. Ben Davies at the back post. Notts are one ahead and the ground is bouncing. I look towards my old man and his face says it all as he smiles and jumps up and down. It's 1-0 and the season is only seventeen minutes old.

The next 20 minutes pass somewhat within the blink of an eye. Hughes and Rodgers are causing chaos for the Bradford backline whilst Charlie is on the sideline barking instructions in a demanding and regimented way.

A long ball direct from the heart of the Notts defence is suddenly hit forwards on 39 minutes. As the ball bounces, Bradford's Zesh Rehmann does not deal with it and Lee Hughes springs to life. He looks up, narrows in on goal and drops a shoulder before slotting home a second just before the break. The all important time in a match, just before half time, and Notts have capitalised. This time everyone seems to have an extra inch in their bounce as the Magpies celebrate their lead. Over in the Jimmy Sirrel Stand, Bradford's sea of gold and claret has changed to something of a still lake. Not a flicker of movement within their ranks, it looks lifeless.

This will do nicely. A 2-0 lead at the break and we can steady the ship in the second half. However, Notts being Notts have other ideas and don't let up just yet. Westcarr's efforts are duly noted as he crosses a timely ball for Hughes on 43 minutes. As if by script, the terrier-like striker bundles home his second and Notts' third of the game and it is 3-0! Dreamland!

It is almost too good to be true. News filters through during the break that the other club from this city are not winning at Reading and it gives us more reason to cheer. I make my way under the stand for some half-time refreshment but soon alter my temptations as the Notts staff fail to cope with the onslaught of like-minded fans wishing to grab a bite to eat.

As I step back up for the second half, Hughes is unlucky not to net his hat-trick when he has two efforts blocked from a narrow angle before firing over. The boy is clearly in the mood for goals. On 55 minutes however, his wait for the elusive third is over when Luke Rodgers is felled by Clarke in the box. Calm, composed and assured, Hughes slots home the hat-trick and at 4-0, the game is well and truly over.

Charlie withdraws the star man on 64 minutes, to a standing ovation I might add, and with it, fellow new-boy Karl Hawley is given a chance to shine upfront. Notts continue to look dangerous too. With each attack there seems to come a chance. Rodgers, then Hawley, before Bishop and Ravenhill all try and get in on the act. Hamshaw replaces Westcarr and Hoult remains unnerved at the other end so it is almost inevitable that on 86 minutes, Brendan Moloney breaks down the right, neatly interchanging with Luke Rodgers and then nets arguably the goal of the game with a shimmy in the box and a neat, delicate chip into Eastwood's net.

A 5-0 victory against one of the more favoured sides in League Two. C'mon You Pies.

In The Summer Time

The summer hit Notts fans like a bucket of cold water awakening us from our sleep. You shudder, you shake, you rub your eyes and you ask yourself *"where on earth am I? Is this a dream? Have I imagined all of this? Is any of it real?"*

Thankfully, this dream was very much a reality and set to become the fabric that held our emotions together from match-day to match-day. Gone would be the days of drafting in some free transfers and hoping for the best. No longer would our main aim be simply to keep hold of anyone who showed the slightest bit of form or ability until we could demand a fee for them.

When the news hit home just what was happening at Notts County, the whole of the country watched on with mixed emotions and reactions. Fellow League Two clubs hated it. Some fans from the other side of the river, if not all, hated it too. Neutrals were intrigued whilst those who'd experienced massive investments wished us all the best for the future. Chelsea and Manchester City fans I spoke with were surprisingly interested and often amongst the well wishes on internet forums and out in the streets.

Notts County's squad at the end of 2008/09 was not the brightest set of players you would find in League Two. On the final game of the season, having lost every league game during April, Charlie McParland fielded a Notts side set for an overhaul even if they were not yet aware of it.

Kevin Pilkington started between the sticks on that final game away at Wycombe with a side of Phil Picken, Mike Edwards, Stephen Hunt, Matty Hamshaw, John Thompson, Gavin Strachan, Myles Weston, Sean Canham and Ben Fairclough ahead of him. On the bench, Richard Butcher, Adam Tann, Matt Richards, Delroy Facey and Jamie Forrester awaited their chance to come on.

With gates of between 3 and 4,000 down at Meadow Lane, the season had hardly been breathtaking and I had managed to take in just over half a dozen games without once seeing a win. Many fans I knew of were more than reluctant to commit to a season ticket for the 2009/10 season and understandably so. In what other entertainment based industry would you consistently buy more tickets for what you ultimately consider to be poor performances?

No one returns on a weekly basis to check out films that they know to be poorly directed in the same way that we would not pay to go to see a band down the road the night after we saw them play poorly in our neighbouring city.

Sport, and from my knowledge of football more than any other, is not privy to this rule of thumb.

"I can't remember the last time he had a good game" or *"Every week he is fucking useless"* are not uncommon statements heard in the stands when Saturday afternoon comes. And sometimes such words are uttered by fans that support some of the better clubs.

A good friend of mine, despite being an Arsenal fan, is pained when you talk about his expectations and hopes for the season ahead. Fast forward to November time and more often than not he has given up all hope. He'll tell you how the club's board do not spend enough cash, or how their manager is more focused with his own personal agenda of grooming the best youngsters and how one or two of the foreign lads just aren't good enough. The same Arsenal Football Club that, from the 92 league teams who play the game professionally in England, are consistently what you'd consider to be the third best side in England based over the past seven or eight years. If he is moaning, what hope do the other 89 sets of fans have?

So for the last five years how has it been to support Notts County? Fucking dire. Four of those five seasons saw us finish in the bottom six of the Football League. Our year of reprieve (2006/07) saw us muster a nose-bleed sort of position in thirteenth.

But despite beating Wycombe on the final day of last term, there was no two ways about it. We had been poor. We had a poor playing staff and the best we could hope for was for them to *"show a little spirit"* or to *"play with some pride"* as the fans in the stands would comment.

If we could afford to bring in better players we would have done but the bare facts are that a club without funds can do little more than tread water and balance the books. At best, such clubs set about releasing players for nothing and bringing in new faces for the exact same cost.

So just how was the pattern going to change for Notts? Well in truth, it wasn't. None of us saw it changing anytime soon and none of us could envisage what was about to happen.

When I first heard about a takeover, I like many others became excited and hopeful for the times ahead. But the news of a possible takeover was just that; a possibility. Football has let me down before when I've expected something to happen (most of the time it is England doing the letting down part).

Notts County Football Club, and its then Chairman John Armstrong-Holmes, were met with an offer from Munto Finance, an investment company said to be acting on behalf of investors from the Middle East.

But it was not until the evening of the 25th June 2009 that we would learn, in more detail, what may be about to happen to our small, family orientated club. Armstrong-Holmes gave just a taster that evening at a fans forum stating *"We do have proof of funds. They are substantial proof of funds. More substantial than this Football Club has seen in its history."*

It was to blow minds from the Clifton estate to Calverton, from the Meadows to Woodthorpe and throughout various other suburbs of Nottingham. It also began to make my mind race here in Loughborough where, since 2005, I had moved and settled down.

"They've calculated how much it will cost to get into the Premiership" said Armstrong-Holmes and he was nonchalant in saying so. As if by magic, Notts were set to be transformed from a poorly run, going nowhere, League Two struggler, into a promotion chasing, trophy hunting, player magnet with sights set firmly on not just the top flight but also European football.

Despite the announcements, we knew very little still about those investing in the club. But many of us cared very little in truth. All we knew after those words from above was that Notts County were set for bigger and better things and I for one liked the sound of it.

Of the vast playing squad that had featured during 2008/09, most were shown the exit door at a time when the rumour mills were merely grinding and acquisitions were purely on the cards. Of the player's who'd spent time on loan with the club during the season, none were followed up with a view to a permanent deal. In the defensive department, long term servant and Football League veteran Michael Johnson retired from the playing staff, Paul Mayo was let go for pastures new in January 2009 in the form of Mansfield Town and Adam Tann was released before he joined non-League Histon.

In midfield, Neil McKenzie also departed to join the Stags down the road whilst Jay Smith, Gavin Strachan and Adam Nowland were all released. Richard Butcher was allowed to leave for Lincoln City at the end of the campaign despite grabbing a handful of goals whilst Myles Weston, perhaps the one bright spark of an otherwise dreary campaign, opted to accept an offer from Brentford during the summer which would mean a tribunal would decide a fee for the youngster.

In attack, there was little to talk about either. Jamie Forrester was released along with Spencer Weir Daley whilst Jonathan Forte, on loan from Scunthorpe, was not asked to return leaving just three forwards in the squad in Delroy Facey, Sean Canham and Ben Fairclough.

The turn-around (especially at this level) for the playing staff is huge. The less money a club has, generally the bigger the turn-around in players becomes. Financially poor clubs generally dish out shorter deals for players. Shorter deals generally means the player is not good enough to demand a longer one and in turn, these short deals are also less-well paid than the player would wish to be on.

If a player improves and shows his worth, the same club can invariably not afford much of an improvement and thus he either moves on for nothing or a nominal fee is accepted prior to his deal expiring which would see the club losing him for nothing. On the other hand, there are those players that are on said deals that do not show their worth and arguably find it hard to have the manager purring over an extension to their deal. At Notts, this was the norm.

With the disappointing season still fresh in the mind, clearly something was happening at the club even if we were not fully aware of it all just yet. Come late May, before Munto Finance, Sven-Goran Eriksson and 'The Project', Notts snapped up two midfielders to bolster their ranks.

Two signings in two days meant that first Ricky Ravenhill and then Neal Bishop would sign for the club from Darlington and Barnet respectively. It would be another two weeks though until the interest at Meadow Lane would begin to light-up though.

On June 4th, Chairman John Armstrong-Holmes told the BBC how the club had an offer in place that was "*substantial*" and from that day on, we did not look back. Pretty soon both Peter Trembling and Peter Willett were appointed to the club's board in order to help move the takeover forwards and some six weeks later, on July 14th 2009, it was confirmed that Munto Finance had purchased the Oldest Football League Club in the World.

Peter Trembling was hired by Munto to help oversee the purchase of the club when their interest had stepped up. Previously involved in the commercial side of business with Everton FC, Trembling was brought in by Peter Willett and when discussions with the previous owners of Notts County reached advanced stages, he was appointed Chief Executive with the view to ensuring the transition would be as smooth as possible.

Whilst John Armstrong-Holmes remained secretive as to the identity of those purchasing the club, Peter Trembling was seen as the public face of Munto Finance during the takeover.

Yet if the plans behind the scenes were hectic, albeit vague, things were just as intense for manager Charlie McParland who was now looking at a much smaller group of playing staff than he had ended 2008/09 with despite a very different kind of backing from up above.

Graeme Lee had arrived from Bradford City on June 30th adding much needed depth to the defence and two days later we learnt that Brendan Moloney would arrive on loan for six months from over the river.

It was confirmed by the Notts on the 2nd July that Myles Weston was to leave for Brentford despite McParland's public comments that it could be the wrong move for the winger. But the blow was softened with the arrival of Ben Davies from Shrewsbury Town at more-or-less the same time.

It was an exciting turn of events down at Meadow Lane and the calibre of the players coming in was a clear improvement on those departing. With some numbers needed to give depth, it was a welcome change that those players being signed were more than mere freebies looking to get a game but now out of contract players in demand wanting to play for us.

Shrewsbury Town wanted to hold onto Davies and offered him a new deal in much the same way Notts wished to keep Weston whilst Ravenhill had an offer on the table from League One side Oldham prior to joining us down at the Lane. All the time McParland would talk and reiterate about the additions he was still hoping to make. Players like Billy Clarke and James Bowditch were looked at and touted but as with any manager, he was struggling to find strikers that were of both of a high calibre and available.

On July 14th Munto Finance were confirmed at the club and with it, the real fun and games began. On July 22nd Sven-Goran Eriksson arrived in town as Director of Football in what was to be the boldest statement ever made by a League Two club and as though it was a mark of intention, Notts then secured deals for trialist and free agent Luke Rodgers, previously of Shrewsbury, Port Vale and Yeovil as well as Lee Hughes, the veteran goal scorer who'd enjoyed spells with West Brom, Coventry City and more recently Oldham Athletic and Blackpool.

Notts went from having an average (or some may argue a way-below average) League Two attack to a front pairing capable of all sorts in a matter of days. A week later the club confirmed their interest in Premier League youngster Matt Ritchie from Portsmouth whilst Karl Hawley arrived prior to the new campaign kicking off for a nominal fee from Preston North End.

Despite more out-goings than in-comings, the squad looked much brighter than before and fans started to dream again. A backbone to the side was starting to become clear and when, after a few games of the season behind us, we secured a deal said to be in the region of £1,000,000 (a club record none-the-less) for Manchester City goalkeeper Kasper Schmeichel, I think it is fair to say that most fans clearly felt we'd arrived on the big stage.

Being a Notts fan during the summer was like having an extra full-time job. To follow the ins and outs, the comings and goings, the news, the gossip, the potential arrivals and the bold predictions meant that much time was spent watching or reading up on the club. Partners of long suffering Notts fans became the new sufferers. The term 'footballing widow' is so true that those that doubt it are not fully aware of how bad the addiction can get.

I stopped cooking when I got in from work, instead watching Central News and East Midlands Today for an hour (basically the same news but relayed on different channels). I went out of my way to find copies of the Nottingham Evening Post that are not so easily accessible in Loughborough and spent hours upon hours trawling articles on the net looking for hints or suggestions of what may be happening.

This was all at the same time as my own pre-season regime began for my own club CSKA Carnabys. I had training sessions to plan, deliver, analyse and reconstruct. I had new players to watch and sign, pre-season games to plan for and fitness tests to carry out. My life was well and truly taken over by the game once again.

When I then decided that not only was I going to live and breathe the beautiful game but I would also document it all in the form of a book, I passed a point of no return.

Away Day Blues

Nothing can quite match a local derby game. Even when you get a chance to meet some of the big guns, a match against a local side, with bragging rights on offer and a short trip into enemy territory cannot be matched. So a trip to Chesterfield on a Tuesday night is one that I have looked forward to since the fixtures were announced.

The clock is ticking at work. My beady eyes focused on it as it ventures closer and closer to 5pm. Bag packed, jacket already on. My cursor hovering over the shut down button as it reaches 16:59 on the computer monitor.

"That's me done!" I shout as I am halfway out the door and bidding farewell to those in my office.

I'm in a real good mood today. After two thumping wins, racking up five goals at home to Bradford and four on the road at Macclesfield, tonight is a chance to make it three wins from three and confirm our intention to all in League Two that we, Notts County, mean business this time around.

We are boosted by the arrival of new signing Kasper Schmeichel who finalised a deal over the weekend to become what has been reported as our new record signing. The Guardian wrote on Friday that *"The fee is believed to have eclipsed the record of £685,000 previously paid for Tony Agana in 1991."*

Despite the wealth of goalkeeping experience within our ranks in Russell Hoult and Kevin Pilkington, the arrival of Kasper has really lifted everyone at the club as it is a huge sign of intent from the new board and management. Arriving from Manchester City, Kasper has also enjoyed loan spells with Cardiff City, Coventry City and Falkirk but now, hopefully he'll make Nottingham his permanent home for the foreseeable future.

A week ago we may have lost 1-0 at home to Doncaster Rovers in the League Cup but Coppinger's 54th minute goal did little to dampen spirits at Notts for there is a much bigger picture this season and the League Cup was just a sub-plot that perhaps we can do without.

It's a shame in a way that the League Cup has become something of a footnote in the game for most clubs. There was a time when all clubs wanted to compete and contest a place in the next round. I remember many a summer holiday, usually the last week before I was due back at school, sat up listening to Notts County on the radio away at some seaside town in the League Cup.

Then, gradually, as money became more and more prominent in the game, the League Cup became less so. One or two of the *"Top, top clubs"* (In the words of Jamie Redknapp) began to rest some of their bigger names and before we knew it, everyone from the top flight was using it to give a road test to their back-up players.

It was like a fever that spread from club-to-club. In fairness, managers like Arsene Wenger used it for a good cause and they proved on a regular basis that their kids could hack it on the big stage. But as the resting-players bug spread, it became more common in the lower league too until now it is viewed as the thing to do. The norm. The expected. As I say, it is a shame, but at the same time, I'd happily accept our defeat to Doncaster if it means three points tonight.

For tonight, somehow, I have managed to persuade my other half that on a Tuesday night she would love a trip down the motorway to take me to watch Notts. To say she has little interest in football is an understatement. She tolerates it for me I guess. She lets me know on a regular basis that she does not approve of how much time I dedicate to it and makes a real point of making it known that she is *letting me* watch or go to games. But for some reason, tonight, she has agreed to come with me and drive us over.

In the days leading up to tonight, I have had warnings from various fans in various places.

"You want to avoid there" they say when pub names are mentioned or places to park are discussed.

Others merely point out that avoiding Chesterfield altogether is perhaps a better option than travelling there in the first place.

"It's a dive" says one of my mates. For the record, he is a Chesterfield lad and fan, born and bred.

As I arrive home and wait for Jade to pull up in the car, I begin to feel nervy and on edge. The journey should take around an hour, although with her driving maybe an hour and twenty. So as it approaches, and then passes, half five, I start to wonder where she is. Calling her mobile does nothing to lessen my nerves as she doesn't pick up and I receive a sixth sense that she is truly annoyed that I am calling her in the first place.

I can imagine it now.

"The quicker you stop calling and let me concentrate on getting home, the quicker I will be with you" she would remark had she picked up. I leave it two minutes and then try again.

Eventually, at just gone 6pm, the car pulls up outside the front of the house and I am slamming shut the front door as the wheels are still grinding to a halt. As I jump into the motor, I am grinning from ear to ear with excitement and anticipation. Her face does not mirror mine.

"I don't even have chance to eat or get changed then?" she says without a glance in my direction and pulling away from the parking space. She is not best pleased.

Her mood is not bettered when thirty seconds into the road trip I turn off her CD and begin searching for TalkSport Radio.

"Erm, I don't think so. My car, my choice" she says as she flicks it straight back. This could be a long hour and twenty.

Not being a driver, I assume the motorway is the best option. It's logical as far as I can see. Loughborough to Chesterfield is not the greatest of journeys but never-the-less, a motorway on which one can put their foot down would, to me, be the best option. Not for Jade.

We argue about the route, we argue about the radio. We have a discussion about the coming weekend and the fact she has a Saturday off. In her world, travelling to Chesterfield tonight has by some twisted logic meant that I should miss Dagenham at home on Saturday and spend the day with her.

"I'm going to the Dagenham game. Come if you want" I say. We don't talk for the next twenty minutes.

As fate would have it, we do not talk until the next argument arises. I, some 25 minutes earlier, apparently won the battle of minds with regards to the route and even though she said her way was quickest, she went for my option.

Women, I find, have a knack for doing this on a fairly regular basis. Argue but give in. Or rather argue and accept your viewpoint whilst not admitting theirs was the wrong view point. Either way you look at it, she has accepted my angle but in doing so, gave her the much needed ammunition that should anything go wrong, I take the full force of the blame. Women are too clever at times.

Anyhow, I did not say too much at the time of noticing her decision. It would have appeared that I was gloating. Nor did I say anything when after two further songs on her CD, she flicked TalkSport on for me. We both just sat there, looked forward and got on with the journey.

"I told you I didn't like the motorway" she says in an angered and agitated tone. Why, I am not sure but she is glancing in here rear view mirror almost every other second and is not pleased about something.

"Well I thought you had decided not to go down the motorway."

I try not to sound confrontational. But I must have done because it only further increased her bad mood.

The car begins to shake and now I can sense what she could sense some 60 seconds earlier on her foot pedals as our little run around begins to be temperamental. There is a bang, a chug and suddenly all power disappears from the motor as a cloud of black smog, reminiscent of a poorly lit BBQ she started in the summer, begins to bellow out of the back end of the car.

Jade panics, understandably. But at the same time, she has managed to guide us into the hard shoulder as passers-by beep their horns and Jade's face looks like the definition of *'pissed off'*.

Now this was probably not the finest moment to utter the following words as Jade jumped out the car and ordered me to do the same. But I am only human. I have my faults and, perhaps, timing is one of them.

"It's only an hour until Kick-off." I should have bitten my lip.

As we glance back at the mess that was a Peugeot 306, there is black soot and car remains going back for some 200 yards down the hard shoulder and outside lane. We sit on the bank as red hot steam pipes out of the car and smoke bellows form the rear. Neither of us wanting to say anything, we pause momentarily. I pick up my phone and call my old man and in turn she picks up her phone and calls the AA.

"That car you sorted us out with" I tell him. *"It's fucked!"*

I go on to tell him where we are, albeit roughly, and in turn that we will miss the game. He is disappointed but with his wise head on, he reminds me it is only one game. Why does it still hurt when someone says that?

The AA advise us that they will be with us within an hour at which point it is 7pm and I begin to fully accept that for me, Chesterfield v Notts will not be on the cards tonight.

I get the blame for the whole debacle. It is my entire fault and she begins to read the riot act.

"You said we should get this motor for nothing from your Dad" she begins. *"You pushed me into going tonight to watch Notts. I didn't want to go"* she adds. *"And it was you who said lets go on the motorway. You know I hate motorways"* she finishes.

Now to all intents and purposes, she is right. But we are broke. The motor we were offered was a freebie, more-or-less, to get us by for a few months. Six or seven months we have had out of it so we can't grumble. As for pushing her into going, I didn't. That is the God's honest truth.

When she saw my enthusiasm last week for the opening day, she seemed genuinely pleased for me that I was in a good mood about football for once. When I joked about her going to a game with me, I was shocked that her reply was a positive one. When I further joked about Chesterfield, she kindly said yes. Again, I was shocked but it took no pressure from my part. She would argue it was only for me though.

As for the motorway? Well let's face it. If a car is fucked, it is fucked. By not going on the motorway we'd have merely prolonged the life span on the car for another journey or two until the exact same thing would have happened but instead of it being light outside and Jade having me in the car, she could have been stuck on her own, late at night and in the middle of nowhere.

So the judge's verdict for Luke; regrettably, he'd say I was guilty on all charges. But I'd argue back.

By 7.45pm (talk about rubbing it in Mr AA) a van pulls up and a short, fat, balding chap motions over towards us on the grass verge.

"What's the problem?"

"Notts are kicking off about now" I tell him only to receive a good whack across the midriff from Jade. She has a wry smile on her face as she does it though and the tension by now has eased off.

She has accepted we are both angry for varying reasons but arguing is not going to help either of our moods so she walks down to the motor to show the chap what the problem is, although it's obvious to anyone with the ability to see, and even without the power of sight you could hazard a guess.

The verdict, which I had already told my dad on the phone, was that the car is fucked. The black stuff that was trailing back along the road that we had driven was diagnosed as being *"lots of parts of the engine"* after closer inspection by Mr AA.

"I can tow you back but it'll cost you a bit because your plan does not cover you" he points out.

"Fantastic" I say. The sarcasm is lost on him. He doesn't care about us. He doesn't care about Notts. He pulls his van up in front of the Peugeot 306 shell, does his stuff and we sit there watching, despondent and reflective as the piece of junk is lifted on the back of his big yellow van.

The first derby game of the season was not supposed to pan out like this. As 8.45pm comes and goes, we take our seat alongside our charismatic, charmer of an AA man and he phones the office to check what the damage will be on our pocket. The fact we have little choice in the matter is neither here nor there. We can't just dump it as we'd get fined and the only option to get somewhere without paying this chap is a service station that would charge the earth in parking fees.

"£110 Ok with you?" he stupidly asks.

"Yeah, great. Can you throw in Notts on the radio with that?" I ask.

"Sorry, can't have the radio on I am afraid. Company policy."

It is a lesson is this. Had I been more patient, I'd have suggested we leave out going to Chesterfield, what with the mad rush from work, and we'd have planned another trip elsewhere, a little further down the line. In one fell swoop, I have managed to increase my partner's hatred of the game and in particular, probably Notts County.

We sit in silence most of the way home, although now things are less tense, despite the silence. I walk through the back door leaving Jade to empty everything out of the motionless Peugeot. I've had enough. My day could not get any worse after being so excited just some four or five hours previous.

Despite all of this, Notts are still in a position tonight to make it three from three. Not long left now surely I think as I glance up at the clock and make a bee-line for the TV remote and the radio. Simultaneously, both forms of media compound my mood into a further, downwards spiral. Notts have just conceded not one, but two penalties late in the day at Chesterfield's Saltergate home.

BBC's Colin Slater is less than impressed. Sky Sports News offers much the same damning views of a tight encounter, yet a non-event. But two rash tackles late in the game and Notts trail by two goals to nil in our first local derby of the season. I am gutted.

Jade walks in, slings a bag on the floor and makes a phone call to some chap who it turns out will pay £30 for the scrap of junk in our back yard. She is nothing if not pro-active. As I sit listening to the final few minutes, she gives me a consoling hug. She is knocked back momentarily when Mike Edwards grabs a goal for the Magpies but the disappointment does not end as the whistle goes shortly after and two Jamie Lowry penalties means that Notts come home with nothing to show for their evenings' endeavours other than a bitter taste of defeat. At least their coach may have an engine.

Away day blues and it's still August.

Marque Signings

Yesterday, at around midday, news reached me that former Tottenham, Arsenal and England defender Sol Campbell had been spotted down at Meadow Lane. Idle gossip does very little for anyone, especially in football. If I had a quid for each time I have been sat, waiting and hoping for such and such a player to sign, or so-and-so to declare himself fit for the big, up-coming game I'd have earned a small fortune.

Back in the day when I first began following football intensely, we had two or three options to source our information. Ceefax and the trusty page of 302 (it used to be the first thing I would check upon returning home from school), the local papers (not always the greatest at revealing the gossip that fans thrive on) or thirdly club call - a premium rate telephone line that I'd call before my mum got home just to hear several options and no real news. I once remember phoning it three times in an evening when I was denying to myself that Mark Draper had been sold to Leicester City. The day after, Notts sold Mark Draper to Leicester and my mum had a phone bill that had gone through the roof and a son who was extremely upset.

Usually however, that for which one hope's for rarely materialises in football so with the rumour mills clanging away with regards to Notts County, I decide to laugh off all speculation and wait to see it for real. Only a few days ago, it was said that Patrick Vieira, Pavel Nedved and Luis Figo were in talks with Notts. League Two Notts County chasing players, albeit older and wiser than in their pomp, of that calibre just seems all a bit surreal.

That said I was then shown pictures of said Mr Campbell arriving in a Mercedes outside the Derek Pavis Stand. Suddenly it hit home that he may actually be coming here. Sol Campbell, for all his qualities, was never a player I regarded as top draw down the years. He was a steady, fairly rock-solid centre half. He was never overly stylish or fashionable but steady he certainly was. However, this is not the Premier League we are talking about either. In League Two, big Sol would be able to control the defence, keep the ship steady and probably help guide the Magpies along the way to success without pushing himself into top gear.

Today is another day though. Sol is yet to be confirmed, fans are not really talking much about the rumour and there is a game against top of the table Dagenham to contemplate. Under the management of John

Still, the Daggers have taken nine points from a possible nine so far with Danny Green grabbing two goals along the way.

In our own camp, spirits are still high though despite the unexpected loss at Chesterfield. At the start of the week, McParland managed to secure the services of Johnnie Jackson on a free transfer from Colchester United to add to the arrival of Kasper and today we are hoping both will make their home debut.

I arrive at Nottingham train station accompanied by my mate Sean and introduce him to the Bentinck Hotel. Sean is a first timer at Notts and also happens to be the stand in skipper at present for my club, CSKA Carnabys. A Villa fan himself, he's keen to see what all the talk is about so we are making a day of it. He's keen to see Lee Hughes in action after my glowing report last week and I have also tipped him off to keep a close eye on Ricky Ravenhill, a player that plays a similar style game to Sean himself.

Notts, for all their hard work and endeavour on the opening day and away at Macclesfield, were poor in mid-week to a second rate Chesterfield. I say that with the littlest of disrespect intended although being a local side, they'd take it. But the Spireites are not going to be one of the top sides in this division for my money. They do not possess enough for a sustained run of form and the club as a whole would be punching way above their weight to expect to put together a promotion challenge. That sounds really disrespectful doesn't it? Oh well, fuck it.

So now with Dagenham on our patch, it is vital we get back to winning ways. As we arrive at the ground, we are lifted by the news that Kasper Schmeichel will start in goal. Like his old man, Kasper is an imposing figure and certainly a larger than life character on first impressions.

Many expected Kasper to make his debut in mid-week away at Chesterfield but Charlie, rather wisely in my view, has kept him for a home crowd to welcome him to the club with open arms. Notts start well and each time Kasper gets the ball himself, he is quick to release and start attacks.

From my seat in the Derek Pavis Stand, The Kop is in full swing and they are making enough noise for the Jimmy Sirrel and Derek Pavis Stands too that are much quieter in comparison. With it once again a warm, August afternoon down at Notts, the atmosphere is great and the feel around the place is buzzing.

In Brendan Moloney and Ben Davies, Notts have two players down the right flank that look vibrant and full of promise and both clearly possess good footballing brains. Davies arrived in the summer from

Shrewsbury Town and despite only being a few games into his career at Meadow Lane, the fans clearly love his ability on the ball.

Something of a late developer, it was not until the age of 25 that Davies first began to make notable steps in the professional game when he signed for Shrewsbury from Chester City. Between 2006 and 2009, Davies netted 30 League goals for the boys from the Welsh border racking up some 111 league appearances during the same time. Why Davies has not played at a higher level seems bewildering after having his presence in the side for just a few games so far.

Notts see most of the possession in these early stages. Things are tight but Notts look at ease. Kasper is commanding and Hughes energetic. The sun is shining and some 100 or so Dagenham fans are here for what Notts fans describe as the Daggers big day out. But the visitors are top and rightfully so. Because of this it is a relief when, on 43 minutes, Davies is the provider for goal hungry Hughes at the back post. The free-kick curled and weighted to perfection. Hughes cuts-loose, free from his marker and in to space. He nods in and dances away in front of The Kop who join him with his jig.

"Let's all do the Hughesy..." they all sing, waving their arms around.

Despite the loss at Chesterfield, Notts are back in business. Now we attack some more. With just a few minutes until the break and with the deadlock finally broken, Hughes appears down the right in space, pulling away from the Daggers back line. He looks up and waits. Not the fastest mover on the park, Hughes' awareness appears to create time and space for both himself and the team mates around him so we are not surprised when on the stroke of half time, he turns provider, this time sliding a neat ball into the box and into the path of Karl Hawley for his first goal since joining from Preston. It is just what was required and now we are two goals to the good.

Sean and I laugh with one another. Like two buses coming along at once, we find ourselves watching Notts with a comfortable lead and in such good fashion too. We know this game is signed and sealed now.

As we break for half time, it is a nice feeling to be able to just sit in a t-shirt in the summer sun waiting for the action to recommence. For all the years I have watched football, I have always felt that a season has a clear beginning, middle and end and this is certainly a new beginning.

The opening weeks and closing weeks, traditionally, always seem to be played in feel-good atmospheres and sun-drenched skies. Maybe it is the feeling of a lack of football there has been or the lack of football to come respectively for both periods that ensures the crowds are better and the fans are in good spirits. No one looks forward to the cold, long and wet winter months with any amount of anticipation. So long may the sunny skies and goals galore at Meadow Lane continue.

After the break, it is much of the same; Free-flowing, exciting football. The team no longer relying on one or two lads or a stroke of luck, we have a side that can play their way out of games and hopefully out of this division. On 63 minutes, Moloney finds Hughes who subtly turns his man before cutting infield. A deft touch later and Johnnie Jackson takes the ball on his chest before guiding home number three past visiting keeper Tony Roberts to give us a resounding 3-0 victory against the previously top of the league club and all with little effort seemingly used.

Sean jumps up and down with me and we share the moment.

"This is great" he joyfully announces and he is right. I'm just hoping and praying this feeling will last.

After the match we have a few beers. The Navigation Pub, more affectionately known as simply The Navi, is busy and full of optimistic Notts fans and for the first time in as long as I can remember it feels like we're close to untouchable.

The following morning, Sean and I will help guide our club to a 3-0 friendly win for CSKA Carnabys against a well fancied side from down the road with Sean setting myself up for a brace. What a great season this could turn out to be.

Coca Cola League Two Table:

	Pld	+/-	Pts
1. **Notts County**	4	11	9
2. Dagenham & Redbridge	4	5	9
3. Crewe Alexandra	4	5	9
---			
4. Bournemouth	4	3	9
5. Northampton Town	4	4	7
6. Barnet	4	2	7
7. Cheltenham Town	4	1	7

There Ain't No Easy Way Out

Notts County v Burton Albion
Meadow Lane / League Two / 05.09.09

We were expecting a few thousand from their lot given that it is one of the biggest games in the history of Burton Albion Football Club. And given the fact that they are from just down the road too, you'd expect a good turn out from them but their following does not reflect it. They've had a decent start to be fair under former Sheffield United, Birmingham and Canadian international Paul Peschisolido. At the start of play they are level pegging with Notts and therefore the three points on offer carries more weight than just some local pride.

Last week was poor. Very non-descript if you like. Travelling away to Barnet is never going to be one of the games you relish as a fan and probably not as a player either but to lose in the fashion we did? A 94th minute goal and one that, in hindsight, should have been dealt with easily, was a painful lesson after the good vibrations felt here down here at Meadow Lane against Dagenham the week previous.

Had the late goal not gone in at Barnet, a point may have looked like a decent return for the trip down south. Win your home games and pick up points on the road. That is the recipe for success at this level and any level really. But former Notts man Ian Hendon had a well-disciplined side ready for us last week and their hard work paid off much to Notts' dismay.

On the trip back I had to discuss with a fellow traveller how there was no easy way out of League Two. I did not wish to discuss the matter for the best part of two hours though. I wanted to be left to wallow in my own self-pity. I wanted to be left alone to sulk or sleep depending on when the lager kicked in. He did not allow me to. If you have ever been to an away game on your own on a train or a coach, I dare say you've been in such a situation. It can feel like a lifetime.

However, today is a new day and we need to get back to winning ways as aspirations of promotion and success in League Two are built on a good, solid home form. It has been so far so good too netting eight goals without reply and two flamboyant wins.

This morning the sun was beating down, promising to deliver another opening-day sort of feel down at Meadow Lane. But now, with kick-off upon us, the sun has gone in behind the clouds and the first signs of the autumn ahead are in the air. Notts line-up strong with Kasper in goal behind Moloney, Clapham, Thompson and Hunt in defence. Ravenhill and Bishop are joined in midfield by Jackson and Davies whilst up top; Hughes and Hawley are paired together.

Unfortunately, there is no sign of Sol Campbell in the match day squad however. Snaps taken of him training in the press suggested that Sol is carrying a little extra weight at present which understandably has gone down like a lead balloon with Notts fans waiting for his debut.

I'd heard whispers that today could be the day we see him appear on the bench but looking around, he is nowhere in sight just yet so our patient wait will continue.

In the Burton side, former Notts man and easy target for the boo boys, Guy Branston features at centre back whilst in attack, another ex-Notts man Sean Harrad starts.

The sides ready themselves and the Notts fans are up for the battle and certainly ready to take three points off Burton Albion. Notts start positively as Moloney ventures down the right in the opening stages and we feel as though we are in control from the off. An early corner is won and then wasted but we look alright. As we are composed and steady in possession, Burton do not dwell on the ball and are much more direct from the left peg of Branston at the back. Clearance after clearance is hit forwards leaving Harrad to chase and pressure, harass and close-down.

Shortly after the wasted chance, Clapham sees an effort from a set-piece hit the wall before more endeavour from Moloney offers Hawley a half chance at goal but the deadlock remains with twenty minutes already on the clock.

The atmosphere begins to dampen and just below me, one or two fans begin to show displeasure.

"McParland where is your plan B? Earn your fucking money!" shouts one bloke who jumped to his feet after a failed attack led to a goal kick.

"Sit down you prick" responds a fan behind us and Sean finds it hilarious.

"Yeah you tell him, prick."

Whilst he may have had a valid point with regards to McParland making changes, twenty minutes into the game is hardly the time to be judging this afternoon's performance. So far this season, it does appear that Charlie likes to make like-for-like changes. Nothing wrong with that in practice but when things are not working out, when the opposition have the reckoning of you and appear to be dealing with all you are throwing at them, sometimes something a little different is needed.

Only a few moments pass when the same fan is called into action again for a good moan. Greg Pearson tests Schmeichel from a tight angle and suddenly there are some sighs and moans from the stands.

Sighs and moans as though lowly Burton are supposed to have surrendered to our greater firepower by now and simply rolled over. Football does not work in such simplistic way. Fans would do well to remember this.

Our own Ben Davies then goes into the book for a late tackle, mistimed and ill-judged according to referee Woolmer. Following this, Hughes earns a free-kick in front of the dugouts as Branston looks clumsy and fails to win the ball from our talisman but neither of the sides is in the ascendency now and the game has become evenly matched in the middle of the park. Jackson turns in the box and fires over and in reply, Pearson works another opening for the visitors only to blast up into the higher realms of the Kop. Towards the end of the half, our hopes are raised when Clapham spots an opening but as his driven effort glides over the bar, our hopes of a half time lead disappear too.

From somewhere, or someone, we need a trigger; a glimmer of magic or a simple spark to kick us into life. McParland's critics are seemingly out in full force now analysing each fault as his own and considering each minute passed as one he has failed to turn the game on its head.

In their white shirts, Burton maintain their shape and their work ethic as the second half gets underway. They press, close down and play to their strengths. Paul Peschisolido meanwhile orchestrates from the touchline, encouraging and inspiring. Charlie screams orders and they look as if they are falling on deaf ears as players continue in much the same vein.

Then, when perhaps one or two more fans are starting to lose their hope and expectations are waning, Clapham turns provider for Hawley in an intricate move down the left. Hawley, with space to run into, glances up and then audaciously chips Artur Krysiak from the corner of the penalty area and we finally have the lead. Get in!

Karl Hawley turns and runs towards our stand, sliding on his knees and jubilant in his actions. The breakthrough. The chance. The points we need are now on the cards.

Suddenly Notts are a different side. Wanting the ball, playing their football, working Burton from left-to-right. Jackson fires in a superb free-kick which is firmly met by the crossbar. As it crashes back out as far as Jackson, we all rise and then look to the heavens in disbelief. Seconds later the ball works its way out to the left. Jackson chips into the path of Davies before a cross is worked into the box and eventually finds Hughes. The man you need in this situation, Hughes swivels, opens his body and he agonises as the ball curls narrowly around the post.

Notts maintain the pressure and it is not long until Burton Albion are on the back foot once more. The Kop is trying to draw the Notts side forward with its enthusiasm and songs.

"Black and white army, black and white army" they sing. Clapham is out on the left. He turns one way, then another. He then cuts inside his man and has a host of targets to aim for. Hawley peels off his man, in space and wanting the ball. Clapham looks up and surely now it will be two. Hawley picks his spot and guides it goalwards only for a defenders foot to deflect the ball wide.

"Gotta take these chances" I tell Sean.

Matt Ritchie, signed on loan from Portsmouth in the week and now on for Ricky Ravenhill, is looking keen and lively on his debut and now Jackson is playing with much more authority from the centre of the park. Notts look like the only side capable of scoring now as the evening draws in.

Hughes continually searches for spaces and is denied several times by the strong figure of Branston at the back. Solid on the ground and even more commanding in the air, Burton have tightened things up and McParland looks nervous from the sideline.

Notts have options on the bench though. The bulky Delroy Facey, the tenacious Luke Rodgers and the pacey Craig Westcarr. They are ignored and left to watch from the sidelines as Notts search to kill the game off. Peschisolido makes two changes on 80 minutes and it is his last throw of the dice. Notts need three points but Burton would take the one.

Then, with 84 minutes on the clock and against the run of play, Burton sub Richard Walker finds himself with a chance in front of goal and with it he breaks Notts' hearts. We are left feeling gutted. Kasper reacts angrily. He bemoans and screams and berates. First goal conceded at home and he is clearly not happy with his defenders.

McParland just looks deflated. He urges his side on but we've been victim of a smash and grab. Seconds later it nearly gets much worse when Sean Harrad motions forward, readies himself and then thumps the ball against the woodwork of Kasper's goal.

Fans are now showing their anger rather than allowing an undercurrent of murmurs to be gently heard. McParland is blamed and players are blamed. It is not good enough so say the fans around me. The Kop continues to sing but less unified and more in desperation than anything. The Burton following are celebrating and feel as though all three points are on the cards.

If fans were expecting this League Two to be a walk in the park, Chesterfield, Barnet and now the Football League's new boys Burton Albion have awoken us to the realisation that it won't be as we have one point, from two bloody games.

Coca Cola League Two Table:

	Pld	+/-	Pts
1. Rotherham United	6	6	15
2. Bournemouth	6	5	15
3. Dagenham & Redbridge	6	8	13
---	---	---	---
4. Barnet	6	5	13
5. Crewe Alexandra	6	5	12
6. Notts County	**6**	**10**	**10**
7. Aldershot Town	6	3	10

A Stark Contrast

This is a rarity. Certainly not something I'd consider an addiction or a habit in the same way my visits to Meadow Lane could be viewed. In fact, going back down the years, my affairs with England on the live stage have been pretty limited.

A few trips to the old Wembley are fond in the memory. Despite the stadium being little more than a shithole, it was a magical shithole with the cramped leg space, poor views, rubbish seating in the lower parts and chaos upon leaving the ground. But it was special. *The home of football,* if you will. The place everyone wanted to visit, play, watch, manage at and report from. Whatever your role is within the game, you wanted it to include a trip to Wembley and for that, the old ground was second to none.

I also saw England at Elland Road once. For the life of me I cannot quite remember why the game was not at Wembley but it was long before any redevelopment work began. It was a random game and just a friendly but it was a chance to see England none-the-less. Since then I have not seen the national team play in person however.

Going into tonight's game, the footballing world is a pretty place to be for me. Notts are looking steady and up at the right end of the table whilst England eagerly awaits this summer's World Cup in South Africa. We top Group Six at present with 21 points, four ahead of Croatia and seven ahead of Ukraine of who could be more of a threat than the Croats given the fact we still have to go to Kyiv and the Croats have played a game more than both ourselves and the Ukrainians.

All of this is by-the-by though because, as it stands, it'd take a monumental fuck-up even by England's standards to not be at the World Cup come June 12th 2010.

Jade and I arrive in London early, hitting the car park for our hotel in West Brompton before midday. It's a red hot today and given the fact it's London, and also that we'd experienced some vehicle issues earlier in the season en route to Chesterfield, we departed Loughborough with time to spare so that nothing could go wrong this time around.

Given that my 27th birthday is coming up, and the fact that I *"already have everything"* I'd want, Jade suggested tickets to a football game would be a good idea for my birthday. Ultimately, it has coincided more with her birthday as two days ago she celebrated her 26th so I feel like I am cheating the system in a way by getting my present today but it is a welcomed break for the pair of us.

Now, first things first; Jade is Scottish. She is proud, to an annoying extent, about her Scottish-ness and therefore today is more than merely getting her to go to a football game. For today only, she is supporting England. Now I am patriotic and I always have been. But the factors that have led me to be annoyed about Jade's Scottish-ness are as follows:

- She believes Scotland accepting they are shit at football is an excuse for being shit at football. She needs to understand it is not.
- She seems to reiterate that she hates England whenever I happen to mention them, watch them or wear a shirt. It's like a result of my actions.
- She hates England despite moving south of the border as a toddler and subsequently not choosing to return to Scotland when she hit an age when she became old enough to choose her city/country of residence. If you hate something so much, would you not do something about it?
- She was educated in England and has worked all her working life here in England, yet she is adamant Scotland is better. Her actions prove it clearly isn't.

I personally have nothing against the Scots, the place or the football teams. I have a soft-spot for Motherwell due a former work colleague of my old man taking us up there to see The Well at Fir Park when I was a youngster and somewhere along the line, my family has some Scottish blood. But the efforts Jade goes to be so pro-Scotland and anti-England annoys me. Anyhow, on that note my moan is over. I am sure you get the picture.

Being here today, for tonight's game which has set her back a fair amount, is something of a minor miracle because of all the above. We take our bags up to the hotel room and contemplate a power nap (you know how it gets after a long journey and hot weather) but instead we dump our stuff and make our way straight back out again. We are only here for one day so we feel we may as well make the most of it.

As we hit Soho on the tube, there are signs already that there is a game on in town. Several Croats sit sunning themselves outside the bars and cafes in the Soho area and they look colourful and friendly in their bright blue shirts and chequered red and white alternatives. Huge, flowing flags cover their tables, the backs of chairs and the shoulders of pretty Croat women dressed in little more than vest tops and flags.

London is busy. The hustle and bustle you read about is evident and as we try to push our way across the crowd surging forwards to exit left on a walk way, we eventually find ourselves needing to cut back against the wave having missed the turn off we had wanted.

A quick dart across a busy street, grabbing Jade's hand to ensure she follows, and we find ourselves at the head of our destination, Carnaby Street. Having been in a band named after the very place for the past four years, it seemed only right that I, as a founder member of The Carnabys, visited the very spot and had a beer or two.

We check out the cuts of the cloth in the vintage stores along the way, eye-up tailored Mod suits that I cannot even begin to imagine affording and then we stop off for a drink as the bars begin to fill with a mixture of London tourists, local workers and milling match goers.

We sit down in a pub just off Carnaby Street and enjoy a beer and some food whilst glancing up occasionally to see if there is any team news on the screens ahead of tonight's game. As excitement goes, I am on a high. Tonight should see England seal qualification after all. Understandably, Jade is not as bothered although in the spirit of things, she is in a good mood.

After a few drinks, we take to our feet and make our way through the even busier streets and head back towards the London Underground in order to make our way to Wembley Central. Despite the game being on, we climb into our carriage relatively unopposed. There is a young couple, also seemingly going to the game, to our left whilst one or two folks in suits look to head home after a day in the city.

You'd not notice there was a game on in this tube if truth be told. Stop-by-stop this changes however. The carriage is hot and humid. It clatters from side to side, jolting occasionally and making us, both not used to such modes of transport, slightly nervous. As it shakes you feel as though you are about to topple over, off the track into the side of the tunnel.

Despite this, we live to make it to the next stop at which point a few more fans jump on and steadily, we become seated with nothing but legs, arses and backs in front of us as the carriage fills and the heat worsens. But now the whole thing stops. The power goes like someone flicking a switch and the announcement advises us that we have reached the end of the line. Some two stops away from Wembley itself. One by one we clamber off and then stand, tightly pressed onto a tiny platform, patient and expectant of the next tube to take us the remainder of the way. I feel sorry for the commuters in and amongst us. Some who perhaps care very little for the game, or England, or even us.

The first tube arrives and we sigh. The doors open and close without any of us penetrating the crowded carriages already full to the brim. The nice, calm, broken-English voice tells us not to worry as there will be another tube along in a few minutes and we wait. We wait 25 more bloody minutes. Those at the front pray for no nudges within the crowd to force them onto the track.

Jade and I don't talk. We conserve our energy in the heated atmosphere, drink the bottles of water she cleverly picked up and we wish we were perhaps somewhere else.

Eventually a tube train arrives with just enough space for the crowd of us to join, albeit in much more cramped conditions. But none of us are risking another wait. Two minutes after we depart, I notice a momentary shot of the Wembley arch and thank whoever it is looking down on me that we are close to arriving and getting some fresh air; if there is such a thing in London.

The streets are littered. Littered with fans. Littered with bottles and glasses. Littered with polystyrene chip trays and empty coke cans. Drunken fans spill into the roads, almost feeling invisible as though no car would go over ten miles per hour in such busy conditions. Then a car does exactly that and some bloke finds himself on a bonnet shouting obscenities. The driver chooses not to shout back but would be well within his right.

It feels like we are in some war zone rather than off to a football game. Take away shops with small little flats above surround us. God knows how those residents feel on match-days. In the sky a Bet365 helicopter circles, advertising to the masses with its trailing banner weaving its way through the evening sky and police helicopters hover some distance away, just monitoring the streets below for crowd problems. The noise generated by the various objects in the sky intensifies the whole atmosphere.

Horses; big, powerful horses with mounted coppers patrol the roads. They tower way above us fans, keeping groups in tow and controlling the movement. Some fans get kicked out of one pub and fall into the next. Some Croats sing aggressively but perhaps it is misinterpreted as their smiles suggest they are here for a good time.

Horns are blown, flags waved and car horns beep. The same young couple we saw on the tube way over an hour and half back suddenly fall back into place in front of us and look more confused and scared than Jade does by the whole atmosphere.

I've been here before mind. Big games. Big crowds. Big occasions. To me it is not a new experience. But the reality of such an occasion is perhaps more frightening than what we see on Sky Sports before a big game with several families smiling for the camera and shouting *"Come on England!"*

Random calls for *"Rooney"* bellow out whilst street vendors push scarves and cheap, knock off t-shirts in everyone's face. We make a beeline, following the signs and heading towards where we can sense the stadium being. You'd think it would be obvious where to head but in the built up roads we stand in, it isn't and it is not until we come within close proximity that we see the ground in full glory for the first time.

It is something to behold. The share magnitude of it! The aura it gives off! Fans flow like a steady stream towards the stadium and my heart is beating. Jade grabs her camera and takes as many pictures as is possible whilst we remain moving. The closer we get, the bigger it appears to become. It seemingly grows grander in its manner and size. When we hit the outskirts I am in awe.

This is something entirely different yet in three days time, I will be watching Notts again, at home, against little old Northampton.

The more Croats we see, the louder England fans become. Clear groups of club fans mix together with pro-Gerrard songs resonating from one select group. Another section chant Frank Lampard songs and call out the skipper, John Terry's, name. United fans simply sing United songs as they feel the need to do so. Something about United fans means they insist on reminding others that their priority is United and only United. Some unnerving vulnerability and insecurity that appears deep rooted in their support. Probably due to the fact that many of them are not from Manchester or even the north west.

As we reach the stadium it dawns on me just how big this place is. Usually, when you revisit somewhere that you frequented as a child, the magnitude and memories are much bigger than the new reality set out in front of you. To some extent, this is because you are a few feet taller and as a kid, everything seems that little bit bigger anyhow.

But if anything, the area seems even bigger than my trips as a youngster.

I am fully aware that it is a new ground. That is not the point I am making. But the area in which we are? Wembley Way, the walk to the ground, the distance from the tube. All of it just seems like another level. And that is before you take in the size of the new stadium.

Keen and eager, we make our way into the ground after a quick photo opportunity with the Bobby Moore statue and once inside, the excitement levels intensify. Even Jade seems rather amazed and excited by the whole thing now.

We make our way up some huge escalators with hundreds of others heading the same way. We are all here in fine spirits and all here to see England seal qualification. As we stand stationary on the smooth motioned escalators, it feels that if there was an entrance to the pearly gates, this is the sort of thing the big man upstairs would have installed.

"This is amazing" says Jade and I cannot help but suggest she is perhaps now more English than ever.

We hit the concourse area and buy two drinks and two hot dogs and in doing so may now need to take out a small loan to get us through until the end of the month. How they can charge the prices they do is beyond me. The hot dogs set us back £8 before we've even entertained a drink. But we are starving and thirsty and we are fully aware that we probably will not hit our hotel until well past midnight.

So we spend the most unjustifiable £10+ in our life (not a lot but on a moral standing, it is a joke) and then savour the taste, or lack of it, before heading to pick up a programme. Wembley is still relatively empty given how it will be by the time kick-off arrives. But we head up to our seats and sit down as we spot, from some distance, the likes of Frank Lampard, Wayne Rooney and Glenn Johnson warming up on the near side.

Across the way, on the other side of the ground, the small corner of Croats sing loud, with determination and passion, waving their flags and generally jumping up and down. They'll be absolutely knackered by the time kick-off arrives.

The whole build up to that first whistle seems to last a life time. Gradually, one-by-one, the seats that surround us fill up. People pass you by, thank you for standing and letting them through and then do the same two minutes later when they decide they need to venture back down to grab a bite to eat but there is no bad feeling. No bitterness or annoyed faces. We are sat up in the area reserved for the armed forces although to glance around, you'd not necessarily think you were in with the stereotypical army types.

There are families, groups of mates, fathers with their sons, and grown up lads with their even older dads. The build-up intensifies and the drama starts to unfold. Dignitaries are announced onto the pitch and are formally given mementos of the occasion or for their efforts in the past. It feels so far away it is hard to tell.

If one thing is more prevalent than anything else this evening, it is the quality of the stadium, the facilities and the views on offer. The old Wembley sometimes left you with a view of someone's head such was the seating incline as you worked your way up the stands. We may be a fair distance from the action up here in the heavens, but we'll certainly see everything that happens before our eyes.

For the first time in a long time, Jade is looking really happy and content. Her job as a carer has caused her to do endless amounts of double shifts and late nights of late and to some extent, she likes it as it enables her to put money away and save for our future. But now she has a few days off from work and because of it, she seems much more relaxed and happy. She smiles more than I have seen in months and it is nice to see. Her eyes gaze around the stadium and she continuously checks I am ok and if I am glad we have come.

"Of course I am" I tell her with a smile at which point everyone rises to their feet and the two teams stroll out onto the Wembley turf.

The Croats are intense over in their corner. It looks as though there is some sort of tribal dancing going off as the songs pour out from their hearts. A continuous bouncing motion and mass scarf waving demonstration greets their side as they make their way to the centre to have the anthems pumped out the speaker system.

They join in, they are patriotic and they are venturing into new things with each tournament and qualifying campaign as one of the more recently established nations in an ever-changing Europe.

Then it is our turn as we hold our heads high and sing as many of the words to *"God Save The Queen"* as each person knows. It is something I have always believed in singing and something I have known from a young age. I'd not say I am pro-royal family or anything like that. But you cannot deny the few moments of solidarity that everyone feels when fans, management, staff and VIP guests alike are standing to acknowledge the song.

It is a real hairs-on-the-back-of-your-neck moment which I often feel is an over-used description for an emotion or particular minute in one's life. But this is one of those moments and upon completion, the whole stadium roars as the captains are called to the centre circle to call the toss.

I feel myself gently bouncing up and down myself, just on the tips of my toes. It's not a song being sung or a celebratory motion that I hope will come later. It is pure adrenaline and nerves. You want to see your nation perform of course. Even more so when it is the first national game you've witnessed in over a decade in person.

As the game kicks-off, it turns strangely quiet in the area we are sat though. The Croats continue to make their noise. Of course they do. Somehow they are still full of energy it appears. Small pockets of England fans all around the ground sing their songs and try and encourage and motivate the Three Lions. But in a stadium this big and this widespread, I guess you have to first accept that the whole ground will not be one intense, ferocious, cauldron of tension and singing.

Pretty soon we have the visitors on the back foot however. Balls are spread from right to left and back again. The full-backs, Glenn Johnson and Ashley Cole, are as advanced a duo that one could ever imagine watching whilst up top, the talisman Wayne Rooney is alive and looking in the mood to get hold of the ball.

There are not more than five or so minutes on the clock when Aaron Lennon receives the ball out wide on the right and then cuts inside, causing panic and disruption in the Croat back line. Looking on, some fans rise to their feet as Lennon comes crashing to the ground inside the box. As if waiting for their queue, the rest of the fans jump to their feet once they see the referee, clearly visible in bright yellow, dramatically sprint into the box and sternly pointing at the spot.

The Croats protest but they do so with little conviction because, even from up here, it appeared to be a stone-wall penalty kick. The offending player holds his arms aloft as he returns to his feet. Praying for reprieve in the way the Italians made an art form in the eighties. But the referee is not interested.

As Josip Simunic walks away despondent and full of self-pity, Frank Lampard grabs the ball and prepares to fire England into an early lead. From the spot, Lamps is one of the best and seconds later we are back on our feet and celebrating as he finds the inside corner of the net and England are off the mark.

England's support is much clearer and louder now. The Croats Head Coach, Slaven Bilic, is animated on the touchline hoping to inspire his Croat boys but some twelve minutes later, we are expectant once again as Lennon receives the ball out wide from a Gerrard pass. This time, as he wriggles his way towards the box, rather than trying to lure the foul he delicately lofts a ball towards the back post and we rise once more to celebrate as Steven Gerrard makes it 2-0 with a well placed header.

England are in full control and I am told as much through the text messages I get from Paul, my band mate and Leicester City fan.

"Lennon's having a stormer" he declares and the whole stadium is now in the partying mood except for a small corner drafted in from the continent. Even Jade alongside me is looking pleased as her smile is a carbon copy of that on any English person's face this evening.

Now we sit back down and feel a little more relaxed and with a two goal lead, rightfully so. It's far from over. Only a fool would think otherwise. But with the way we've started, it's hard to imagine us letting this stranglehold on the game slip.

For much of the remainder of the first half, England keep the ball well as fans all around the stadium sing their songs and we enjoy the atmosphere. With each passing minute we don't add a third, the Croats become a little more apparent in the far corner but they are making the most of a bad situation rather than expecting a comeback.

Half time comes and goes. I am eager for more though. Not content with a 2-0 win, I want to see England make a signal of intent to Europe and the rest of the world. When David Beckham trots out from the dugout to warm-up the whole stadium offers a standing ovation whilst on the touchline, Fabio Capello stands like a school teacher or chess master. Either way he is masterminding a very successful qualifying campaign which is beginning to draw ever-nearer to a positive ending.

Sometimes, when early goals are scored, I think the loss of tension and anxiousness can lead to a more subdued atmosphere. When you win a game at the death, on the edge of your seat with your heart pounding, it lives long in the memory. A crushing 5-0 win can sometimes feel less dramatic, especially when the hard work was done early doors and the game was never in doubt beyond an early goal or two.

It sounds insane doesn't it? I prefer a tightly fought win than an easy, stress free encounter though. Ok, perhaps prefer is the wrong term. But I remember them for longer. It's the same with a clubs league season. I think most fans would rather win a Play-Off Final in extra-time than a win automatic promotion by finishing in second place. But once you are in that Play-Off situation, there are no assurances.

On 59 minutes the stadium lifts itself once more as Lennon again proves to be the tricky obstacle which stands between a tighter defence for the Croats in the second half and one that will fall by the way side once more. Lennon is bright and on his toes, skipping past one man and then the next. Rather harshly and abruptly, he is felled some 35-yards from goal however and we rise to our feet, angry and adamant that a foul has been committed. We pause, the referee pauses and, as we find ourselves ready to shout and appeal further, Gerrard drives a ball out to Johnson and play is waved on with it being advantage England. With Johnson running at his man and England players pouring forward into the box, the anticipation is there from all quarters of the ground as Lennon brushes himself down and picks himself up.

Johnson does a neat step over following his positive run at his man and then delicately chips a ball back from the bye-line onto the head of

Lampard who glances the ball across goal into the bottom corner sealing the move, the win, the group and qualification in one swift movement.

The cheers and appreciation shown is less dramatic this time. As I pointed out, the game is won. The tension has evaporated and eased off and at three goals to the good, we now know that the fate of both teams in front of us is all but confirmed in the morning papers.

Now Croatia look despondent and lost on the big stage. England players on the other hand all want the ball. They all want a chance to impress. Gerrard makes it 4-0 on 66 minutes when some sloppy play in the Croat defence sees England pounce. An over hit ball for Rooney is rescued with a high, lofted cut back and a third headed goal of the game is nodded home making it two apiece for the two central midfield men who cannot supposedly play in the same side.

Jermaine Defoe and David Beckham both get in on the act as we applaud those departing and those making their bow. We cheer loudly as we pass the ball amongst our backline. We seek more though. We demand more as 'God Save The Queen' and 'Rule Britannia' roars out around the ground. Jade, still sat smiling and in awe at the stage in which is laid out before us, continues to check I am enjoying it.

"Fantastic night" is the only response I can summon to do the occasion justice before, against the run of play, Arsenal's Eduardo, subject to some serious booing this evening, grabs a late consolation on 71 minutes.

Eduardo was at the centre of a cheat-storm a month or so ago when, playing for Arsenal v Celtic, he was involved in one of the clearest acts of simulation (diving) we've seen in recent years. Fans all around the stadium remember it and, to be fair, he has probably got off lightly considering.

Tonight is not about being anti-Eduardo or seeking revenge for Croatia knocking us out of the Euro 2008 Qualifiers though. Tonight is all about doing a job for ourselves and on 77 minutes, we see Wayne Rooney cap off a fantastic night when he drives home from the edge of the box following a poor clearance by the Croat keeper.

The stadium is raucous now. The volume is beyond anything I have experienced before as every touch by a man in white is celebrated with equal measure. Jade and I remain seated, soaking up the volume and happiness around us, taking in each second of the success we have seen before us as England play their way firmly into our hearts under the guidance of Fabio.

A 5-1 win over Croatia is such a different story to the last time they were here. But that does not matter now.

Upon leaving the ground, nothing can take away the shine from what we have seen this evening. Sharing it with Jade means I have done so with someone who is not overly bothered about the success of my national team. But she enjoyed it, celebrated it and joined in as though it meant as much to her, quite possibly because of how much it meant to me.

It's cooler now outside. The temperature has dropped a little and the paths that lead away from the famous stadium are chaotic and grinding to a halt not long after we leave the ground. The journey away is always more daunting and less appealing than the trip on the way in for obvious reasons.

Drunk on euphoria and tired from the energy that went into the day itself, we only want to be in our hotel now. We want to be crashed out in silence. No noise. No bustling our way to get to where we want to be. Just there and alone. We wish to be back in the hotel that we can neither remember the name or exact location of as we start to rack our brains.

The tube journey away is long awaited but we are far from being in the final carriages that will leave Wembley. We get in one at the third time of asking after being packed once more onto a small platform with too many people per square foot. But now it is louder and more intimidating. More of a boisterous crowd with some bellies full of lager from an evening's drinking. It seems idiotic that the chants are now of a different nature.

Anti-United songs, anti-Lampard songs and anti-Croat songs are sung. Songs about Germans and songs about the IRA reeled off too. Gone are the good-feelings amongst all men. Now the club mentality seems to have crept back in.

"Stick your Blue flag up your arse" sing a section of West Ham fans to a lad donning '8. Lampard' on the back of his shirt.

As though tonight never happened, we are apparently no longer England fans together but fans of various clubs who just happen to share the same space. As we find a small space on the tube, I wish we hadn't. A large group of blokes, crude, ignorant and pissed-up, stand beside us. They talk freely in the surrounding area filled by women and more importantly little kids with painted faces. They go below the belt with the clever comments and outrageous suggestions and argue so loud that those waiting on the platform back at Wembley can probably still hear them as we hit the first stop.

Eight stops later and still they stand, now even less aware of those around them as two begin to argue and one throws a punch at a younger member of the group. No one around them wants to intervene, myself included. Doing so would be non-wise for any of us but the whole incident puts me on something of a downer after a great night. I stand between Jade and the crowd, shielding her as they move around, elbows and all, falling into folks and making no apology for their actions.

"Do you think he's a cunt?" one of them asks rather loudly and aggressively. He's directed the question right at me and the one he refers to turns and looks at me waiting for a reply.

"A bit" I state as the tube pulls into the next station and I have that uneasy feeling in the depths of my stomach.

"It's a good job this is our stop then" says the chap who asked me as he pushes his mate out the doors and they start singing the German Bomber song. I just breathe a deep sigh of relief and Jade and I take a seat as she attempts to doze off on my shoulder whilst our tube inches closer to the area that we know our hotel is.

By 11.50pm, with a pizza box in hand and aching legs, we find our hotel although it wasn't where we remember leaving it. A great game and on the whole a good day. That's my England fix for the next decade or so I guess. In a stark contrast, it'll be Torquay at home on Sunday for me. Come on you Pies.

World Cup 2010 Qualifying – Group 6:

	Pld	+/-	Pts
1. **England**	**8**	**26**	**24**
2. Croatia	9	14	17
3. Ukraine	8	8	15
4. Belarus	8	4	10
5. Kazakhstan	8	-13	6
6. Andorra	9	-30	0

"Sulzeer Jeremiah Campbell has left the club..."

23.09.09

"Sol is a tortured soul."
Kelly Hoppen (interior designer and ex-girlfriend of Sol Campbell)

As quick as that, it was over. Say hello and goodbye to the Notts County career of Sol *'bloody'* Campbell; laboured, lack lustre, off the pace, unfit and defeated. Granted, it could have been a different story on the day. But it wasn't.

We went behind midway through the first half when Morecambe's skipper Jim Bentley headed the opener for the home side. Until that moment, it had been bleak and that goal was only a sign of what had been on the cards. We may have had the presence of Sol in defence but we looked as vulnerable as we had in any other game witnessed in recent weeks.

Despite Ben Davies hitting a venomous volley early on, we had looked much more ordinary than the eight point gap between ourselves and them would have suggested after just seven league games.

After the break, another set-piece and another header meant Morecambe were 2-0 up and Notts were now playing catch-up. On 71 minutes Davies produced a moment of magic, turning on the edge of the box and driving a fine effort home to make it 2-1 but in the end, we were left relying on Kasper to come forward for a corner and nearly volley us level with a dramatic, late, bicycle kick. His shot went just over however and with it, our hopes of taking anything from the sea side were dashed.

And there you have it; another poor outing by Notts on the road. Come Saturday evening, the biggest question mark I had was about the lack of an impact Sol made at the back though.

"He looked off the pace" I heard one fan saying as we left the tin shed stand at full-time, still bewildered and confused by what we had seen.

Was Charlie under pressure to play him? He didn't look anywhere near fit enough and if anything, he came across as the weak link in the back-line. But the whole episode just made me left wondering what was going off.

When Notts signed Sol Campbell I am not sure, deep down, what I really expected. At a bare minimum, I expected he'd control the back four, marshal, talk and dictate his way through the games and be a stand-out marker for leadership and encouragement. None of that was evident though, albeit his first showing. For a man with supposed presence and ability, it was most concerning that twice we conceded headers from set-pieces. As with any new signing, time is needed (although he'd already had a fair share of that in order to get himself match sharp) but the performance was just not good enough.

So today? Yes I am shocked. As I took to my seat at work, I was none the wiser. Then *she* spoke.

"So what do you think of Sol. He loves Notts so much he's only played once."

If I am honest, I care very little for what she says on the game. She thinks Steven Gerrard is amazing because she fancies him and is about as clued up on the game as Andy Townsend. You see, this lass in my office likes to try and wind folk up on various subjects and I often seem to be a priority target. Should I care for what she tells me? Of course I shouldn't. But when I am in an irritable mood, I guess I let people get the better of me.

I feel slightly guilty for mentioning the fact that it was a *she* that said anything in the first place to be honest. There is another lass on the other side of the office who knows her stuff and is genuinely an avid fan, albeit of Spurs. But I can't stand people, female or otherwise, who try and pretend to know more about the game than they do. It's like those 'England' fans who suddenly appear during big tournaments and know nothing about the game. It just gets to me.

Her half-a-story does not draw me into talking however. I refuse to get into conversation and discuss the issue but instead log on to the BBC website and investigate for myself. There it is, aptly in black and white. Sulzeer Jeremiah Campbell has left the club by mutual consent. Not even a full month into his five-year, multi-million pound deal, he has backed out. Jumped ship or bottled it for want of a better phrase.

As I read on, I know there is going to be much more to come from this little story. Most of the footballing world was gobsmacked when he was confirmed as a Notts County man at the back end of August. I joined those in my surprise at the time. But now?

We have to put it all into context of course. Sol Campbell was, and is, regarded as a top flight player. Does he feel he has short changed himself? Maybe this is the case. Does he feel he has a chance to still make England's World Cup squad as has been suggested? I'd question this based on my own views but if he has the self-belief, again it is possible. Does he have a history of making odd decisions? Well the career notes would suggest so.

- Summer of 2001
  With his contract expiring, Sol Campbell is offered a lucrative deal to stay with Tottenham which will make him the highest paid player at the club. Sol confirms he will sign a new deal and states he would never sign for their local rivals Arsenal. As his deal expires, Sol Campbell leaves Spurs on a free transfer and turns up at none other than Arsenal. Spurs fans, understandably, hold this against him for the rest of time and in 2009, the Daily Mail declared Sol Campbell as football's biggest ever traitor in their 'Top 50' survey.
- February 2006
  Having had a nightmare 45 minutes at Highbury for Arsenal against West Ham, Sol fails to come back out after the break and instead goes home, not watching the rest of the match. Team-mate Robert Pires states that Sol had *"A big worry"* in his private life and despite training nine days later, Sol missed first team action for the ten weeks that followed.
- August 2006
  Sol Campbell signs for Portsmouth Football Club after having his deal terminated with Arsenal mutually so he can pursue a challenge abroad. Sol was said to have discussed a termination with Arsenal in order to try something new and it is believed that Turkey, and Fenerbache in particular, was to be his choice of destination. Arsenal boss Arsene Wenger is confused stating *"It is a big surprise to me because he cancelled his contract to go abroad. Have you [England] sold Portsmouth to a foreign country? No."*

For anyone not entirely sure at what I am getting at here, Sol Campbell has consistently made decisions that have both shocked and also perhaps been morally the wrong choice (in my view of course) given the circumstances on offer. So when he departed Portsmouth at the end of his contract, he had several options, so we are led to believe by the press.

Hull City was said to be one potential destination for Sol but it appeared every man and his dog turned down a move to Phil Brown's side during the summer. Also confirmed to be in the running were the other Magpies, Newcastle. Relegated last season from the Premier League, and trimming their squad down for life in the second tier, signing Sol on a big deal would have appeared a tad illogical considering what they were doing as a club. Despite this, apparently an offer was made but perhaps not with enough zero's to entice Sol up north to help the lads "*doon the toon*" to get back up to where they feel they belong.

So Sol was left with one or two options. Perhaps a limited selection but as soon as one Sven-Goran Eriksson made the phone call, surely it presented itself as the perfect solution? We were teased with the stories of his imminent arrival. We expected the name to be confirmed and we heard whispers on the old grapevine. However, it never happened as quickly as perhaps it should have, mainly due to the fact that he took some persuading as we've since learnt. When Sol did eventually put pen to paper though, who were we to question such a bold statement from a League Two side? Ultimately the biggest statement of intent from a side in the lowest division since...well since Sven himself joined.

What does the future hold now for Sol Campbell though? Well his character will come into question for one. I fully expect a whole host of former team mates to jump to his defence and tell us what a great guy he is and I am sure nobody within Notts will discredit him. Football is funny like that. Within the coming days I am sure Harry Redknapp and Arsene Wenger, to name just two managers, will tell us that Sol must have had his reasons and that he's a top guy. But do they really expect it to wash with the Notts fans that welcomed him aboard? What about the same Notts fans that did not moan when he took a prolonged period to get to match fit or those that had the name of the former England man on the back of their shirts?

Come the end of the day, it is announced that Notts County supposedly did not deliver on certain things Sol was promised. What exactly, I am sure we will learn in due course. However, it is the Notts fans that have been let down. Sol signed for five years last time I checked. He didn't even manage five weeks.

The FA state that Sol Campbell cannot sign for any other club until January due to his contract termination and on a personal level I feel minimal sympathy for him. If he did not want to be with us then I bid good riddance. I am sure, in due time, more will come from this little charade. Either Sol, or maybe the club, will be confirmed in the press as being in the wrong. For now though, I guess we will have to wait on that front.

The whole episode was all the more frustrating too after last week's victory over Northampton at home. Despite going behind early doors, we eventually hit Northampton for five with Matt Ritchie, bagging a brace in his first start for us and Lee Hughes grabbing a hat-trick to give us a 5-2 win.

Talk about taking one step forward and two steps back.

The talks down at the pubs where Notts fans drank were not entirely focused around Sol Campbell in the evenings that followed the loss at Morecambe however as a couple of us had began to read the odd article or two in recent weeks with regards to our new owners, Munto Finance.

It was perhaps naive to try and shut ourselves off from the tales that were set to creep into the press about Munto and, ultimately, the beneficiaries of Notts County Football Club. At the same time however, we are not in the business of looking too deeply into the management and day-to-day running of our football club either.

It appears the Football League are to delay announcing that Munto have been ratified as per the *'Fit and Proper Persons Test'* which has become all too common a test within these shores in recent years. If you need to do tests to check someone is legit, I am guessing there are enough characters that have fallen under suspicion to make such things a necessity.

Concerning for any of us willing to accept there may be a problem, we are aware that Leeds United have had ownership issues in recent times surrounding the ultimate beneficiaries behind the business vehicle Forward Sports Fund that owns their club. The website twohundredpercent.net reported how *"Leeds chairman Ken Bates doesn't know the 'ultimate beneficiaries' of Leeds' owners, Forward Sports Fund despite being their 'UK representative', to the extent that he pleaded it in court."*

If history has a tendency to repeat itself, it appears we have not had to wait long for a new club to have less than transparent owners taking over at the reigns. When former Chairman John Armstrong-Holmes initially announced the prospective takeover at Meadow Lane, he categorically refused to tell us who it was taking over at the helm. If these stories continue to seep through the woodwork, I imagine there will be a few fans that start to demand such information though.

The Football League announced that ratification was unlikely to be announced until October 8th 2009 when the board next meets. Until then, we will nervously wait.

Coca Cola League Two Table:

	Pld	+/-	Pts
1. Bournemouth	8	9	21
2. Dagenham & Redbridge	8	10	19
3. Rotherham United	8	6	17
4. Barnet	8	5	15
5. Aldershot Town	8	4	14
6. Rochdale	8	4	14
7. Shrewsbury Town	8	2	14
8. Notts County	**8**	**12**	**13**

Three and Easy

Given the fact that last time we had had an evening kick-off away at a local rival the car packed in and Jade and I argued for much of the evening, I decided not to suggest Lincoln away tonight. I felt it was perhaps best to not even propose, joke or hint at me and her making the short journey to Lincolnshire for a game against an Imps side that are set for a tough season.

The fact that we'd lost three away games on the bounce would not have strengthened my argument and nor would the fact that *"they'll be up for it"* given the fact that former England, Chelsea and Blackburn striker Chris Sutton has recently taken over.

So I am kind enough to pass on the opportunity for Jade and I to travel across the Lincolnshire border on a mild Tuesday night. Instead I go alone. She won't mind though. She won't even know if I can blag a lift back before she finishes work.

Despite the losses at Chesterfield, Barnet and most recently Morecambe on the road, at home we have still been very much on fire. We put five past Northampton (another local-ish game) and then three past Port Vale either side of the Morecambe defeat meaning that other than the small blip against Burton Albion, we have been pretty untouchable on home soil.

Despite Sol Campbell's exit, a further addition was made yesterday in the form of Ade Akinbiyi on a free transfer, giving hope that we'll simply have too much in attack for most sides in League Two this season even if we may look Sol-less at the back. From the squad point of view, I am sure there will be a few more twists along the way this season but on the whole, we still look in good shape.

In football much can be said for the twelfth man and the impact the fans can have. Why else do people ask *"Where is it at?"* when you query who'll win tonight's game between Chelsea and Everton?
"I'd fancy an upset at Goodison but not at Stamford Bridge" many will say. It's the same the world over.

There are exceptions of course. Away from home, free from the pressure of a home crowd and an expectant stadium demanding you attack, players can play with less weight on their shoulders. Sometimes home fans that are simply waiting, wishing and willing the visitors to roll over and die can have an adverse effect. When an early goal does not come, or worse still you fall behind, a disgruntled home crowd can be just as damaging as a good home crowd can be encouraging.

Fortunately, tonight, we witness firsthand what an early away goal does to the home crowd. Silence. Deathly silence and dropped heads. That 'here we go again' feeling. The stark realisation that tonight is to be a long night. Not in our corner of the ground though.

I feel arms and bodies clambering up against me as we take the lead. My own jumps are confined to a tight small space and restricted by others pushing downwards as flailing arms reach across me and celebrate. There must only be fifteen seconds on the clock but we are one up already. We are one up and away from bloody home too.

Close to the pitch, and tightly pressed into a small corner of Sincil Bank, we are over the moon at the nature of the early break that's allowed Luke Rodgers to burst free and slot home from just inside the box. What's more, I literally got to my seat as a Mike Edwards header was launched forwards to set-up the goal. Talk about cutting it fine.

"One Luke Rodgers, there's only one Luke Rodger!..." sing I and at least a thousand or so more as the forward wheels away after netting his first of the season. "Walking along, singing a song, walking in a Rodgers wonderland."

I should have been here with time to spare but arriving on queue in such fashion? Well I can't see how I could have topped my entrance.

It is going back some years now since I visited Lincoln and my memories of it are somewhat clouded. Perhaps I did not have many a memorable game here or maybe I just did not visit as much as my dad and I speculated the other night when talking about it on the phone.

The Notts fans are certainly intending to make this one last in the memory as our end is in full voice and only getting louder and prouder with each passing moment. We look composed and in control on the park. In the stands our noise fills the darkening Lincolnshire skies as the City fans sit back and watch their side chase shadows. It is not a pastime anyone enjoys when your side are being made to look inferior. It's like men against boys.

I'm on my feet again and I've hardly had a chance to catch my breath. We sing and turn and we point at the Lincoln lot. We taunt them and they try and stir a song or two but cannot muster the numbers needed to outdo the travelling band of merry men (and women) from Nottingham.

We continue to celebrate our lead and then we celebrate our keeper, Kasper Schmeichel. In his all yellow keeper kit, he stands out in the distance starting moves and dictating play from the back. For the first time ever, I think I am watching a play-making goalkeeper but little is asked of him in the early exchanges and we do not pause to sit, although there isn't really choice in the matter. It's a case of stand up tall, which at 5ft6 I struggle to do, or miss the action.

Mike Edwards, over in the far corner, switches play to Brendan Moloney via our skipper John Thompson. Moloney searches for Hughes in an advanced roll and those standing up around me anticipate some action up our end. The continuous clattering of chairs folding upon themselves bangs around us as the few that are standing already are joined by the rest. Hughes seems to miss the ball though, instead dummying the pass and allowing it to run through to Rodgers. Call it carbon copy, call it well executed and call it route one. Anyway you call it we're 2-0 up and again I am being drowned in arms and bodies and I celebrate with jubilant Magpies in the away end.

Rodgers found himself in acres and he slotted home cool, calm and crisply despite the desperate lunge from the defender. The ground is surreal with so much movement, energy and a huge release of tension from such a small quarter. The rest of Sincil Bank motionless, lacking spark and seemingly left for dead.

"*We are going up, say we are going up...*" cry our visiting section.

All my frustrations from Barnet and Morecambe along with that empty memory of Chesterfield from the motorway fade to the back of my mind. There is something about having hope that enables you to get by from week-to-week when following your club. Despite one loss, you know you can right the wrongs next time around. Two losses and you all know you have further time to put things right. Your brain works over time.

Maths lessons come into practise in the real world, tallying up how many more points can be dropped based on those who were promoted last season. You focus in on how many points you are off the top and, given the fact you know you can beat them home and away, how many points you could theoretically be ahead of them following that said six points. It is all if's and buts'. As the table stands or how it'd be if you excluded goals in injury time or where you will be once everyone has played each other once? It's all pure speculation that keeps us going on those long, drawn out, boring days we call non-match days.

No speculating tonight though. No clocking up the points in the head and working out the best or worst case scenarios this evening. There is no need as we are two goals to the good away at a local rival and we look strong and compact all over the park, oozing professionalism and focus. Surely we are set for three big points.

The Notts following remains on-song and almost feverish in its vocal support. The best following I can remember since...well just the best following I can remember.

Despite the love for games at Meadow Lane and the positives that a home game brings, as a fan you cannot beat a real good game on the road. You feel like you belong. You wink and nod and speak with faces you recognise. You share jokes, sit and sup a pint in pubs and give views on the new boy up front and the manager's latest decisions.

At home, it does not happen to the same extent. Perhaps it is something to do with being in the minority or the siege mentality of being on someone else's patch. I can only dream of how it must feel to be in a small away following that wins at somewhere such as Old Trafford. I love the underdog feeling when you are outnumbered by home fans. When you are outnumbered on their turf in unfamiliar surroundings and enclosed in the smallest area of the ground with police all around you despite the behaviour being impeccable.

But we like to taunt. Who doesn't? So we tell them straight.

'We are going up! Say we are going up!" and the songs continue. We bounce on our feet and cheer as Rodgers' name is released over the speaker system.

Come 45 minutes and finally, after what felt like four hours, I get chance to breathe and rest. My heart pounding and adrenaline pumping through my veins, I am in a fantastic mood and for once it is away from home.

Half time, for anyone who is not a regular down at their local club, is like pausing life. For fifteen minutes you are not immature, excitable, aggressive, nervous, arrogant, brimming, deflated, antagonising or the loudest individual in the local post code area. For fifteen minutes you just rest and reflect. You sit back, watch the half time entertainment pass you by, read your programme and listen out for the other scores around the country.

Maybe a beer, maybe a pie or maybe a piss. If you are quick enough or lucky enough to plan your time, you may manage all three. Tonight I just sit down because I am shattered though. A long, arduous journey here by train and it'll be a fairly long one back too unless I can find a mate who I know is here tonight and lives a short drive from me.

At 2-0 though, this game is not finished just yet. We need to come out and kill this game off and it is a sentiment I share with some young lads sat behind me who spent part of the first half on my back. They appear to be what I have come to know merely as 'chavs' these days. Twenty years ago they would have been considered as stereotypical, young, hooligans just by their dress sense and hair and wrongly so. Nowadays, with hooliganism documented far less than before, they are just young lads who I'd be unlikely to talk to in the street or down the pub. But they are nice enough lad's none-the-less and they probably think I am just some hippy guy with my mop-top hair and winkle-picker shoes (if they know what the terms even mean). In a packed stand, men and women from all walks of life and with contrasting backgrounds and histories all mix on a level playing field however.

As the two I am speaking with are joined by a third with a pie, I receive endless apologies for the over-zealous nature of his celebrations in his young, Nottingham accent that I must listen to intently in order to understand.

"Don't be soft. I'd have done the same to him in front had you not been stopping me" I say pointing at a frail old chap in front. I'm joking of course although by the way the old boy reacted, he'd have not cared either.

The second half is a tight encounter. It starts off tight and changes very little as the big hand on my watch ticks closer towards the three points we must earn tonight.

Jimmy Greaves may have said it was a game of two halves but my word, did that statement not do enough to demonstrate the case tonight. Jubilant, buoyant, loud and rapturous in the opening 45 minutes, now we appear to encompass the opposite characteristics. We sit back, quiet, nervous, patient and drained of vocal support. We make a go of it once in a while (the three youngsters behind me trying more than once to instigate a rendition of *"This City is ours, this City is ours...."* but it just doesn't happen for whatever reason.

If anything, Lincoln are the most likely side to score as the game enters the final stages. Kasper's right hand post receives a thud from a Shane Clarke pile driver and in doing so we begin to become more agitated and quiet with a further 20 minutes still left on the clock.

Other than Clarke's strike though, Lincoln's efforts do not test Notts too much. We look as though we are hard to break down. Much more so than we were in previous away games too which is pleasing and so far, no schoolboy errors have arisen that have literally gifted sides the points in the three games on the road that preceded this one.

"Not long now" says one of the lads as we are standing in the final moments. The Wheelbarrow song is raised from the away corner and the black and white shirts on show are comforting. They make you feel like you are at home.

We are in the dying moments now and despite being a distance away from home, it feels great to be here, at their gaff, taking all three points.

"We are going up..." we sing as a high ball is taken down by Ravenhill with a deft touch. *"Say we are going up..."* as he loops the ball back towards goal and into the mixer.

"Gamble on it!" I shout, hoping Hughes finds himself with the ball in the box. Away at the far end of the ground, a crowded area leaves us confused and grasping for a clear sight. The ball breaks away from Hughes who turns and appeals at the referee but as it breaks, we rise, jump and....yes it's there! We scream and shout and laugh and bloody well love this feeling! Little Luke Rodgers has pounced on the loose ball to grab his third of the night, Notts' third of the night and a goal that makes it three points on the night.

Sharing the joy with strangers and smiling with random people the young lads jumping on my back are declaring their love for Rodgers now and they look ecstatic. Then, out of the corner of my eye, I see my mate dancing around on the stairs towards the exit and I know my night has just gone from fantastic to perfect as he spots me and shouts me over to see if I want a lift back to Loughborough. Absolutely.

It's an interesting journey home, to say the least, mainly because for the first time I am listening rather closely to someone else's views on the whole thing so far. My assessment to date is frustrated but satisfied I guess. Indeed it would have been nice to get a few more points on the road but it is at home where good foundations are laid and from there we can then build. And it is at home that Notts have been faultless.

"Charlie hasn't got a clue" explains my mate. *"Game after game we are left losing a little more ground on the others at the top."*

I must say, it comes as a shock that someone is so blunt about the whole thing given the fact we sit just five points off the top and have netted a handful of goals more than anyone else in the country.

"Too many draws you see" continues my driver as we press on into the dark, late night sky. A negative view perhaps given tonight's 3-0 mauling of Lincoln City.

From above, the whispers are that Charlie will be given time, at least for now. He was the man the new owners saw fit to support when the takeover took place so it would seem somewhat rash to go making changes now, especially after such a commanding win on the road. Only last week, Peter Trembling spoke to the BBC with regards to how Charlie's position was under constant review however:

Of course we've got to review all the time whether he's the right man for the long-term job. He's under pressure; we spent a lot of money so it goes with the territory.

We are under the spotlight. We haven't started in the best possible way but sometimes it takes a while for things to gel.

"Perhaps he is on borrowed time but as long as we win games like that, he'll be fine" I say to my mate as we head down the motorway sitting sixth in the table after ten games. *"I guess it's a game at a time for Munto though"* knowing October will prove to be a very telling month in the calendar with five games and a trip to promotion chasing Rotherham in the middle.

As we arrive back in Loughborough it is smiles all round though as I notice that Jade's car is not in the drive. It means I have managed to get away for the night to support my club, spent a fair amount of cash (which she'd suggest was a waste), return home without her even realising I've been gone and what's more, it is the first win on the road in six weeks. Away games can be horrid affairs when they don't go according to plan. I tell you now though; they are bloody terrific when they do.

Coca Cola League Two Table:

	Pld	+/-	Pts
1. Bournemouth	10	9	24
2. Rochdale	10	9	20
3. Dagenham & Redbridge	10	8	20
---	---	---	---
4. Rotherham United	10	7	20
5. Shrewsbury Town	10	6	20
6. Notts County	**10**	**17**	**19**
7. Aldershot Town	10	7	18

Trial by the Media

I read that some fans were dubbing this as the biggest day in the club's history. The Football League were set ratify the club's takeover. Ratification for Munto Finance, the investors, the board, the money and the entire kitchen sink.

The whole situation has been dragged backwards through a hedge in recent weeks by the media and if truth be told, many Notts fans have been both tired and angry about the whole episode. I find myself somewhere in the middle however. I feel somewhat lost in the columns, articles, pages and internet message board threads in recent weeks and trying to make any sense of any of it is like trying to finish a jigsaw made up of half of Meadow Lane and half of that other great Nottinghamshire sports ground; Trent Bridge.

It appears that the press (and certain areas more than others) are circling like vultures waiting for a timely collapse of 'The Project' as it has been dubbed by Sven and the board. Rival fans that were gutted two months ago now sense something else on the horizon and if truth be told, since Sol walked out, the press has not been great for the club.

The ever-increasing influence that the press has within the game is as prominent as a big-money flop at St James Park these days. Once the press gains momentum on a story, very little seems capable of stopping it and in turn, it can be the reasoning behind fans agony and despair.

I have managed to Sky+ both BBC East Midlands Today and Central News on ITV each and every day in recent weeks. I do so in the hope that any news that does not filter through to me during the day will be caught at tea time. I am spending an unhealthy amount of hours sat up watching Sky Sports News or reading posts from 'plympie' or 'muntopie' whilst browsing the Notts County forums and I know just as well as Jade does that it is doing nothing for my health or relationship.

"If you are not down at Notts, you are reading about them."

Very true is her statement I hasten to add but I do not agree with her. That's like admitting you have a problem. I don't have a problem. I simply have a hobby. Maybe more of a passion? But I don't have a problem. Honest. Really I don't. I insist.

When it finally hit home that I would never play professional football (The penny did not drop early enough given my steady but limited ability), I found myself new hopes and ambitions. Those ambitions led to a dream that I'd one day be a football writer. Not a journalist but a writer. I think there is a clear distinction between the two.

Whether it was newspapers, magazines, fanzines, programmes or books, I spent much of my teenage years taking in as much information as humanly possible. During the period from 1995 to around 1998, I had reached a level of understanding and knowledge about the game that I could recite all 92 Football League club's in alphabetical order at a fair speed. In the top flight, I could name all twenty clubs squad's (including position, squad number and approximate age) and as a season wore on, I'd be able to back track to any evening during the campaign to tell you the score between Newcastle United and Coventry City, who scored the goals and in what order. It was like my brain had become a sponge for anything related to the game (coincidentally, I was single throughout school).

I also wish to add that facts do not instantly mean knowledge or understanding. Just because I could recite all the finer details, it did not give me instant awareness about the game. But this was also something I had always made a point of developing even from a young age. I don't simply see a game with goals but I always see patterns in play and the smaller details that coaches may have worked on behind the scenes during the week before a big game. I ended up managing for the first time at the youthful age of fifteen and officially took over a club just a few years later. I just continued to absorb as much as I could, eventually going on to do first my FA Level One coaching badge (basically how to set up cones) before taking my Level Two a few years later.

I was forever writing reports on games or articles on players and I remember earning the place of *'first letter'* on the letters page of the Nottingham Evening Post back in 1996 explaining why the City Ground was chosen to host games for the forthcoming Euro '96 tournament based on the proximity of the ground, the facilities on offer and the ethos of the FA sharing games around the country and that it was not based in any way, shape or form, on the grounds tenants being amongst footballs elite. For a fourteen-year-old, it perhaps came across as quite sad.

I educated myself further with Friday nights sat with my dad watching Match of The Seventies (The seventies are to football what the sixties were to music for me) whilst A Question of Sport with Bill Beaumont and Ian Botham was enjoyed from an age when most of my mates were busy banging about with toys and making a mess of their mum's new carpet.

Fast forward a few years on and the routine had not changed. I may have swapped A Question of Sport for some Sky Sports show and I may have been reading Total Football instead of Match magazine but I was still the same. Still hungry for more details, information and football knowledge.

At school I was nicknamed Statto after the Fantasy Football TV shows factual bible of a bloke whilst I was touted as the *"most likely to become a Manager"* (which I did) and *"least likely to find a girlfriend"* (which I didn't). Whilst my mates were out on the local parks drinking cider, trying cigarettes and finding their way around a girl's bra strap for the first time in their mid-teens, I was sat at home writing reports for the Fantasy Football League I ran at school (I made an absolute killing one year with over 40 lads in my year taking part including one of the teachers), or watching re-runs of The Greatest Ever Goals or The George Best Story.

When rumours were amidst for the first time that a girl was pregnant in my academic year, I did not bat an eyelid for I had no understanding on how it could have happened. Who'd want to mess about doing things like that when there was Championship Manager (The cause of death for my own Fantasy League business) to play at home and a garden complete with homemade goal posts and net, in which I was able to hone my skills against my younger brother Kieran?

Many years later, my dad would suggest I was eventually over-saturated by football.

"We're spoilt nowadays on TV. How many games are actually any good?" is his view. I believe it is a little pessimistic really. If every game played between Liverpool and Newcastle was 4-3 (My word those were two amazing games), then that is when we'd become ultimately bored and spoilt. For every seven-goal thriller, there are 1-0 scrapes and for all the build-up in the world, the media cannot change that.

I am the sort of person that can say *"that was a decent 0-0."* Not many people can. Why does a ball crossing a line as opposed to be tipped over the bar make it technically a better game? It doesn't. Missed chances can make a game just as exciting as can solid defensive displays (Although I can see why some people disagree).

So for me, my footballing intake through the media has always been a huge part of my football enjoyment. It is only now, with Notts County in the mire so to speak, that I dislike the media-in-general.

Is it a dislike of the media or is it that I dislike what they say? Maybe it is a combination of the two. Perhaps once the truth is out with regards to our owners I will sit at ease more and read news articles with a laugh and a joke but whilst everything is in the balance, including my day-to-day happiness, I will reserve judgement.

I cannot help but find myself being agitated by something that I always wanted to, and still do in some respects, be a part of. My misery is caused by hacks that are doing their job. They have a role within their companies to report news and people such as Matt Scott at The Guardian have been doing just that. Some say he has an agenda against our club. Some say he is stirring things up. I'd like to think that anyone wishing to have a career that is sustainable, credible and fruitful will attempt to write in an open, frank and honest manner however.

Scott's revelations in the last few weeks have been directed more at the ownership and the faces behind the scenes more than Sven, Hughes and the Meadow Lane crowds. Unfortunately (in some ways), Notts County is now an attractive source of conversation which in turn has meant that Scott, along with writers at The Sun, The Mirror and The Mail have felt a need to have their two-penneth worth. It neither means they are right or wrong at the moment though does it?

Nathan and Peter Willett, two names we know to be involved with the Munto, are subject to several aspersions from Scott in his Guardian columns. The main person to feel the force of his questions and probing though is Russell King, supposedly not involved with the club any longer but someone who was acting as an advisor for Munto when seeking to purchase the club.

Understandably, the Football League want some clarity to this because the chap has had question marks made against his character in the past. Also under scrutiny is the nature of Sol Campbell's arrival and then departure and also the type of deal he was supposedly tied to whilst a Notts player. Scott has suggested that the contract he had, partly with what he claims to be a third party company, had not been within Football League rules. So again it is a cause for concern.

Today was to be the day we gave a sigh of relief and asked ourselves what all the panic was for though. Either that or we would be refused the seal of approval from the Football League and we would learn of our alternative fate.

Come the close of play, we had received neither judgement. Late in the evening, Notts announced that discussions are on-going and that further information has been requested by the league. Notts fans call the local phone-in and are angry, bemused and angry further still. They see it as a vendetta against the club. Uncle Colin (Slater) on BBC Radio Nottingham tries to calm fans down. He tries to reiterate that the hierarchy are encouraged by the progress and we are left non-the-wiser.

An official club statement read:

> *We welcome and are encouraged by the Football League's response regarding the further information we have submitted to them. We wish to reiterate that we have been happy to comply fully at all times with all requests which have been made by the League in relation to these matters. In terms of the final additional outstanding issues mentioned by the League today, these are receiving our immediate attention. All Notts fans, we are sure, will be delighted to hear that the League is looking to conclude these matters in the near future.*

None of this would have happened in the Seventies now would it? I bloody well hate the media.

Poor Old Torquay

Notts County v Torquay United
Meadow Lane / League Two / 11.10.09

Back down the Lane after what feels like a long term sentence away. However, the whole theory of only going to a few games is starting to disappear out the back door so my weekly fix has not been too bad. I went down to the Bradford game on the opening day with the view of perhaps going to a fair few games when I could. Fast forward to the start of October and one evening this week was spent with Jade and I arguing because I'd mentioned that any plans for Boxing Day this coming Christmas would have to take into account my trip to Notts County v Grimsby Town at Meadow Lane.

Personally, I feel this to be a perfectly reasonable request from me, a reasonable and well balanced young man. My partner disagrees and an off the cuff comment is made with regards to my addiction to football being well and truly back.

Sean has missed the last few games and due to this, I decided to go Lincoln away all on my own having originally penned it in as an away day trip with the lads. Following Lincoln, we felt a little robbed four days later when a late goal from Elvis Hammond denied us all three points at Cheltenham after Rodgers had given us the lead with his fourth in two games. Less worryingly, we then saw defeat in the Johnstone's Paint Trophy after we lost on penalties following a 2-2 draw away at Bradford with Craig Westcarr and Delroy Facey both scoring during normal time.

Upon Sean's return from Cyprus, he is buzzing to get back down Notts though. So this week will see Torquay in front of the Sky cameras and then a trip to Rotherham who I hear have a soul-less ground with a half decent side. It'll be one of the League Two games of the week that is for sure, so the next seven days is set to hold a fair amount of twists and turns.

Also joining us down Meadow Lane today is band mate and CSKA midfielder Paul. He decided spur of the minute to join us earlier today after we lost a 2-0 advantage which meant CSKA drew a game that was in the bag and thus missing out on top spot in our league.

Today's game is live on the box and it is a Sunday evening but the lads were happy to pay £20 for our tickets and make an afternoon and an evening out of it. You have to sometimes don't you? It was hoped that today would be a bit of a party day. We had hoped the Football League would have given our new owners the green light and ratification by now. We had hoped that the club would have slashed prices to try and entice fans in for the cameras and stop them being armchair fans who, after all, could watch it for free in the comfort of their homes or local pubs.

Notts have opted against this however, in turn causing some concern that the Sky viewing public might see a half empty ground. To make up for this, the club have given some 5,000 tickets to schools and colleges and this is all well and good but it does not really benefit the fans of who have been coming for each game so far this season. Beyond that you have the fans that have loyally been down for years on end. It would have been a nice gesture. Unfortunately, such gestures do not exist in football all too often.

I guess that with Notts County being where they are though, the free tickets to the schools could be, in the long term, a good investment. As any fan from the other side of the river will bore you with the details, the Reds have the bigger divide of the Nottingham paying public these days when it comes to attendances although it wasn't always the way. Come May however, with a big promotion push and a few extra new comers, there is no reason why Notts could not be hitting 10,000 per week. It is hardly a massive void for us to make up on our rivals from the other side of the Trent.

So with numerous kiddies being encouraged to come down to Meadow Lane, many maybe for the first time, hopefully the club will make one or two new addicts for the coming years. Children are the future and all that palaver.

The real burning issue remains the clubs ownership at present though and it is something that none of us fans can deny. It's a tale that has begun to create tension in the stands, stories in the papers and some hatred from our opponents who already hated us because of the takeover happening in the first place. The fact that rumours now suggest the company (or rather its owners) may not be legitimate business people, appears to have heightened the anti-Notts movement.

The club continuously tell us on the local radio phone-in that we need not worry. Peter Trembling, our Chief Executive and the mouth piece for Munto Finance, seems confident that all issues are set to be resolved and it is merely a matter of time until the necessary checks are complete and we can get back to worrying about the next home game rather than the next tabloid expose.

On the pitch? Well the added incentive for this Sunday evening Sky date we have with Torquay is the fact that our rivals in and around us at the top have all played so we know exactly where we will stand come the close of play should we pick up the three points as expected. That said, nothing at this level is a given right as Hereford proved last week taking points off Bournemouth. Sometimes the lower clubs will conjure up a surprise or two.

To my delight, at the eleventh hour, an offer is made to me and my fellow match goers by a kind chap by the name of Ian who has come by some extra tickets. He doesn't have to, but he offers me the tickets for free. It is the kind of gesture that reminds me that Notts is a family club. A community sort of club. One looks out for one another and vice versa.

It is a strange atmosphere come kick-off though. A few beers, grab a programme and a scan of the names. The cold begins to set in and winter is upon us. I notice as much as my feet feel the cold. Rewind just a few weeks and it was seemingly hot summer days against Bradford and Dagenham. But they are long gone now. Winter is well and truly on its way.

As we take to our seats, the Torquay lot sit, quiet and alone. They have, understandably, only brought a small handful of travelling supporters. They are the real hardcore, ardent fans. They have come 230 miles for four or more hours on the road to see their side, currently without a win in six games. They are hardcore all right. Their efforts are a real measure of passion. Tell them it is only a game. Tell them they are fair-weather fans. Tell them their team are awful. Would they listen? Would they hell as like.

As a full-to-the-rafters Kop Stand erupts, singing in full bloom whilst Torquay seem jaded. They are over in the shadows and looking very, very lonely. Even their clever little songs about Notts fans not being here when we were shit would not be heard today. Even the banter will be missing this evening. The Notts faithful let their voices ring out. The Wheelbarrow song echoes around this stadium. We may have had to wait an extra day this week for match day, but now it is here we are delighted.

"Come on you Pies" they sing. *"Come on you Pies!"*

Sven-Goran Eriksson is given a song as is the hero of the moment Mr Peter Trembling who appears to be fighting off the media accusations single handedly.

"One Peter Trembling, there's only one Peter Trembling!"

Thank the heavens that he is ours think most fans as he continues to deflect attention away from all that is apparently going off behind the scenes. As the sides walk out, the cameras pan across our faces. The fans rise and the raptures are lifted. And poor lonely Torquay sit, apparently waiting for what the rest believe to be inevitable.

Charlie McParland has sprung a surprise or two today. The fans sing his name and he gives them a waves. He does not milk it though. He never does milk the chants does Charlie. Tommy Johnson takes his seat on the bench alongside him, the teams do the pleasantries and the Sky cameras are beaming the images all over the country and beyond. Notts finally get the chance to show Mr Joe Public just what is happening here in middle England. Here on the banks of the better side of the Trent.

Luke Rodgers is again given the nod ahead of Karl Hawley and rightfully so. He's bagged a few goals of late and is now a man with confidence. He has fire in his belly and looks ready to go. Craig Westcarr is given a rare outing on the right flank with several forced changes to the side that played here at Meadow Lane last. Moloney is away on Under 21 duty and Johnnie Jackson has a slight knock. But this is Torquay. Six games without a win. Six games without so much as a victory to cheer. There is only one club below them in the whole of England's professional game. Time for Notts to show everyone just what is happening perhaps?

The game starts lively. Ball down on the deck. Slick passes and neat interchanges. The grass looks good, the surface sublime. Charlie has Notts playing with an intention to do the surface justice. Kasper builds from the back as young Daniel Jones, on loan from Wolves, is getting forward at each opportunity from left back.

"*Come on you Pies, come on you Pies!*" sing the Kop as attacks build. Ritchie and Davies are the men at the middle of most things good. There is only one side out there this evening and only one side in the running. The boys in black and white are in fine form.

Notts break again and again. Ritchie and Jones work in unison down the left stretching Torquay. Stretching their side and pulling them apart. Poor Torquay with one man alone up top and waiting for a ball that never arrives. It's one-way traffic here in front of us and Notts do not appear to be letting up. Then a deep cross to the main man Hughes. He rises well and picks his spot. He arches his neck back in order to gain purchase that connects.

"*What a save!*" I imagine the Sky man in the gantry proclaiming as Hughes' powerful header meets perfectly with Michael Poke's gloves in the opposition net.

Notts are in full swing by now though. Surely the wait will not last too long. Notts break with pace once more. Poor old Torquay with their run of defeats, their lonely figure up top and a handful of fans watching on. Poor old Torquay.

The passion and adrenaline from the Kop is now in full force. Trembling is again credited as being of the *one* variety. He waves to the fans as does Sven. Sven raises a hand from way up high in the Pavis Stand. Down on the touchline, the ever-so-different manager raises a gratuitous hand for his own song.

"Charlie, giz a wave, Charlie, Charlie giz a wave".

The Kop inspire Notts. The Kop encourages. Notts attack in numbers and in style. The ball is crossed and a Torquay head meets the flight but it is not a solid clearance however and ready to pounce is Craig Westcarr arriving on the edge of the box. Purposeful and composed, Westcarr opens his body and places the ball into the top right corner. The net bulges and the fans all rise to their feet. The release is there and with only twelve minutes showing on the near-defunct score board, the Magpies are once again flying high at home. I turn to Sean and Paul and we jump and cheer. What a way to show the rest of the country I think. What a performance so far.

Notts continue in the same manner. Overlaps, interchanges, neat passes and tidy moves. Hughes looks hungry for a goal whilst Luke Rodgers is working hard and creating space and openings. Kasper Schmeichel continues to yell orders as with previous games but in fairness, he is called upon to do very little.

Notts have plenty of footballers in this side. An obvious statement which is all too often not true at not only this, but many levels of football. Did Wimbledon have many *footballers* in their side back in the nineties? Did a pre-Wenger Arsenal have many *footballers* amongst their back four? This Notts side has enough to cover the two teams today.

The waves of black and white continue to stem forward, probing and searching for a second goal. Ben Davies looks one way, looks another, picks a pass and finds a space. He dictates the play from the middle of the park, a role which, until today, he had been absent from as he has been asked to play wide. But today he is proving his value from the centre of the park. Showing what he is made of. Raising his stock so to speak. Jones and Ritchie do the same working together down the flank with their partnership forming, and being nurtured by one another.

Ricky Ravenhill pops up on the edge of the box to win a tackle and is felled.

"Fucking disgusting" scream the fans as the offending Torquay man comes to his feet. The referee stands, almost apologetic in having to award the free-kick. The anticipation levels increase. Half hour or so on

the dusty old scoreboard. A good time to double the lead we think. Show the cameras and the country what we're all about. Ben Davies steps up, angles his body and exhales breaths of confidence. He approaches, he leans and he whips at the ball, curling it and watching on as the ball glides over the Torquay wall and into the top corner. What a strike! What a finish! What a player!

It is 2-0 to the Magpies and my word does he look like he enjoyed that. He runs Kop-wards, around the back of Poke's goal and sprints along the front of the stand and joined by his team mates.

"Come on you Pies" indeed.

The ground is buzzing now. The fans are in a buoyant mood and understandably so. Within two points of the leaders once we can seal the three points here against poor Torquay. The foot is released off the gas now. Notts slow the game down and maintain their ethos. Charlie continues to bark, players warm-up on the sideline and those out there in the shirts are doing the fans proud.

A few minutes until the break and all around me look towards the time. They begin to slowly wander to bars below us. Off for food, drink and a half-time chat. Check the goals on the monitors and see how classy that Ben Davies strike was.

Torquay force the issue for the first time though. Breaking down the left, a ball is drilled at pace and Davies protects his face. The referee does not agree though and handball is given. Notts must stay focused. Nothing stupid now please. Let's see the half out. The defence ready themselves and Kasper orders them about. The hands go up from the Torquay kick taker and the delivery is good. It is not the greatest but it does enough to suggest there is a sniff. Thompson misjudges whilst Edwards just doesn't judge at all and in nips Ellis to prod home from close range. Kasper is furious and rightfully so. Should he have claimed it? Perhaps. Should Thompson and Edwards have dealt with it? Certainly. Either way it is 2-1 going into the break. Silly Notts concede against poor Torquay who are not so poor now.

Down under the stand and the drinks are in as replays are shown. Davies' free-kick was of the highest regard and fans give a half hearted cheer as the replays shows the ball hit the back of the net. Peter Beagrie and Neil Warnock in the studio share their eternal wisdom but we all know Notts must focus now. They must get back in control of the game. The stand above gives off thunderous sounds as the fans make their way back up. Beer only just received in my hand, there is a rush on now. I leave my drink and head back up leaving Sean and Paul to it.

Up the steps and into the darkness. Within the last fifteen minutes the skies have darkened and the cold weather has laid its mark even more. It'll only get worse from here until the winter now. Cold football nights. Dark, cold football nights that will need to be lit up. But the lights don't come and suddenly Torquay have more hunger. Their last six games on the spin mean very little now. This game is all about confidence and suddenly they have it. Their handful of travelling fans start to sing a bit more and as they grow in confidence, the Kop becomes a quieter, more subdued place to be.

Charlie screams, balls are lost and possession turns over all too quickly for a side that are looking to go just two points off the top.

"Come on Notts, get a grip!" shouts a disgruntled fan and I hear his fears. So too do those around me. No longer anticipating a rout, a win will be gratefully received by one and all but it is our visitors who look most likely to increase their tally.

A break on 55 minutes and there is sloppy defending and desperation in the ranks for Notts. A block and an appeal from the Torquay lads in the area but this time the referee waves away penalty claims. Notts are on the knife edge now though and we can't keep living like this. We need to kill them off.

Balls spread from side to side as Ritchie and Jones continue to get forward and Ben Davies tries to dictate the tempo. It all comes a lot harder now though. Much more of a game on our hands and the fans sense it. Torquay sense it too as does a nervous Charlie McParland. Will changes be made? Activity on the touchline seems nondescript.

From somewhere Notts need more impetus and fight. More composure all round. But they do not find it and they continue to let the boys in yellow ebb their way into what is now a well balanced game of football. No longer showing the Sky cameras what we are all about are we? No longer making the mark we had hoped for. It was glorious football for 43 minutes but nervous and edgy ever since.

I, like the whole of the home support, sit much quieter now. No longer singing every song and smiling and laughing, we all sense the inevitable being, well inevitable. Karl Hawley is introduced in place of Rodgers but it will do little to change the way of the game. The pattern will remain and Notts' style will continue. But Charlie knows best. We must trust him. Not get on his back. Torquay are breaking up the play all-to-easy now though.

As time is ticking, Torquay force the issue and another set-piece goes their way. A deep, deep ball into our half and deeper still into Kasper's area, we see a knock down by Hargreaves across to Mark Ellis. There is a scramble in the box. An almighty scramble. It causes havoc for our defenders and as Ellis turns on the ball, Notts are looking like a desperate group as they get across to try and block. Tim Sills arrives late in the box and makes a poor connection but poor connections are unreadable. And so there it is. It is 2-2. What a blow. What a way to give away such a lead.

The fans are not happy now. Westcarr is removed but again the change is like-for-like. Matty Hamshaw comes off the bench to play wide right and the shape of the side remains. Can he conjure anything? Can he deliver a telling contribution? Torquay break again though and a chance at the back post causes further panic in our ranks. It is widespread panic all over Meadow Lane now. What has happened? What are we doing?

Notts hit back and try and press the boys in yellow. Notts huff and puff and try to blow down the Torquay backline but they stand strong and tall. Ritchie fires an effort high and wide which troubles Michael Poke none whatsoever. Notts are no longer in their stride. They are holding on as much as Torquay now. Jones suddenly appears uncomfortable on the ball as possession becomes loose and passes are lacking. A point appears to be a destined reward now.

One last chance surely? Davies creates again, feigning a shot and finding Hawley. The ball is blocked but only as far as that man Hughes. He readies himself, looks up and drives an effort at goal. Poke is equal again though as his gloves nip the ball over the bar. It just won't come but Notts won't give up. Hamshaw finds Davies in space and with time. He looks up, puts plenty of whip and pace on the ball and the height is perfect. Hawley rises, Hawley glances and Hawley agonises as he crashes the ball against the foot of the post and another chance goes begging. A let off for the Torquay boys but they'll argue that they deserve it now.

Notts are falling short at the very last. So close yet so far. I was on my feet. I was raising my arms and ready to celebrate.

"I thought that was in" says Paul.

I could have sworn the ball was in the back of the net too but it wasn't to be. Two points dropped. Two points now gone and never to return. Poor, little Torquay. Not so poor with an unexpected point in their locker now though are they.

The fans boo. The fans give little in terms of appreciation. The full-time whistle spreads around the ground like a bitter taste you fail to get rid of. It will be a long trip home for that small group of Torquay fans. It'll seem even longer for me.

Coca Cola League Two Table:

	Pld	+/-	Pts
1. Bournemouth	12	8	25
2. Dagenham & Redbridge	12	10	24
3. Rotherham United	12	8	24
--			
4. Rochdale	12	9	23
5. Notts County	**12**	**17**	**21**
6. Aldershot Town	12	9	21
7. Barnet	12	6	21

"Charlie Out, Charlie Out"

It is the day after the disappointing evening before. So Notts are not top of the table and nor are they within two points of the leaders but the Pies are still up there at the business end of the division. However, today is another day for the rumours to circulate. By midday, the word on the street is Charlie may not see the day out as Notts boss.

Despite this, it is taken with a pinch of salt. After all, McParland has fought off such rumours for many weeks now. He has had the wolves at the door so to speak since day one of the investment arriving at the club. For the second time this season Notts have failed to take maximum points off a side that have only just arrived in League Two from non-league football though. For the second time this season, Notts fans are questioning what the Manager does to earn his money when things are not going so well.

Bradford, Dagenham, Northampton and Port Vale. All four games were comprehensively won. Hughes bagged eight goals in those four games alone. The players did the hard work. They turned on the style and got the fans purring for more.

However against Burton Albion, and again yesterday against Torquay United, not everything was going according to plan. Nor did it away at Chesterfield, Barnet, Morecambe and, to a lesser extent, Cheltenham.

There is a growing concern at the club. A split between the fans of what is the right way and what is the wrong way to progress. You have the *"fickle fans"* as Charlie called them last night in a post-match rant. I doubt that went down too well with some but in fairness, he was right. Football fans (not just Notts fans) are fickle. When things are going well, they are on the whole a happy bunch of followers. When things are not so rosy, understandably they voice their concern. For the fans, margins are so small. Fickle, fickle fans. Charlie is not sure what the Notts fans want and to be honest, nor am I.

As mid-afternoon arrives, word has now spread that Notts County have parted company with Charlie McParland however. He has left the club, or rather the club have asked him to leave and now the debate springs as to whether he has been treated fairly or harshly.

Four points off the top and only twelve games gone in a season which has so far produced the best football that the fans have witnessed since many can remember. Charlie is *"One of us"*, state one faction of the supporters. They ironically forget that for the best part of a decade he had been involved with them lot over there coaching and also managing them with a degree of success, albeit short term.

Those of whom are pro-Charlie would tell you that his departure will be another little bit of history and another bit of the clubs soul leaving us. They want someone who is Notts County through and through to lead the club on the upwards journey through the Football League. The same fans forget that the legendary Jimmy Sirrel had no links or affinity with the club before his arrival at Notts. They forget that Neil Warnock had no ties with Meadow Lane when he walked into the job after being appointed by Derek Pavis. Fans, as some put it, are fickle.

McParland, his supporters would tell you, signed some quality players during the summer. I would agree with that. Well I would agree that Notts County have signed some quality players. But who actually signed who is neither clear nor necessarily important. Schmeichel, Moloney (loan), Graeme Lee and Matt Ritchie (also loan). Then there is Ricky Ravenhill, Neal Bishop, Luke Rodgers and Karl Hawley as well as Hughes and Sol...well you know the rest.

What matters is that these boys have added quality to the club. They have added some much needed bite, class and ability to a side that were closer to falling out of the Football League last May than finding their way onto Sky Sports News or the back page of The Sun.

Those of who are less-inclined to share their fond memories of Charlie will tell you he was poor last season. He did very little for the club prior to the new men above him coming in and at the time, Notts could afford no better, attract no better and had no better options. They will tell you that despite the club getting the ball down and playing some good football this term, Charlie has failed to influence games once the players have stepped over the white line. Yes he can pick eleven good players. Can't we all? But when those eleven players do not function as well as one would hope, or the opposition manager makes tactical changes to thwart their impact, Charlie fails to have another option. He simply does not respond.

"McParland where is your plan B? Earn your fucking money!" shouted a disgruntled fan not too far from me on September 5th. Notts were stuttering against Burton Albion and eventually stalled and drew 1-1. On that day I felt that fan was both premature and overly critical of Charlie. His concerns were voiced with little more than twenty minutes on the clock. But now, looking back, perhaps he was just pre-empting that Charlie was in a precarious position already. It is not that he wouldn't make the right changes but more so that he couldn't.

Upon leaving the ground last night, fans were heard murmuring about why new boy Ade Akinbiyi was not used. I was not one to comment. I felt that perhaps he was not fully fit and his naming amongst the substitutes was more of a gesture to get the big man involved in the first team affairs than anything else.

However, other fans were not too kind in their allowances and again many viewed his no show as a simple sign that Charlie was going with 4-4-2 and would not risk three men up top or consider removing Lee Hughes from the park.

They are two view points with a very large divide. Was Charlie McParland ever going to last in the post? Of course he could have. Had Notts been top, steamrolling League Two and firing on all cylinders, then the man would have still been at the club, picking the side and making the decisions. Ultimately, this is a results business and the powers that be feel that McParland would not assure the club of exactly what it was they needed to be assured of; League One football next season.

So as the bookmakers tell one and all of whom the next man at the helm might be Notts fans can only sit and dream. Several years ago, the potential candidates would have been a shortlist for a top club job in the Premier League or dare I suggest it, the national side. Sven-Goran Eriksson, Glenn Hoddle and Terry Venables are rumoured for starters. David Platt, Steve Coppell or Roberto Mancini. This is not Fantasy Football. This is real life.

My gut instinct says Neil Warnock, now at Crystal Palace but formerly a Notts' hero. He guided the club to the very top flight that we now dream and believe to be within our grasp. No nonsense and straight-talking, perhaps he is an outside bet given the circumstances and the fact the new boss has to work with a Director of Football. But all the same, I would at least give him a call and sound him out as his situation at Palace is not exactly great given their financial problems and transfer restraints in the Championship.

My gut instinct, along with every other Notts fan, also says no thanks to David Platt. He is a former Red and just not what the club are after. Never liked the things he said on TV and never cared much for him as a player. No!!!

After that, who knows? Steve Coppell or Alan Curbishley would be sound bets as would Peter Taylor. Someone that knows the lower leagues and knows how to get a club out of it would be invaluable. But the candidates fitting this sort of description could be very long indeed.

In Peter Trembling, once again, we as fans and a club will trust to do what is right for the team.

With off-the-pitch matters still an issue for those running the club I think the mindset was to replace Charlie now, rather than delaying the inevitable and take some of the focus off of the other saga's surrounding the football club. It may also be argued that if Charlie was to be going, then it may as well be done now rather than later and whilst there is a smell of instability behind the scenes, we may as well get all the issues resolved in one go rather than one at a time.

I would not have been opposed to Charlie being given more time but now he has gone, I am quite excited about what the future could bring.

For the time being, we learn that Dave Kevan and Michael Johnson will be placed in temporary charge as a caretaking duo whilst the board search for Charlie's successor. Kevan, with the club as an Assistant since 2007, spent virtually all of his playing days split between ourselves and Stoke City if you exclude a handful of games out on loan in between. Having been here since 2007, he knows the club fairly well so it appears to be an astute choice given the circumstances whilst promoting Michael Johnson alongside him, we have someone else who is as in touch with the club as anyone having played for us over 100 times over two spells and has been part of the coaching set-up since his retirement at the back end of last season.

Beyond Dave Kevan and Michael Johnson? Well time will tell I guess.

"Who owns ya?, Who owns ya?"

As Charlie's expected departure came and went, we are now wondering just what the limits are for this football club. From the outside looking in, it would appear that those up above want big things for the future. Just how much truth is there in the rumours that have been touted about I'm not sure? But suddenly talks about Luis Figo or Pavel Nedved coming out of retirement or David Beckham ending his playing days here do not seem so absurd. In fact, it was reported that one of Sol Campbell's major concerns were promises not being kept with regards to Roberto Carlos being signed in the weeks that followed his own arrival so the attraction must be there to some extent for such attempts to be deemed realistic.

Despite Sol jumping ship, very little seems to have changed with a view to the ambitions of the club. We read on a daily basis about the latest developments at Meadow Lane and the latest targets. With Sven in the comfortable seats, just how much pulling power he could have still remains to be seen. Even if we swapped our Swede for Ulrika Johnson in the boardroom, I guess the colour of the money is, and will remain to be, the main pulling power.

Of late, Notts fans have become edgy for reasons other than those on the pitch. The summer happenings came like a whirlwind with new found hope and optimism all around us. In fact never before was the mood at this club so good. I mean never!

But the cause for our edginess in more recent weeks has not been down to Charlie's decisions from the dugout or our expectancy that Hughes will score three every game and Kasper will never concede a goal ever again (that is the stuff of outrageous dreams).

Our concerns and nerves have grown from the media. The media that have chosen to press buttons that irritate club officials and to some extent fans alike. Now commonly viewed as Notts County's major critic, Matt Scott of The Guardian is almost penning daily updates on the club, the ownership and the vague faces behind the investments that have been made.

So should we be worried? Perhaps we should. Perhaps the whole thing is too good to be true, it will all come falling down and Kasper, Lee and the rest of the squad will grab a shower, pick up their boots and wave at the rest of us as they go and pick up a club in League One or the Championship at which they'd be more than capable of doing.

On the other hand, perhaps the concerns are unfounded and they are simply just some articles and suggestions put together to try and create a story around something that, despite the media frenzy at first, no longer has a story other than the one that is played out on the grass.

First and foremost we are football fans. So what is the issue? Well the issue is all the doubt I guess. All the mystery surrounding Munto Finance and the guys who are funding the club appears to have gathered pace of late. Doubts have a way of niggling away at you don't they? At first they plant a seed in your head. You pretend it is not there. You try and ignore it. Suddenly the seed is fed life however and gradually becomes more prominent. It will continue to grow and you have no way of stopping it. You either block it out, which is tough, or you let it in and assess it for yourself. It's like insisting to yourself that you are going to be sacked at work or that that Mrs is having it away with some bloke. The more we tell ourselves it is happening, the truer it all seems in the mind.

I've never really cared about who owns my football club. The concerns I have held down the years have been who will score the goals, who will provide the defensive stability and who will pick the side? With this summer's events still very much in the present however, I can't help but take it all in of late.

Add to the mix the fact that the Football League have yet to give the club the green light with regards to the takeover, the fact Sol Campbell left as he felt *"promises"* had not been met (but failed to shed much light on such promises) and the feeling that McParland's days were numbered regardless of form, and you cannot help but enquire as to what is going on behind the scenes.

We are led to believe that we have been purchased by a company that has Middle Eastern and European based families at the helm. Munto Finance is a subsidiary of Qadbak Investments Ltd; a British Virgin Islands registered company which first came into public prominence in July when the takeover was first spoken of.

Exactly who these investors are is less clear and now we perhaps only raise questions ourselves due to what we've been fed by various media sources and in particular, Matt Scott.

On September 24th I heard the news that Scott had written a piece about a certain Russell King and his involvement in Notts County and the takeover. The initial story did, in fairness, not stir too many concerns or worries for me or any Notts fan I sit with, drink with or talk to.

King was said to have played a major role in the negotiations between Munto and The Supporters Trust which gifted their shares to the new owners back in the summer of 2009. Scott also stated:

"A source close to a senior figure at the club had told The Guardian that all contract negotiations about joining Notts County were conducted by King and Nathan Willett, one of King's associates."

The source added:

"King, Willett and Munto appointed Trembling. They are the representatives of the companies that brought the club. But you always come up against a brick wall when you look to find out who owns Qadbak."

Now they say any publicity is good publicity and, at this point, fans would be forgiven for not really caring where the investment was coming from. It was more 'Thank god it is here' rather than 'Only god knows from where' for most fans.

A day later however, we heard that the Football League were set to look into the clubs affairs after suggestions were made that Sol Campbell's contract with the club had violated the league's ruling on salary caps and money laundering.

Scott revealed that Blenheim1862, the holding company of Notts County Football Club, only had a contract for £7,000 per week with the former England man but that £33,000 per week was to be paid to Sol by Swiss Commodity Holding AG, a company that had Sol as one of their ambassadors in much the same vein that they had Sven as one.

Incidentally, Swiss Commodity had two named Directors, one being King's associate Nathan Willett and the other being his father, Peter Willett, who'd been named on the papers submitted to the league with regards to being a Director at Notts.

Now as I say, normally I'd not get entangled in such stories. When I fell in love with football I did so for the players, the art, the skill and the passion. Holding companies, investors, off-shore bank accounts and named and unnamed directors never really did it for me.

Now, with all this coming out in the press and my love for the game reaching an all-time high (for love see addiction), I wanted to know what was going off? Who was messing around with my club and my dreams?

Now in the days that followed these unravelling myths, and given the fact that the Football League were yet to give us our much desired ratification, I started to listen for news with even more anticipation but also some fear along the way. Deep down I longed for stability that was not forthcoming.

The problem nowadays is that to fully understand a football club and its ownership, you have to understand business. Gone are the days in which families run football clubs, passed down from generation-to-generation and kept within the community.

At the back end of September, rather quietly and under the radar, Notts County released a statement declaring that the families that had invested in the club were the Shafi and Hyat families. The Guardian wrote:

> *The Shafi family and the Hyat family – who are based in the Middle East – have both agreed to be named and the club have confirmed that they have extensive business interests throughout the Middle East, Japan, Kazakhstan and Pakistan with real estate investments in Europe, the Middle East and Asia. They have invested in Qadbak Investments, one of whose subsidiaries, Munto Finance, brokered the deal to buy the club.*

A quote was supposedly given by Anwar Shafi through the clubs official statement declaring

> *I can confirm that the families have a significant holding in Qadbak and are very pleased with the diversified range of assets we have invested in. But we are a private business and do not wish to comment any further.*

At the time, I remember reading such press statements with a sense of relief and optimism. Although these investors were not shouting from the roof tops, it was a positive step that meant the clarification was perhaps not as far away as we'd feared.

However, days before we welcome Torquay to Meadow Lane, Scott was once again revealing cracks in the story that we fans did not want to hear:

> *The mystery over Notts County's ownership deepened last night when Anwar Shafi, who Qadbak had tried to recruit to become involved with the company, said that he had nothing to do with Notts County. Shafi explained that representatives for Qadbak have attempted in recent weeks to recruit him "with a view to employment as a spokesperson or with an ambassadorial role" but that he had turned them down.*

> *Notts County yesterday declined to comment on any of the issues raised by Shafi, but instead issued a statement purporting to be on behalf of the Hyat/Shafi Family Trust and its head, Sardar Hyat. It said that the trust: "Condemns any attempt to interpret their wish to continue to conduct their business affairs with discretion and privacy as in some way hallmarked by an*

intention to deceive the public as to the nature of the underlying interests in the family trust and the companies in its ownership. The family are well aware of the operations of Qadbak and its interest in Notts County Football Club and have never sought to conceal that interest from anyone."

In the space of ten days or so, it appeared that we went from knowing exactly who our owners were before going back to square one and not having any clarity at all to the situation.

As we readied ourselves for a trip up north to Yorkshire for a top-of-the-table clash with Rotherham, we were left without a manager, without a secured future with regards to our takeover and without a clue as to who was going to be in charge on the touchline in a week, month or even a year's time.

Away at Rotherham (in Sheffield)

Rotherham United v Notts County
The Don Valley Stadium / League Two / 18.10.09

"If it weren't for Saturdays, managing would be the best job in the world. You get that horrible feeling in your guts and your head is going round."
Ronnie Moore (speaking in 2006 when at Oldham)

"Away tomorrow. Sean and I making a day of it...I can't wait."

Jade did not share my enthusiasm as I told her of my plans. An away game at one of our fellow early-season contenders. Away days are great. I may have seen Notts on the road already this season but this is the first proper one in my mind. Travelling up, a few beers and banter on the way and going with one of my mates. It sure beats travelling alone to places like Barnet or Lincoln.

It's an early start and out on the road, grabbing a bite, catching a train, catching a bus, catching a tram and catching a cold. All part of the away day rituals. I wake early and flick through last week's programme as I wait for Sean. Last week was a disappointment. Last week was a let-down and last week was dropped points. It is as simple as that really.

All the media intrusion and behind-the-scenes rumours about just who owns the club has been just as disappointing, so today it's nice to put all of that to the back of the mind and enjoy some football. Today is all about a fresh start without Charlie. We'll give these players another chance to impress and another opportunity to perform. To show they care and to show they will fight for the club.

"Come on you Pies!" says Sean as I open the door to him.

We sit on the 10am train from Loughborough to Derby. A packed train. Shoppers, weekend trippers and students. Bloody students.

We sit and laugh. We talk about football. We watch a student lad try and latch onto some lass he likes the looks of. Talk more football, show our tickets to the inspector and spot a fellow Notts fan.

"How do?" with a nod and a wink.

Football, football, football. It is all we talk about on our short trip to Derby. We see Pride Park, we see some early Derby fans readying themselves for their local derby match with Leicester City. We talk about Charlie, we talk about Sven. We forget about Charlie, we talk about Tommy Johnson. We think back to the days of Tommy Johnson in the late eighties and early nineties. We talk about times when football was different. Dare I say purer? We arrive at Derby and we wish we hadn't.

After finding out the connecting train to Sheffield is delayed, we then fail to find anywhere worth noting outside Derby station and thus are starving. We refuse to pay £3.99 for a bacon baguette at one of those expensive food outlets within the train station building and therefore wait. Instead? We talk about football.

Eventually, some 40 minutes later than hoped, we jump on a train to Sheffield. We see some Hammers fans connecting to Stoke. We see more Derby fans heading for Leicester and some Notts fans heading our way.

Later than planned, we arrive at Sheffield. More football talk, two cups of tea and many student passer-by's later, we hit the Steel City. Not so much steel as modern art as we are welcomed by what looks like a big piece of metal with water pissing down it. What a waste of money. Heading for a tram and not finding one as expected, we walk along the tram line until we hit the city centre and find an information board. Now we see Sheffield Wednesday fans (granted not many), a fair few Notts fans but no Rotherham supporters.

We stand, we wait and we watch. Tired and ready for a beer, we are fully aware that Villa-Chelsea is on the box and our intention was to be watching it. The tram is delayed. Then delayed some more. The delay continues until the crowd at the side is too big to contemplate all getting on. They all still try. It's hot and crowded. It is unbearable. It feels as bad as being on the London Underground last month when I saw England-Croatia. We jump off a stop early to avoid paying and being crushed to death. To avoid being crushed to death and bored to death at the same time by the Notts fan of whom has decided he wants to become our new best friend. He seems intent on proving to us that he should be the new boss and is hardly coherent with a drink fuelled mind giving us his views.

We follow the tram and walk the line. We keep up with it and arrive at the stop we wanted just seconds later. The Don Valley Stadium is the least likely place on earth for football. Ok maybe not quite that unlikely but it is no football ground. We search around looking for a pub. A pub with Sky? A pub with beer and Sky? Our search drags. We wander into the town (I use the term town very loosely) and we are feeling depressed by this point.

"It's like the fucking twilight zone" says Sean and whilst hushing him, I agree. Dead end streets, boarded up buildings. Abandoned! They appear neither loved nor cared for. They are neither a home nor refuge by their appearance. We step inside five public houses in total and spend less

than ten seconds in each. A few stares, glances and frowns are sent in our direction.

"Fuck this!" says Sean and before we know it, we're back at the first pub we entered that appears to be the most appealing of the lot. A few Notts fans are at the bar, they serve food, they have beer on tap and Sky Sports News is on the box. Ok we're not getting to watch the Villa-Chelsea match but at least we'll see updates. However, the beer is flat, it is poured into plastic cups, food is no longer being served and the place is freezing. Still, it's an away game. It's still exciting.

"Come on you Pies" ring out the songs from in the back room by one or two of our lot.

We sit and talk. Talk football and talk little else. We down a few shoddy drinks and we depart from the Cocked Hat eager for some entertainment, some life and maybe some drama. We walk around the stadium with a few Notts fans. The sun is now shining and the atmosphere is now lifting a notch. We pay on the gates, hand over our cash and push our way through and arrive under the stands. Well normally you would arrive under the stands except this being the Don Valley, the ground is not exactly that way. It's primarily an athletics arena so any normal layout appears to have gone right out of the window. We buy a drink, take a walk and mingle. The Notts representation is looking good today and the bar is packed. There is a crowded drinking area and big queues for the toilets. Old friends make small talk with one another, old faces reacquaint and new friendships are being established. A good following and a good mood as well as a good away win and we'll all be happy.

We take to our seats. Our lowly, pitch level seats and I am not best pleased. It is rammed though. As full as it can be in the Notts end and the fans eagerly await the emergence of the side and our caretaker management team of Dave Kevan and Michael Johnson. To our left, one stand is pretty much full of Rotherham fans. We're stuck, tucked away in the corner. Between us and the pitch, a running track. A fucking running track and a blasted speaker turned up full volume pumping out awful music. Awful music and a northern announcer, reading t' names for t' Millers.

I feel like jumping over and pulling the cables out. We're literally yards away from this speaker and it is not letting up. To our right? Nothingness. To the far side? More nothingness. And in the opposite corner. Absolutely fuck all.

"They only open up half of t' ground" the older steward tells me. *"Killing crowds playing here."*

As the teams walk out, Notts are set out differently with no Luke Rodgers or Karl Hawley included. More cautious it appears. More fearful than any Notts side I have seen so far this season.

It is Schmeichel, Thompson, Jones, Lee and Edwards. Jackson, Bishop, Ravenhill and Davies with Ritchie and Hughes.

Ritchie, as the game starts, appears here, there and everywhere. As they stand, it looks like a 4-4-1-1 but from our angle, your guess is as good as mine. The far end is literally that. Far. Schmeichel is hardly visible in the distance. I stand up and give a *"COME ON YOU PIES!"* and with it the chant carries around our stand as a few hundred join in and those around me look annoyed. Probably pissed off they have a loud mouth close by.

It takes some ten seconds before we receive the expected *"scabs, scabs, scabs"* in response. Highly original from a Yorkshire side I hasten to add. It is highly original indeed. The irony comes in the form of it being twelve, thirteen and fourteen year-old lads giving the verbal abuse. For those of you from a younger generation, a scab is the term used with little affection aimed at someone who crosses a picketing line. From my experience, it is a term used directly at the two clubs from Nottingham for the cities part in the strike action of the mid-eighties for working miners. Considering my age, I have very little recollection of the period although I was knocking about as a toddler and only a year or two away from my first ever visit to Meadow Lane.

Like a stigma that will not disappear or fade, Nottingham will always be viewed upon with judgement by those who did strike in the north, as many Nottinghamshire miners continued to work. At the time, my family would have known many of those who felt they could not strike. Those that had mouths to feed and bills to pay that felt they had to continue with their jobs and so, to this day, fans of Nottinghamshire clubs still receive unwanted grief on behalf of those hard-working, family orientated men who merely felt they were doing the right thing.

At first, as I am told by my dad, the whole Yorkshire v Nottingham rivalry was something of a raw subject in the years that followed. Many of those who went on strike in Yorkshire felt that the men of Nottingham had turned their back on fellow miners in returning to work. Now, as the years have gone on, it's sung or rather chanted, in a derogatory manner which I doubt many of the fans in question really understand in any way, shape or form.

My own grandad worked in the pits when he was younger and purely based on his and other family member's stories; I know that such a job was not done for love. It was a tough place to be and a hard way to bring in much needed money. For this alone I think all those that ever had to spend time down in the mines are due a certain amount of respect and tarnishing their efforts with such remarks every time a Nottinghamshire side meets a Yorkshire club begins to seem a little futile after a while. I am not saying that those from Yorkshire were in the wrong to strike either. I am simply saying that everyone had their own decisions to make without others casting the first stone.

Anyway, back to the game. Rotherham do not appear to have a singing section here at the Don Valley, just a quiet (but full) stand of fans.

However, despite a few early Notts songs, the crowds settle down rather quickly as does the game into a dull, uneventful half of football. Edwards sees a header hit the bar midway through but it's a case of close but not close enough and with that gone, so does the half. It disappears. Uneventful and uninspiring with an awful atmosphere.

You sit and wait. You anticipate the second half and you hope for a better 45 minutes. It'd be hard for it to not be the case. In fairness to Notts, they are more positive as the game gets back underway, showing hunger for the ball and dictating the play. Unadventurous and equally unconcerned, Rotherham, now managed by club legend Ronnie Moore, sit back, absorb the pressure and play for a draw.

"Nil-Nil all over it" Sean says. I agree but I don't speak. I sit with a small, dissatisfied smile. The type you saw Lineker make to Bobby Robson when Gazza got booked back in 1990. A different emotion though and a totally different game. League Two Notts trying to break down the Millers. The Millers that are miles away from their home.

A Rotherham player sees red and Notts press some more. Rodgers is introduced and sparks Notts into life creating an instant opportunity. Now seemingly camped in their half and piling on the pressure, we look to have a purpose about us. Their keeper, looking double the age of anyone around him, continues to defy though. Davies and Jackson try and probe the oppositions defence and they show persistence to try and break them down. Rotherham show little interest in breaking forward though and this means Notts have more to get past. Late, ever-so late, Notts break in behind. Rodgers in the box looks up and slots home from close range. Finally a breakthrough and a goal. It's a feeling of pure joy...then we see it disallowed.

Absolute despair just seconds later. We stand and we make our way up the steps. We want a head start out of this dive. Out of the Don Valley and away from Sheffield as the play stops and a solitary flag on the far side waves in the linesman's hand. Away days? I fucking hate them.

We head up and out sharp-ish and one or two fans have the same idea. Across the track and onto the tram platform, we stand and wait as some of the young Rotherham boys remind us of our Nottinghamshire-Scab history once more. We really appreciate their effort but show no response. Drained after a poor 90 minutes of football, we stand silent. They may be used to the drivel that we've all just witnessed but at Notts we've witnessed over four goals per game at home in the league so far.

Following your team should never feel like a wasted journey but today? Well it is an anti-climax shall we say. Big day out turned into anything but. We check the time and know we can make a train earlier than the one intended if we are quick. Mainly down to the fact he has had a few pints, Sean decides we should run once we get off the tram.

It sounds like a good idea when he says it but in Sean, I am running with the fittest member of the CSKA squad. Not a great way of measuring my own fitness on a cold October evening in my winkle-picker shoes against Sean in his trainers. It kills me. My chest hurts and I feel more than just fifteen years older than I was when I last ran after a game to catch an early train. He turns, whilst running, goading me and telling me to hurry. I physically cannot go any faster as we nip in and out, weaving our way through crowds of folks walking in the opposite direction.

We hit the station with seconds to spare. No fellow fans alighting, unsurprising given the speed at which we have made it here, I am hungry but now also feeling a little sick as well as emotionally drained.

Shit day all around.

Coca Cola League Two Table:

	Pld	+/-	Pts
1. Bournemouth	13	9	28
2. Dagenham & Redbridge	13	11	27
3. Rochdale	13	11	26
----			
4. Rotherham United	13	8	25
5. Notts County	**13**	**17**	**22**
6. Aldershot Town	13	8	22
7. Shrewsbury	13	4	21

On The Spion Kop

Something of a first today or at least I think it is. I am sat alone in the middle of the stand and awaiting the action. I am awaiting the three points at home. But still I am all alone. All alone yet surrounded by hundreds. Sean cannot make the game today and the old man is busy working and I neither try nor wish to try and tempt anyone else down.

Tempting someone now, with the season in full-swing, would probably frustrate me. I want to enjoy the game. Not explain it. Not name each player, deliver a verdict, tell them of their form and explain their style. Today I want to sit (or stand) and watch the game. Alone, I make my way through the turnstile. Alone I buy my programme, venture up the steps and search for a seat. Today I am in the Kop. Not only the first time this season. Not just the first time since it was given back to the home fans. Today I am in the Kop for the first time in well over fifteen years. For the first time ever, I am watching my club on my own at home.

"Come on you Pies!" cry the chants as I make my way across a row of seats with twenty minutes still to go until kick-off.

The Kop is, for me, a romantic part of Meadow Lane. In fact just as it is for fans of various clubs all over the country, the Kop has some sort of spiritual draw to it that is hard to explain. Growing up, I would spend a fair amount of time stood on the old Spion Kop with my old man and uncle Danny. Before the days of season tickets, where we would later upgrade to seats that were no more than a wooden bench in the higher reaches of what is now called the Derek Pavis Stand, we would pay on the gate to stand on a concrete mound behind the goal down at Meadow Lane. Lines and lines of men at varying heights, randomly staggered over the vast cement structure. Some leaning on steel bars sporadically placed at various points. Some youngsters, such as I, perched on top in order to gain further vantage over those around us.

I assumed that everyone had a Kop such was the normality of it. Liverpool, seemingly on TV as much as anyone when I was little, had one of their own. Obviously they had the most famous and most talked about Kop of all. They had 'The famous Kop atmosphere' and 'The spirit of the Kop'.

Perhaps more through coincidence, a lot of grounds I visited in my early days as a football fan also seemed to have Kop stands. Highfield

Road, Filbert Street, Bramall Lane, St Andrews and Prenton Park were all part of early away day memories and all came with Kops. Each club was pretty deliberate in their acknowledgement of it too.

I visited other grounds on my travels but simply chose to assume that one end was the Kop end but perhaps no one talked about it. As it turns out, with Wikipedia as my fountain of knowledge, there are only a handful of Kops the world over, mainly in England, with a random one at the Parc des Princes where Paris Saint Germain ply their trade.

Here at Meadow Lane, there was always an extra edge in the Kop though. Divided by nothing more than a wire fence in the late eighties and early nineties, the Kop at Notts encompassed both the loud and lively home fans as well as the enemy. Away fans were packed into what was a very tight area, equating to a third of the stand. They were like caged animals chomping at the bit and I can see why football in the eighties had so much pent up anger and aggression involved within it. Treat people like animals and invariably they become one.

One of the scariest memories of such an occasion was when Manchester City scored late on in a league game down at Meadow Lane and as a result, we saw a mad rush of fans break through the front barriers and invade the pitch. It was nothing shy of moronic and for many years that followed, I always assumed that Manchester City fans were worse than your average set of fans. There they were running amuck on our pitch. They were taunting the home fans that stood behind the advertising boards, goading players with their celebrations and trying to give the police a run for their money. It was one of the first times I actually remember being a bit scared though and, as a youngster, it initially came as a shock. Never before had I seen such anti-social behaviour. I was not brought up in the most affluent of areas but there was never much trouble in my early years where I grew up in the Meadows. My schools had a pretty safe environment and the local Meadows Club (situated at one end of the Meadow Lane ground) on a Saturday night had a great family environment with everything from the Birdy Song and Agadoo to cheap pop and bags of crisps for the little un's.

So suddenly watching hundreds of seemingly angry men shouting obscenities and clearly trying to cause trouble was a landmark moment. I couldn't understand it. I also remember that same night overhearing my mum telling my dad that perhaps I was still too young for football. I wasn't. She just didn't understand. Looking back now, I fully appreciate the angle she was coming from though.

I have good memories in the Kop too though. A not-so glamorous FA Cup tie, back when I was still a new-comer to the game, saw a Notts side compete at home against Wigan Athletic. It was back in the days when Wigan was still primarily a rugby town and nothing more. It was prior to the era of the JJB Stadium or Dave Whelan and long before top flight football or high profile managers arrived in their north-west town. The game itself was nothing special either. It was an ordinary, going-through-the-motions sort of game. Notts would be eventual 2-0 winners that day but, with the game still poised at 0-0, my uncle Danny showed me a little surprise he had in his coat pocket for when we grabbed the first goal of the game.

Notts pressed and from memory, Tommy Johnson opened the scoring before wheeling away from the Kop, arms aloft and jubilant in his manner. At this precise moment, Danny threw, full throttle, a toilet roll pitch-wards, narrowly passing by the heads of two policemen at the bottom of the stand and into the goal mouth.

Back in the late eighties it was something I recall happening fairly often. Sometimes on TV and sometimes at the far end of a ground I had visited rolls appeared as fans celebrated. But this time it was my uncle and it caused a minor enquiry at the time in the Kop at our friendly, family orientated club. The referee halted play as the unravelled roll spread throughout the penalty area and a hapless keeper, with a little help from a steward, attempted to pick up the soggy mess that had presented itself to the crowd with Notts now on top.

The policemen were not best pleased. Up they marched enquiring amongst fans as to who the culprit was. Who'd dare throw such an object towards the playing field? More importantly, who had just managed to miss their heads? Fans looked around, bemused, confused and cryptic in their response. They searched bags, coats and bodies until they arrived at uncle Danny.

"Some fucker up there" pointed my uncle.

He appeared as angry as the pair of coppers. He shared their annoyed expression and as a result, they worked their way up the stand leaving Danny with a spare roll tucked away in his pocket ready for goal number two. I had never laughed so much in my life and for the first time ever, I think I realised that at football, I was allowed to act and behave differently than at home.

"Don't tell Mum" said my dad with a wink.

Unfortunately this sort of Kop no longer exists (I don't mean one from which we throw objects but more a stand from which we are allowed to actually stand). Instead of concrete mounds there are now well built, structured seating enclosures. Where there was once standing room only, there are signs and announcements telling us that standing is the last thing on the agenda. For cold, damp, uncovered spaces, we now have plastic seating with ample leg room and a roof covering us from the elements. As I have said before, in some respects changes can be good but in others not so much.

Opposite me today is the small outline of the Family Stand at the Meadow Lane end of the ground. It is much smaller and seemingly insignificant compared to the rest of the stands here at Meadow Lane and therefore looks a little out of place. Above the skyline of the stand I can see the City Ground across the river and the Trent Bridge cricket ground. Sitting here at the very top of the Kop, higher than I've ever been before here, it makes me realise just how close they are. Just ten seats to my right the drummer of the Kop is banging away. He's trying to create a racket, get the fans going and create an atmosphere. I'm glad I've sat here though. It is much livelier already even if a tad loud.

As I look around however, there are plenty of seats left. Perhaps the Kop just looks fuller when you are sat over in the Pavis Stand. Bang goes the drums and bang go the nerves. We need the points today after three consecutive draws in the league.

"Come on you Pies, come on you Pies!"

To my left are a few hundred Crewe fans gradually take to their seats, tying down their flags and hoping to rustle up a song or two in the process. To give them credit, we know they are here. Bang goes their drum and the atmosphere builds some more.

By 3pm, Notts are ready. Ready to put to sword this Crewe side that are on the slide. Manager Dario Gradi is back at Crewe as the boss and hoping to perform another miracle on low budgets and a prosperous youth development system but Notts will be too good today in a decent atmosphere.

Schmeichel, Thompson, Jones, Edwards, Lee, Ritchie, Westcarr, Davies, Jackson, Hughes, Rodgers. It's a decent side fitting back into a 4-4-2 and has plenty of attacking options. Notts need to get back to winning ways we all know it.

Notts start patiently, stroking the ball around looking for options. Fans are fickle aren't they Charlie? Too right fans are fickle. Craig Westcarr has his doubters. They moan and groan, groan and whine. To be honest, they have had a point. He has looked lost at times and uninterested.

"Sven-Goran Eriksson, Sven-Goran Eriksson" sing the Notts faithful. Well, at least the Kop do. The rest of the stadium watches. Sven waves, we cheer and Notts start on a new crest of attacks.

Davies and Jackson are instrumental and central of all that is positive about our approach. Westcarr continues to frustrate but Notts look comfortable. An early chance arises when Hughes finds space in-behind the Crewe defence but it is wasted. Not good enough to break the deadlock ourselves, Crewe decide to have a crack against the run of play. Direct and down the middle, they break with pace and suddenly a chance is fashioned but Schmeichel's goal remains intact as the ball rolls wide.

Notts are committed to the cause however and are clearly up for the challenge. Michael Johnson and David Kevan guide the troops from the touch line.

"One Neil Warnock, there's only...." sing a small select group of fans to my left. They're pretty obvious on where they lie with regards to the new boss and I'm with them.

Graeme Lee is booked for an over-zealous tackle in the middle of the park minutes after he broke from the back and had a chance to take a pop at goal but Notts still look assured. Ritchie is energetic and Jackson pops up like a wise head, orchestrating from the middle.

Then some sloppy play from Crewe midway through the half in their final third creates a buzz for the home support. Jackson finds Rodgers and Rodgers pounces. One touch, two touch, bang! It is 1-0 and we launch ourselves from our seats. I jump and cheer with blokes I don't know. I discuss the goal and share their delight. Notts are back and looking good. Good old Luke Rodgers answering his critics and proving he is more than just an aggressive bag of energy.

Moments later, Crewe attempt to strike back. Kasper Schmeichel, just like his old man before him, stands big and tall however, using his body and blocking well. In doing so it gives more life to the Notts side as Daniel Jones, from left back, seems to break forward as often as Notts have attacks. He delivers a dangerous cross and somehow Crewe's backline manages to scramble it away before a Hughes header is well saved and Davies sees an effort blocked from eighteen yards. We're on top now though and looking bright.

"Come on you Pies!"

As the sides feel their way towards the break, it is still just the solitary goal that separates us. Somehow, despite chances, openings and opportunities, the game is still only 1-0.

"Westcarr is a lazy git" says one man. He's not happy and the groans seem more purposeful with each mistake he makes.

Edwards at the back is strong despite an early, miss-timed tackle. But Notts are, on the whole, good value for their lead and that is exactly what they do going into the break.

It's a tense day here at Meadow Lane. We know points are a must if we are to maintain this assault on League Two but in the back of our minds, we know we must kill off Crewe and their small (but loud) following.

The second half is much the same. Half chances here, half chances there. We sing louder though and try and push Notts onwards and upwards. But this is no foregone conclusion. Schmeichel tips over from a Grant effort as the visitors press. They bang their drum loud and their side give themselves ample opportunity to get back into the game.

Notts defend a scrappy corner but survive as Edwards continues to prove to his doubters that he can survive this club revolution, and command the back. Notts are now easing themselves back into this game.

"Come on you Pies!" we sing, *"Come on you Pies!"* but we're somewhat more apprehensive now.

On the hour mark Luke Rodgers is alert to give us reason to cheer. A long diagonal ball finds Hughes who instinctively fires across the face of goal. From this end of the ground it looks to be on its way to the back of the net and when Rodgers taps home after a burst of pace, the whole ground erupts. I stand and look, trying to grab a glance between the arms and bodies. I spot the flag though and Crewe are let off. Rodgers must have drifted offside at the far post.

Moments later a second wave moves forward. Rodgers and Hughes motion into space creating a gap down the middle from which Westcarr looks up. His touch is a little clumsy as he shifts it out of his feet and then, without warning, bang! There it is.

"Lazy Craig Westcarr" laughs one man behind me but credit where credit is due; it was a strike and a half. Cutting inside, he released a thunderbolt of an effort and we have extended our lead.

Notts now look in complete control and Crewe hearts are surely deflated. Far from being inferior, they have, for large parts of the game, been equal to us but we have the players that make the difference in the final third and we sing and rejoice in the spirit of the day.

The Kop feels as though it is cruising to three points now. I join with those strangers that surround me, enjoying the moment and being thankful. Unfortunately, as I look back down to earth, Thompson is stretching in the box to put his head on a cross. Looking on, he is adjudged to have pushed inside the box and Crewe are gifted a chance from the spot to pull one back.

"It'd make it a tight fifteen" the chap next to me points out and don't I know it.

Former Everton youngster Steven Schumacher steps up for a one-on-one with Kasper. The Great Dane stands big, trying to psyche his opponent out. It must look like a small goal with that sort of presence blocking your way to the net. I hope Schumacher agrees.

He approaches the ball and hits it firm and direct to Schmeichel's right. We pause, anticipate and hope. Then we celebrate as though it were a goal as Schmeichel saves well, clenches his fists and earns the plaudits.

Without being overly convincing, Notts have won a game that last season they'd have failed miserably in. In the closing stages we are robbed of a third when Ritchie hits a sweet left footed effort only to see it cleared off the line but we'll take this. A 2-0 win at home but more importantly three points ensuring we sit fourth and just three points off second placed Dagenham. We're in this for the long haul.

It is a good feeling when I arrive by train in Leicester to meet Paul after the game. We have ourselves a charity acoustic gig tonight at The Musician in Leicester which is our first public offering since we played The Cavern in Liverpool back in May. It was not until tonight that I realised it has been so long since we performed live and I guess that is down to, in parts, the way football has been so encompassing over recent months.

Whereas our other band members could take or leave the beautiful game, Paul and I love it and so much of tonight (with just the two of us performing) is spent talking about Notts and in turn Leicester's forthcoming away game with Reading on Monday night prior to and after our thirty minute set.

Leicester have only lost one in their last eight going into the Reading encounter and we cannot help but speculate about how good a weekend we could have in London if our respective sides made it to Wembley for the Play-Offs. Although it would prove costly, we agree we'd go and support each other's side. I'd love it if they could be beating another East Midlands side under the Wembley arch. On Monday night they will see off Reading with a 1-0 win lifting them to fifth in The Championship.

Coca Cola League Two Table:

	Pld	+/-	Pts
1. Bournemouth	14	11	31
2. Dagenham & Redbridge	14	11	28
3. Rochdale	14	10	26
----
4. Notts County	**14**	**19**	**25**
5. Rotherham United	14	7	25
6. Barnet	14	7	24
7. Shrewsbury Town	14	6	24

Pushing It

I am buzzing today. On a personal front, I have five goals to my name so far this season but the more notable achievement is, as manager, I have guided CSKA to within just a few points off the top of the table and we sit second from fourteen in the Alliance League Division Five.

It's been a decent start to the campaign so rightfully so, we celebrated today's win as a team at the local pub just minutes away from our home ground. If truth be told, I was frustrated that I was not amongst the scorers in a 5-2 win over LK Old Boys but the bigger picture means we're looking like a very good side at present and one that could potentially earn promotion.

We tumbled in, had a few beers, talked about the game and then had another beer for the road. It's all part of the Sunday League culture which all too often our lads do not incorporate. It is partly due to the fact that we have lads that travel from various parts of Leicestershire rather than all coming from the same suburb or community but at best we only gather for a quick one after a game despite having a great group of lads.

The same group of lads are also beginning to settle down in their personal lives as am I, I guess. Rewind two years and the average age of the squad was around 23. Given the fact two years has elapsed it is perhaps surprising that the average age has gone up by five years. I ousted the trouble makers (a few young ones with ego's) and replaced them with good, sound characters and have so far ensured that we have no big heads or lads with ideas above their station.

We also have lads who, in recent years, have married. Three instantly spring to mind. Others? Well they're moving in with partners, trying for kids, getting mortgages or in the odd case, acting the clown as though they are still eighteen. Step forward Mr Seany Ward.

To a man, they are readying themselves for a more settled future and that is a good thing for all concerned. As I say, it does mean that spur of the moment drinking sessions or random nights out are few and far between, so after today's win, and given the fact we knew three points had guaranteed us second spot for the time being, we managed to entice one or two more than usual down the pub.

Today is also a day that Liverpool entertain United at Anfield in the Premier League. Because of it, everyone appears to be in a 'day of football' type of mood and come along happy to dissect our own match before departing to their various homes to watch the game on the box.

However, I remember far too late what my alternative plans are. Dinner with the in-laws was penned in with Jade's very words this morning being *"I've told my Dad we'll be over about half twelve"*. I did not say anything at the time but this was highly ambitious given the club's home ground is a good thirty minute drive from my place in Loughborough. Give or take fifteen minutes, she'd be fine.

However, as I glance at the Sky Sports News screen above the fruit machines, my heart momentarily sinks as I realise that I have neither text Jade or ensured that I am back as early as possible. It is 1:40pm and that means we are already over an hour late and I am still 30 minutes or so from being home.

As I trudge in just after 2pm, knowing the game has already started at Anfield, I know I am going to be in for a rough ride.

It's not that I don't think about things. Or perhaps it is exactly that. I am not sure. I seem to think about certain things far more clearly than others things. I don't care for United and I care even less for Liverpool. At least with United, they have some sort of right to have an arrogant, cocksure attitude. A vast amount of Liverpool fans still talk about their club as though they are dominating English football like they did in the eighties. They need to wake up and realise they are not. Maybe if one or two realised that Blackburn Rovers have won more titles than them in the past twenty years, they could begin to accept where it is they stand in the modern game.

I flick the TV on and instantly, from upstairs in the front bedroom, I hear a shout from Jade. She is not frustrated today. Frustrated would be her most common mood with me of late given how football is gradually taking over my life. Today she is fuming and understandably so.

Not only did I get to enjoy Notts' win over Crewe yesterday without the stress or nagging from my partner, I've then shot off on this fine Sunday morning to leave her, off work and at a loose end, to play football and then go down the pub. This time, I have pushed things too far.

"Why did you not have your phone on you?" she demands to know as I trot upstairs, caked in mud.

"I forgot. I left it in the car" is the reply she gets. If you read between the lines, this means, *"I did have it on me, I merely forgot to send you a message."*

"Just get a shower. We're already going to be late. Dinner will be ruined" she fumes and off she goes downstairs, clearly not wishing to be on the same floor of the house as me, never mind in the same room. She passes

me without a glance of eye contact or acknowledgment. She doesn't even ask how we (CSKA) got on this morning. It is incredibly rude of her.

I would not say I clean myself thoroughly. It's more a case of running my hand over the mud which allows the visible dirt to wash away down the plug hole. But it feels cleansing and anyone who plays park football will know that come the autumn and winter months, such showers feel fantastic after a tough game and you really feel as though you have put a shift in as enough soil to fill a large plant pot washes away from the skin.

Within minutes however, I am out, drying myself down and getting dressed as quick as my little legs will allow. As I glance out of the window from my music room drying my hair (I think my obsession with my music room has also been a source of annoyance of late), Jade has already started the engine out the back and my phone, now on charge, is flashing.

"I'll be with you in two" I insist but I doubt my own predictions.

The drive from Loughborough to Melton is much longer in the mind than any previous trip to her old man's place. The mood is frosty and she is still angry. She is completely right to be in such a mood but this does not stop me from pleading with her subtly to accept that I am sorry and that I made a genuine error.

To make matters worse, we can't tune the new car's radio into the football, I forget my phone and therefore unable to check for updates and I only remember upon pulling up at her dad's house that he does not have Sky Sports and therefore I'll be unable to watch the 4pm kick-off or see the goals, if there were any, in the earlier game.

I choose not to gloat as we walk into the dining room and learn that dinner is far from ruined. It's not even ready. I knew it wouldn't be. Her dad and his Mrs' are never what you'd call punctual with their plans but this suits me fine and always has done. Why restrict yourselves to exact times? There appears to be little point in doing so. I like their laid back approach.

As Jade apologises for our delay, they fail to even notice the fact we are late. For them, it matters not one jot and I hope that Jade joins their view. However, I have a feeling she won't let this one go for some time yet. **Alliance League Division Five Table:**

	Pld	+/-	Pts
1. Trinderbox	5	41	15
2. **CSKA Carnabys**	7	5	13

Backe To The Future

Selected Odds on next Manager of Notts County:

Peter Taylor	5/2
Sven-Goran Eriksson	4/1
Roberto Mancini	5/1
David Platt	7/1
Steve Coppell	10/1
Neil Warnock	16/1
Kevin Keegan	20/1
Glenn Hoddle	20/1
Sol Campbell	50/1

What you instantly spot from the above list, after laughing at the suggestion of Sol Campbell coming back to Meadow Lane in a managerial capacity, is that there is only one Swede on the list and that his name is not Hans Backe.

I must admit that I had readied myself for something, shall we say, more exciting by the time the announcement arrived. For all the big names and experienced managers who had been linked with our vacant post in the weeks leading up to the appointment, I was hoping that the successful applicant would eventually be chosen for the right reasons rather than his or her media appeal (Hope Powell was suggested in some circles hence the 'her' comment).

We saw all sorts of names banded about as the bookmakers revelled in the latest news from Meadow Lane and whilst some fans would have been purring at the thought of Roberto Mancini, fresh from success with Inter, or former England Managers such as Sven, Kevin Keegan or Glenn Hoddle roaming around the dugout, what was really needed at Notts was someone who knew the lower realms of the English game and, more importantly, would know how to navigate our way out of them sooner rather than later.

Hans Backe fitted neither category. He appeared from nowhere like a racehorse backed by no one, galloping up alongside the railings to overtake all those who threatened to be first past the winning post.

Looking back, it should not have been too much of a surprise when Backe was handed the post. Having previously enjoyed successful stints in Scandinavia with the likes of Djurgarden, Hammarby IF and AIK, the Swede would eventually go on to enjoy his biggest successes in

Denmark. In his first season in 1998/99, he led Aalborg to the Danish Superliga title before his tenure at FC Copenhagen from 2001-2005 resulted in three Superliga's including a treble winning season in 2003/04.

From there, Hans Backe found himself moving to Greece with Panathinakos before a short spell ended prematurely just months into the 2006/07 season. But it was from here that his path would begin to carve its opening to Notts County when, in 2007, he was appointed assistant manager for one Sven-Goran Eriksson at Manchester City.

As Sven lost the job at Eastlands, so too did Backe but when the more high-profile name of the duo was offered the job of Head Coach for Mexico in 2008, Backe followed keeping together the small Swede team of Sven, Hans and former England Assistant Manager Tord Grip.

So now, with Sven's role within the game slightly different in a Director's role, the arrival of Hans Backe at Notts was perhaps on the cards from day one.

Speaking to The Guardian, our new man in charge said:

The first target is definitely to get promoted – not necessarily to win the league but certainly to finish in the top three. With the right type of players there is also the possibility of getting promoted from League One next year. The Championship will be the tougher one but we have to win Leagues Two and One first. That is the target without a doubt.

If the name of the new man was not enough to win fans over, the comments he was making in interviews was certainly giving us enough positivity to believe in the intentions of not just the board but the new man in charge.

When Sven phoned me up a couple of weeks ago I said I'd definitely go for it. It is something really new for both of us, to start in this league and build something. That was the key attraction. I feel hungry and really motivated. My record as a manager is pretty good so this doesn't faze me.

On Saturday October 31st, with interest in the club still high, Notts County stuttered to a 1-1 draw with promotion rivals Shrewsbury Town in Hans Backe's first game in charge. Notts looked lacklustre and tired with the same eleven men that had beaten Crewe seven days previous.

A late Graeme Lee goal on 85 minutes ensured Notts continued their unbeaten home record but in drawing, it meant a chance missed to pick up points on those above us.

Coca Cola League Two Table:

	Pld	+/-	Pts
1. Bournemouth	15	7	31
2. Rochdale	15	14	29
3. Dagenham & Redbridge	15	11	29
4. Notts County	**15**	**19**	**26**
5. Rotherham United	15	7	26
6. Chesterfield	15	3	26
7. Shrewsbury Town	15	6	25

"Should Have Come in a Taxi"

Notts County v Bradford City
Meadow Lane / The FA Cup 1st Round / 06.11.09

Tonight is another first, or at least I think it is. Football on a Friday night is rare in this game and, as far as I can remember, it has never happened for me. Tonight is the start of what can hopefully be an exciting story within a story. It is the start of an FA Cup adventure for all League One and League Two sides so tonight, Notts and Bradford will get the First Round Proper underway along with Bristol Rovers v Southampton and Huddersfield v Dagenham elsewhere.

For me? Well I just want to get through tonight to start with. We could have been handed easier ties than this one whilst tougher ones were also on offer so, after the 5-0 mauling on the opening day and the 2-2 draw and penalty shoot-out defeat in the Paint Pot Cup at their place, we can hopefully keep the edge we have over them and progress tonight.

The dream is ultimately progressing to the Third Round and getting one of the big boys down here at Meadow Lane but as I say, there are two games between now and then so first things first.

Six days ago we welcomed a new manager to Meadow Lane and, given the fact it was his first game in charge since being announced, perhaps the fans cut him a little bit of slack after it took a late equaliser from Graeme Lee to ensure we did not lose at home in the league for the first time this season. Today I am not so sure the fans would be so forgiving however. We must get back (or backe?) to winning ways.

As we arrive in the city it's already dark. The cold is setting in and commuters, students and labourers alike, mix in and around the station as their week comes to an end. The street lights glow, the buses pass us by with the splashing of puddles enhanced by their heavy tyres and winter is fast approaching making no apologies as it does so.

The clocks now firmly back and Christmas being planned by millions all over, tonight has a good feel about it as we make our way down to Meadow Lane. We grab some take-away food to accompany our walk and then wish we hadn't when we arrive at The Navi to see them putting food on for cold match goers out the front.

A few beers, grab a programme, take a seat and talk football. It has been a long week but Sean and I have looked forward to this one. The pub is empty but fills pretty quickly once we are in and settled. Fans are

116

in a rush to finish work, get home, grab a bite to eat, a shower and get down to the game in time for kick-off. Rush, rush, rush.

"Friday night? Awful night for a game" says one fan but I quite like it. It's a little bit different. Nice way to start a weekend if you ask me.

We stroll down to the Kop, get inside and get another beer. Now it is chillingly cold. The feet go cold the quickest. Then the hands that hold the plastic cups. Youths mingle and are served at the bar making me feel old whilst young teens appear excited and opinionated. Stewards deny one or two drunks, the crowd begins to thicken below the stand and the fireworks start to crackle to our right as numerous bonfire parties around the city start to light-up the weekend sky.

We take to our seats as the drum bangs and the fireworks sparkle some more in the air.

"He plays on the left, he plays on the right, that boy Westcarr, makes Weston look shite!" sing the faithful. Westcarr was poor last week though. I admit I am not his biggest fan. I can't see what he brings to this side at present. He needs to up his game considerably. If he can change his fortunes, I'll be the first to sing his praises but he needs to do it soon.

The atmosphere builds and the Kop fills out. To our left is Bradford's following. There is less claret and amber on show than there was a few months back. More like coats and scarves now and a much duller image it is because of it. A small following sit patiently and are quieter than their last visit too.

"5-0 and your back for more, 5-0 and your back for more" sing the comical Pies to our right. Bang, bang goes the drums. Spirits high and hopes for a Cup run on everyone's mind. The teams are read out. Hoult, Bishop, Edwards, Hunt, Clapham, Ravenhill, Jackson, Davies, Ritchie, Hawley and Akinbiyi.

New boss Hans Backe has opted to rest a few lads and try and rotate. A risk but one he must view as both viable and worthwhile. Therefore we'll not be blessed with Kasper, Graeme Lee, Daniel Jones or Hughes. Meanwhile, Brendan Moloney is not available for selection in the cup due to the terms of his loan deal.

The teams are out and with more fireworks raining down on the city, the game gets under way. The Kop is in an effervescent mood and all players get their songs from the Kop directed at them. We out sing, out support and drown out the few hundred travelling Yorkshire men but I give them their dues for the journey they have endured on this cold, wet evening in November. Since they came here back in August, they have done ok for themselves. They put together a bit of an unbeaten run and have certainly shown more promise than they did back on August 8th.

With all this jumping and shouting, singing and standing, we see little of the opening ten minutes. There are *"oooh's"* and *"ahhhs"*, brief moments where we take a seat but on the whole, possession seems to be changing hands every few seconds and neither side gets a grip on the game.

The tempo is quick and some may view it as being end-to-end and action packed. Frustratingly however, neither side appears capable of any prolonged period of possession so our viewing is all the worse for it.

Up and down, up and down, we continue to rise to our feet and sing songs. More so than any home game so far this season, it appears that there is a section of us that fancy creating the atmosphere this week rather than waiting for it to happen.

However, misplaced passes slip off the greasy surface and into touch as spirits are dampened around us. As the half continues the vocal ones among us become more scarce and rare. Over on the touchline, Backe stands for much of the half, pointing here and there and remarking to Kevan by his side, he gives the impression he is analysing rather than instructing. Meanwhile, one fan nearby happens to mention that Charlie did neither. It comes across as rather harsh.

Just as the atmosphere becomes diluted to the mere sounds of explosives in the distance, Notts break with a sudden spark of energy and pace to their attack.

With Bradford back peddling and Notts throwing numbers forward for the cause, the Kop rises once again, starting at the back and working its way forward like a wave gathering momentum. We venture inside the box and in doing so, the ball falls to Ravenhill just inside the area. He strikes with intent and we jump with excitement. It is blocked well however but the ball ricochets back as far as Ravenhill once more who has a carbon copy moment as he drills the ball towards goal, this time seeing the keeper make affine save.

We remain stood up however as third time lucky, Karl Hawley now finds the ball at his feet and despite his initial shot being saved, it squirms under the keeper and into the back of the Bantams net.

We let off some cheers of relief and delight. A combination of the two for sure but we are just glad the breakthrough has come for ourselves after a tight, close half of football.

There was very little before or after worth noting and as the break arrives, Sean and I run down to try and get a beer before the queues populate. Notts have the edge so we can enjoy our pint that little bit more during the break. A slender lead it may be but the beer tastes better for it.

Fans gather in small groups. We see friends and families tightly knit together to fight off the chill whilst young couples hug to keep each other warm. Old men rub their hands and stamp their feet as a group of coppers gather and talk, seemingly unaware that there are a few thousand fans now in and amongst them.

We don't exactly anticipate the second half after what we have just seen but the warm pub after the match will be a delight. We knew it would be cold this evening and so did the small Bradford following that made the effort. All for a good cause though. After all, it is The FA Cup.

We hear the sides returning to the park and we, along with a few hundred others finishing their pints sup up and make our way up the concrete steps and back towards the stands. It is a timely decision as Johnnie Jackson is already imposing himself on Bradford as we arrive back in our seats. He finds Hawley on the edge of the box and goes for the return. The midfielder takes the ball in his stride, shifts it from right to left and then slots past Eastwood in the Bradford goal.

"Get in!!!!!"

Jackson may have been calmness personified but we are anything but.

The next round is now firmly in our sights and Bradford's travelling contingent look less than impressed. We're now up for a few more beers and making a night of it as the Kop comes back to life.

Despite the best efforts on the pitch, the game is not really action packed though. More of a huffing and puffing sort of game than one with endeavour or end-to-end drama.

"Come in a taxi, you should have come in a taxi, come in a taxi" we sing at the quiet, desolate away end. The rain decides to hammer itself down on Nottingham and we are grateful we are under cover as we sing our way to what should be a first bit of success under the new manager.

Westcarr and Rodgers are introduced to the game in place of Ritchie and Akinbiyi and just when we appear home and dry, Bradford break with pace and precision. Before we know it, Boulding strikes a neat finish past Hoult despite the keeper's finger tips nearly denying him and with nine minutes still showing on the clock, the game is not yet over. The last thing we wanted was a nervous end to the game and the potential of a fourth meeting with Bradford in just four months with a First Round replay up north.

They press and probe whilst we sigh and hope. Nail biting our way towards the 90th minute and watching on as Hans brings on Facey in place of Hawley to waste a little time. Notts County's number 22 comes on to great applause from the fans and instantly closes play down to which we appreciate the effort and show our gratitude.

Moments later, with fireworks still sparkling in the rain filled skies, the referee puts his whistle to his mouth and allows us through to the Second Round and a step closer to a meeting with one of the big boys.

We are up on our feet, down the stairs and out before the players even reach to the Kop to clap and wave. It is a gentle jog down the road, into The Navi and a pint ordered before even Sky Sports confirm the game is over. A good night lies ahead now regardless of the wind and rain.

FA Cup Second Round Draw:

Bournemouth will host.......Notts County. And that concludes the draw.

Stressed & Wound Up

Bury v Notts County
An Emotional Crossroads / League Two / 14.11.09

I was winding Jade up. Well at least she thought I was. A trip up north to Gigg Lane was firmly on my agenda and a weekend away was on hers. *"How about up north? Say Greater Manchester?"* She is unaware, or rather uninterested, as to the whereabouts of Bury or its ground and this I jokingly use to my advantage.

She was insistent that this would not become yet another weekend taken up by football.

"You've been three Saturday's running. Can you not just give me one weekend of your time?"

I chose not to point out the Bradford game was actually a Friday. It's more the point she is making rather than the exact facts.

Of late, jobs (hers) and social lives (mine) have ensured that time together has been, at best, limited. Limited just like it was in August. Limited in much the same way it was before the Wembley trip. And now it is seemingly limited all of the time.

It has not helped that after three months or so of the season, and with my memoirs of the campaign gathering pace, I have had an offer to release a book with an independent publisher from the west midlands.

For me, it is welcome news. My ramblings, thoughts, observations and idea's may now actually reach a wider audience. It's an exciting prospect for me and I cannot help but show my enthusiasm as my own project writing about the club's 'project' builds pace.

Jade has not met the idea with as much delight and enthusiasm as I have though. I don't think it is by any means selfish or anything like that but she is aware that if I am spending more time writing on games and travelling up and down the country, our time together will become increasingly rare.

It does not have to be the case though as I point out. I simply plan to write when she works and my spare time will become my time for working on the book. Despite this theory, we both know it is not going to be that simple.

"I need to go to the Bury game."

"Why do you need to go?" she asks over emphasising the 'need' in her speech.

"What if I miss something? It could be important for the book."

It's met with deaf ears but more importantly, it is met with a look of despair and acceptance rather than defiance. Jade has supported me in my dreams and ambitions for the past few years. When we met I was already in a band and it was a long term hope that one day, me and the lads would make a success out of it and be able to do it as a living. I was not wishing for eternal fame and fortune. Just to be able to make a modest living from it and do something that I and the rest of the lads enjoy.

There was a massive part of her, despite her support, that deep down hoped I would not achieve the ultimate success that I wanted from my music though. For her, my success would see a detachment from one another. I'd spend more time *"all over the place"* as she put it whilst she felt she would continue a normal lifestyle with me flitting in and out when my diary suited.

She was also somewhat scared that fame, even if just minor, could lead to other options so to speak. Women, I find, are insecure at the best of times. Give them what they see as reasons to be insecure and suddenly you are looking at a whole bigger issue altogether.

Personally, I always felt her fears were unfounded. And fortunately, of late, they had faded. On the band front things had slowed down. We had recorded an album earlier in the year but if truth be told, it has been one massive financial disaster. We recorded up north in a lovely place called Hebden Bridge in a studio that had all old sixties gear and technology. For us, it was perfect and was set to become our defining moment.

Whilst we were there, over the course of some nine or ten days, fifteen potential album tracks were recorded which we were more than happy with when we listened back on the final day in Yorkshire. Unfortunately, we then made the mistake of leaving the production and mixing to our producer who by this point, we felt knew what we were about and what we needed from this LP. A week or so later we were unhappy with the first mix received for three tracks and six weeks later, after numerous calls and listens, we were distinctly unhappy with the whole thing. £4,000 of our own, hard earned cash was gone and the producer did not have time in his diary for months to work on it further. Even when his diary may eventually permit it, additional costs would be the order of the day.

To cut a long story shorter than I have already started telling, we tried to have it remixed locally with someone less well known, and ultimately cheaper. We then sent samples to Liverpool to try and have another producer, and someone we respected, give us his own mix but by this point costs had become uncontrollable. Paul and I, the two songwriters of the band, were broke beyond our initial fears and it got to a point where our respective weekly shops were heavily restricted and we became disillusioned with music altogether. You cannot live on bread, milk and scotch eggs. Trust me, I've tried it.

Jade never wanted this to happen. Not for one second. As this unfolded over the early parts of 2009 and spread onwards into the summer months, we found ourselves with more time for each other despite our financial issues. This was something she enjoyed. It's also something I enjoyed too but it had happened for the wrong reasons and for me, it had come at a cost both financially and personally.

I can see now why she felt more secure about us at that time than ever before. I was ultimately unhappy with the hand I'd been dealt in life. Other than having Jade, nothing was going right anymore.

So why the issue about the book? Like I say, I don't think the book is the issue. It's more the time I put into it and what falls by the wayside in order to accommodate. Had I said *"I have this offer to write a book so, in order to focus on it, I am going to stop managing CSKA",* I presume she'd have been delighted. But I didn't. I decided the best idea would be to go into the whole thing full throttle. I'd take it on without a second thought for anything else and try and simply balance it with football, my continuing visits to Notts and the rare band get-togethers we'd have. Jade felt like she was an afterthought. I know it was not the ideal scenario. The one thing that has suffered since I began upping my input on the writing front has been us. Me, her and our time alone together is what has really suffered.

Every relationship is different and I have come to accept this more than ever of late. I have had girlfriends by where every spare moment was spent in each other's company. It's unhealthy. Some would say fans have unhealthy relationships with their clubs. You hear the stories of the fan of who has not missed a game in thirty years. Or the fan that had to turn down an invite to his own brother's wedding for a home match against Wycombe or the couple that split up because the wife wanted to marry on Cup Final day. There is such a fine line between being a fan, enjoying the game and taking great pleasure in it as a hobby or being obsessed, agonising over games and living for the next 90 minutes of action as though little else matters.

Growing up, I used to eagerly anticipate the fixtures coming out during the summer months for the season ahead. I used to calculate how many games there would be prior to my return to school. I'd torture myself with the fact that 50% of the games I'd see before school recommenced were already over by mid-August, knowing that with each passing match, I was a step closer to my first day back in the classroom.

I guess I still do it now in some respects. Breaking down my weekend and outlining my plans. Working out how much football I can take in during a single weekend and being pessimistic as the minutes tick before I lay my head on the pillow on Sunday night in order to ready myself for my nine-to-five office job.

So forgive me if I try and take too much in. Forgive me if I want to watch as much football as possible or listen to The Beatles all night after the games have finished for I don't really enjoy other parts of what you'd consider the real world. Work is a means to an end at the end of the day. It's a wage and nothing more. I have other interests that I feel contribute to defining me as a person and I always try and make the most out of them. I guess I know I don't quite have the balance right though and the fine line for my relationship with football has been crossed a little on many occasions.

"If you want to go Bury, you go Bury. I give up" she says resentfully. The penny has dropped that I am not joking and I am not overly bothered about spending the day at home just doing nothing or going away somewhere to simply walk around shops we can't afford to shop in or go for meals we cannot justify spending money on.

However, the situation is rather different now and the mood has changed dramatically. Simply walking out of the house now and heading over to Notts to get a lift up to Gigg Lane would be unforgivable. It's not that I don't understand her frustrations. More the fact I wish she didn't have them. Perhaps I wish she had more happening in her life socially which made my social events irrelevant to her. Maybe I just long for the day when she tells me to go to the game as she is off out anyway. When that day arrives, it may then be me feeling left out though?

After letting the dust settle on the whole discussion, I pop upstairs and run her a bath. I apologise sincerely and suggest we don't go away for the night and nor do I set-off for Bury. Instead, maybe we could pop out for lunch later this afternoon. It's a gesture that builds bridges instantly. She suggests we head out around 2pm which means I will not be able to listen to the commentary but this was the last thought on her mind. She is no longer playing mind games. She was simply not thinking. I choose not to pull the wind from her sails and I agree. I'll have to make do with text alerts this afternoon despite my longing to be up north.

Am I overly harsh or perhaps too selfish? I never felt as though I was but, of late, with Jade's issues becoming more commonly aired I have begun to question my own characteristics. On second thoughts, it may be stress. That must be it. I have been stressed of late. Although my job now seems safe (or as safe as it will ever be), I have been agonising over recent weeks about several other issues and not just mine and Jade's ongoing discussions.

In the CSKA Carnabys camp, all appears to be going well with a serious title chase on the cards and my own form seeing me grab the lion's share of the goals. I am currently enjoying the squad selections less than last season however as the squad has improved immensely with the signings I have made. As a result, the quality of the players I leave out has been of a high calibre meaning frustrated squad members are getting little opportunity to prove their worth.

It is at Meadow Lane that I cannot escape from in reality though. The real anguish and fears lies within those four stands. It feels like a chore supporting Notts at times but with all the recent hype that has surrounded my club, I am now in a position where any concerns remain at the forefront of my mind.

Next Wednesday the club is once more faced with the possibility of a winding-up order, only this time, the momentum behind the case is appearing to gain pace. Despite the notice being served to the clubs parent company Blenheim1862 (now owned by Munto), the debt still exists. According to Matthew Scott's article for The Guardian, a source close to the club stated the petition was in relation to debts relating to PAYE and VAT submissions dating back over two years.

On November 10th, Notts County refused to comment on the issue whilst it was widely reported that at the time of the initial takeover in the summer, those involved in the supporter's trust who had wrote off almost £400,000 in shares were assured such debts would be paid quickly.

Now, with the threat of being wound-up looming large, fans are left wondering where exactly all the money is that has been promised and why the fans have not been given assurances. On the 11th, our chief executive Peter Trembling eventually spoke out to assure fans in an understated interview on BBC East Midlands Today explaining:

> *The club has resolved its dispute with HMRC and HMRC is not proceeding with its application for winding-up. There are residual legal formalities as a consequence of the petition but I am pleased to say that the club's business carries on as usual.*

But what did this mean? To your average fan, it appeared to be business talk that appeased the media vultures but left us none-the-wiser with regards to all the investments we, as a club, were expecting to see.

So in the past few days, most of my conversations with my old man and fellow Notts fans have been all based around the petition, Peter Trembling and what the future holds. In some circles, Trembling is being touted as some sort of legend. The guy that is sticking up for the club, putting the hacks straight and making the fans aware their concerns are unfounded.

Others are starting to suggest there is no smoke without fire and with every new, negative, anti-takeover story that emerges, the doubters become more vocal and more common in numbers. For now? Well in Trembling we trust but frankly, we do not seem to have an alternative other than a very bleak, potential non-existence of a future.

When I try and explain all this stress to Jade, she has a look which seriously appears to doubt my sanity. Understandable I guess. My stress levels are not helped later in the afternoon however when, at 3.20pm, I check the latest scores and learn we are trailing 2-0 away at Bury.

"See. Bet you're glad you didn't go now" laughs Jade. A stupid comment if ever I heard one but you can't say she doesn't have a sense of humour.

An enjoyable (but somewhat tense) meal passes us by and, as we return home for Final Score, I reluctantly accept that 3-3 away at Bury may not be a terrible result given the respective positions at present. After Hughes pulled us back level with a brace, we managed to concede again after the break only for Matt Ritchie to equalise late in the day to make it 3-3.

A point gained on the road leaves us in a somewhat strange position though, being unbeaten in four games on the road but being disappointed in having not won in the last three. Today has been a stressful day to cap off a stressful week come to think of it.

At this point, I guess it is a good job I am completely unaware that tomorrow morning CSKA will win an eleven goal thriller but nearly throw the whole thing away after leading 5-1. That'd be just about unbearable. But as I say, I am unaware of this at present so my stress levels are not tipped over the edge just yet and Jade and I can enjoy a quiet night in.

Coca Cola League Two Table:

	Pld	+/-	Pts
1. Dagenham & Redbridge	16	12	32
2. Bournemouth	16	7	32
3. Rochdale	16	13	29
----
4. Rotherham United	16	8	29
5. Chesterfield	16	4	29
6. Notts County	**16**	**19**	**27**
7. Shrewsbury Town	16	6	26

It Never Rains But It Pours

Rochdale v Notts County
Spotland / League Two / 24.11.09

"The only problem with Rochdale is that, unless you are a home fan, you get to go there only once a season"

John Ladd (The Guide to Football Grounds)

Football has felt like a bit of a chore in the last week or two. Not through lack of enjoyment or even lack of effort. It has just become frustrating. Frustrating to watch. Frustrating to follow. Frustrating to play. On Saturday Notts played out a rather dull and dour 0-0 encounter at Meadow Lane with Aldershot to follow draws with Bury and Shrewsbury in the two league games that preceded it. The game itself had little to write about and given the fact the home form on the whole has been great, we can perhaps forgive a little. We've come to expect more though. In fact we have started to demand more.

On Sunday morning my side, CSKA Carnabys, had a perfectly good opportunity to go joint-top of the Leicester Alliance League Division Five but, rather foolishly, declined the offer. A 3-2 defeat away at the side struggling second from bottom meant we were left wondering *"What if?"* as, with more games played than our rivals, we failed to narrow the gap at the top to a mere goal difference. And all this after a massive 6-5 win the week before feels like a bitter pill to swallow right now.

It was typical Sunday League sort of stuff. A game played in a field with gypsy caravans surrounding us, dogs unleashed and roaming free and shit on the pitch (the muck not the players). We turned out with a near-to-full-strength squad and I admittedly thought we'd have enough on the pitch if I rested one of two lads (myself included) and so I made a few changes.

Despite my replacement bagging two, the overall flow of the game meant we were battling it out in their style rather than our own. So trailing 3-2 with ten minutes left on the clock, I made a triple change which I saw as a last roll of the dice.

However, the gamble turned out blank. My inspirational winger, and chairman of the club, Irish Chris was sent off just moments after going on for telling the referee to piss off and then both I and the other sub that came on had late, half chances to make it 3-3. Jay and I both missed. We lost and we went home wet, cold, windswept and pointless.

So now here I sit. Wet, cold and windswept in another part of the country awaiting another game of football that I am praying will not prove to be as pointless. Notts County away at Rochdale. I set off shortly after lunch having worked a half day in the office and made my way up, by train, to the North West.

I'll be honest. Had I not got the ticket in my back pocket I'd have probably given tonight a miss. I have been in a foul mood for a few days now (all football related) and in turn I feel rather run down and under-the-weather.

Jade and I managed to argue for the duration of Sunday night about this very trip and perhaps I should shoulder the responsibility for not telling her sooner that I had purchased the ticket.

"I thought you were working" was my initial plea. It did not wash.

However, it was a genuine plea. Rochdale had not come up in conversation in the two weeks leading up to this game and quite frankly, I saw no reason to agitate her more than I already had done in recent weeks what with attending seven games in around 40 days prior to tonight. You know how it goes don't you? If you can keep to your plans without the other half knowing, why tell her and wind her up? I had failed to consider the fact that even though she was down to work, she'd then get home hours before I returned from Spotland but again, I will be honest. I was not thinking.

"I got out of work to spend some time with you" she stresses. That felt like a dagger. Quite clever of her too if you ask me because of late, she has been working every hour God sends and in turn, that has wound me up. She would rather work six or seven days a week to try and save up for a holiday or a new car whereas me? Well I do the bare minimum required. That means no over-time, no extra job to bring in more cash and no curbing of expenditure on a Saturday afternoon.

"You just keep doing what you are doing if it makes you happy." And with that she left me to watch Match of The Day 2.

So as I await the teams coming out, I drop Jade a text message. I view it as a subtle apology. She interprets it as something totally different. I highlight the fact that I am cold, damp and on my own, albeit it amongst loads of Notts fans. I admit that I did not enjoy the three hour train journey or the three changes at Sheffield, Manchester and Manchester Tube respectively and I say, with a slice of truth buried in there, I would rather be curled up on the sofa, with her, in the warmth.

"Serves you right!" I get as a reply. Maybe I deserved that one.

Rochdale have lost three on the bounce here so tonight, given the way things are in the league, we need three points to reaffirm our intentions for a promotion slot. Eight points off top of the table Bournemouth is quite a gap at this point but from the small crowd here at Rochdale, there is nothing to suggest we are in for an easy ride tonight.

Now when he wrote about Spotland in the Guide to Football Grounds, I suspect than John Ladd was perhaps a neutral writing about the pro's and con's of the North West and what the clubs had to offer. Sat here right now, I can firmly say that this trip alone is enough for me and my quota of Spotland for this season and beyond.

As the game gets under way it does not take long for the Notts contingent in my corner of the ground to make ourselves known.

"*County! County! County!*" we cry as the sides feel their way into the opening stages on what appears to be a fast and wet surface.

Notts are without Lee Hughes up top so former Leicester, Crystal Palace and Sheffield United man Ade Akinbiyi starts for Notts with the tank that is little Luke Rodgers alongside him.

The first notable chance falls to Rochdale's Will Atkinson in the early stages when a short corner catches Notts unawares at the back. A neat little turn and a slight sight at goal later, Atkinson fires a fine effort towards goal and nearly gets a reward for taking a pop when a deflection leaves Kasper Schmeichel scrambling across his goal mouth to tip just wide of the post. A wake-up call indeed is needed and in our Danish keeper we have someone willing to dish it out as he barks instructions and berates our defender's sloppy approach.

But we are not left waiting too long for Notts to respond and against the run of play, Neal Bishop clatters the cross bar with a header from a Ben Davies cross to give us some inspiration and hope for the game ahead.

"*Come on you Pies, come on you Pies!*" we call in a ground where we are clearly the loudest once we up our own game.

The skies are dark though. Floodlights begin to show some spots of rain dropping towards us and as I anticipate the cold skies opening up, I zip my jacket up and bed myself in for the next hour or so.

Akinbiyi shows his first sign of class in a Notts shirt before the half hour mark, flicking neatly to Westcarr who in turn finds Moloney. It is a swift, flowing move which one by one, sees fans rise to their feet. With each neat, intricate touch, we gather more and more hope. Young Brendan Moloney finds himself in the box and suddenly he has time and space. He angles his body and turns from the desperate legs of Rochdale defenders making last ditch tackles and as I rise on my tiptoes, so do those around me.

"Pull the trigger" we think as he hesitates and eventually, as the ball settles, a flailing leg manages to block the right-backs effort and Notts earn just a corner for their escapade down the flank.

Minutes later we see big Ade turn provider again. Davies plays into Bishop before he plays a fine, threaded ball into the target man Akinbiyi. He holds off his man well and guides the ball into the path of Rodgers who is alert, sharp and instinctive. Rodgers draws a tackle and we rise instantly to appeal for the free-kick in the dangerous area just outside the box.

"Come on ref. That's filth" I hear bellowed down my ear. The ref shows no sign of acting on it though as the ball slides into the feet of Westcarr. We now rise again, this time with hope instead of anger and fall back upon our seat as the winger's curling right foot effort goes wide of the target.

The game opens up as our spirits lift despite the cold temperatures. Rochdale fans begin to stir and sing and Johnnie Jackson is sloppy in the middle of the park, losing both possession and his feet at the same time. Dagnall breaks and suddenly Rochdale spring to life as does Spotland. The player ducks and dives his way past Lee and Hunty before drilling a fine effort at goal as we pause. Then we breathe a sigh of relief as the ball hits the underside of the bar and comes back out for Moloney to bang away into the stands.

The game is now moving at some pace. Both keepers are on full alert and each goal mouth is getting its fair share of action. With just four points separating the sides, a victory carries great weight this evening and both sets of fans know it.

"Could do with grabbing one right now" says the old chap in front as he turns and nods at me. Poor bloke must be as old as what my grandad would have been had he still been with us. He looks about 80 years of age and sat out in this weather, all these miles away from home on a dark Tuesday night, I admire his commitment.

There are 35 minutes on the clock and Notts are now pressing. Looking to make the wishes of the old man in front come true, Moloney puts in a teasing cross only to see the ball cleared. Jackson reacts quickest though and wins the ball back just outside the box. We remain standing from the initial cross but now Westcarr is found out wide and has more time and space to pick out a man. He glides a well paced ball, with precision and intent, bang into the corridor of uncertainty teasing both defenders and attackers alike. Ade comes close but marginally misses the ball as does Rodgers before Ben Davies pops in at the back post and pressures O'Flynn into turning the ball into his own net.

We turn to one another with smiles of delight. The youngsters to my left, the old bloke in front and the middle-aged couple to my right all delighted with the stroke of fortune as the players turn away to celebrate. We are in a fantastic mood now and as the rain begins to intensify, we welcome it upon us as our concerns are lifted from our shoulders.

"*Deserved that*" points out the old bloke.

"*Too right we do*" as I pat him on the back.

For the next few minutes, the atmosphere in our end is good. The game slows down a little though becoming long, direct and without thought. More in hope than anything else, Hunty knocks a long aimless ball that is instantly returned on 40 minutes into the feet of Dagnall. The Rochdale forward turns, or rather is allowed to turn, and then accelerates past Bishop and between Hunty and Clapham as though the pair are not even there. Unfortunately for Notts, Clapham refuses to accept the fact they were seemingly set to be beaten and lunges in before, from a distance, we see Dagnall's arms flap and the forward falls to earth in the box as Kasper boots the loose ball over the stand opposite.

No doubts in the minds of the referee and his assistant on the far side of the result here though.

"*Bloody typical*" declares my new friend in front. He is not best pleased as the youngsters around us shout obscenities at a ref that, in fairness, has probably made the correct call.

We stand, almost praying for a positive outcome. Despite Kasper's presence between the sticks, Dagnall is still the favourite to beat our keeper from twelve-yards and, as if by script, he slots the ball low to Kasper's left to make it 1-1.

"*Only had a few minutes to hold on pal*" I remark as I get up to make my way for a cup of tea.

The bright lights now exaggerate the power of the rain falling from the northern skies but it is the turn of Rochdale's following to care very little for the weather as they look set to head in all square after it seemed certain Notts would have a slender half time lead.

"*Fucking idiots!*" screams a rather over-zealous young lady as I reach the steps to make my way underneath the stand. She's angry and is keen to make her point known in her broad Nottingham accent. I turn and look across as Chris O'Grady latches onto a long ball with Hunty and Graham Lee falling over each other yards behind him. O'Grady, as cool as you like, bears down on goal and rounds Kasper before poking home from close range. From here, I cannot believe how easily the game has turned in the matter of seconds.

"What happened there?" I ask as I wander down the steps alongside two strangers.

"Dunno mate" I get as a response with raised eyebrows and taught lips. *"Fuck knows!"*

The tea tastes shit. The concrete floors absorb the freezing cold temperatures but, from above, it sounds like the rain is letting up. I call home but I need not have bothered. I call a mate too and he's not best pleased.

"Colin [Slater] said we were poor in the build up to second goal."

"I didn't see it. Well not the build-up. But we could have been three ahead by then."

The second half gets underway and from the early signs, we appear to have more urgency. Davies sees an effort deflected wide and straight away he makes a beeline for the corner flag to get on with the game. John Thompson, on for Stephen Hunt at the back, looks steady and more resolute in the early moments and there is enough to suggest we can get back into this. Dagnall, against the run of play, sees a free-kick drift wide of the mark but those around me are growing in confidence despite a breakthrough still not coming by the hour mark.

Karl Hawley and Matt Ritchie are both introduced and the dynamics of the game alter slightly. Clapham watches on in agony as he drags an effort wide from inside the box before Bishop and Davies both have efforts blocked from in and around the edge of the area.

"I'd take a point young'un" says the old chap in front.

"Me too pal."

We enter the final twenty minutes and Notts still press. The rain we had earlier in the night now fades into insignificance as a torrential downpour comes in from over the opposite stand and sweeps around the ground in the swirling winds. I am drenched. I have little cover.

I glance around. Familiar faces of whose names I don't know. Folks from my neck of the woods all watch on with equal hope but ever decreasing optimism. A ball is swung in from the right but the flight is lost in the elements. Davies finds himself in space on the left but as he turns and volleys, the effort is blocked and handled.

"Penalty!?!?!?" yells the animated old boy in front. Hundreds jump and appeal with him. I prefer to watch on, almost reading our fate before it has happened, before the referee gives his decision. The sides play on and Davies is furious.

We sit back, soaked and frozen. Rochdale have short journeys home in order to dry off. I'll be soaked well beyond midnight.

"Come on Notts!" we encourage but the attempts now appear more desperate than patient.

The referee glances at his watch not once, but twice. The home fans whistle but still play continues. The rain is almost horizontal now, coming in directly at us. Full force and at full speed, we are as exposed as Kasper was for that second goal. The roof of the Willbutts Lane stand drips like a constant leak, condemning those below it and saving very few from the sky above.

Bishop lofts a ball into the box and Hawley loses the flight of it as Heaton comes out to claim in the Rochdale goal.

"That's your lot there" I am told and within ten seconds the whistle goes to confirm it.

Not good enough tonight. Not good enough at all. We had them there for the taking but once again we have showed a lack of killer instinct to finish them off on the road. What a way to cap off four dreadful days of football for me.

If I thought I would keep to my own threats, I'd vow to never go away from home ever again. I'd tell myself it is a waste of money and a waste of my efforts. I know I will fold the next time the chance arises though. Trips such as Torquay next May are now going to carry far more weight and pressure than perhaps we or the players would have hoped.

Title chasing Notts looked more like Play-Off maybe's tonight. Now I have to hope Jade will come and fetch me from Sheffield train station at 1am. Fingers crossed I guess. Otherwise, I'll be using wet clothes as blankets in a few hours time.

Coca Cola League Two Table:

	Pld	+/-	Pts
1. Bournemouth	18	8	36
2. Rochdale	18	15	35
3. Rotherham United	18	12	35
4. Dagenham & Redbridge	18	11	33
5. Chesterfield	18	6	32
6. Bury	18	0	29
7. Notts County	**18**	**18**	**28**

A Prior Engagement

One, two, three. It is as simple and easy as that. Goal after goal and the Magpies are back on form on their own turf. On fire and now on a high. Luke Rodgers opened the scoring on twelve minutes before Hughes on fourteen and Ben Davies on seventeen ensure Darlington are firmly put to the sword. We've killed them off good and proper in the opening stages.

If we continue at this rate, we could bag double figures tonight but we all know that won't be the case. Why does it never happen? Not even once or twice. In recent years I remember Manchester United hitting Ipswich 9-0 at Old Trafford with poor Craig Forrest helpless in goal and just the other week Wigan were battered by Spurs 9-1 in a game that, had Spurs been that bit sharper, could have been much more embarrassing for what was a poor Wigan outfit.

There appears to be an unwritten rule in football that, at some point or another, a team eases off when score lines begin to get a little ridiculous. How common is it to see a side race into a 3-0 lead and in the second half just keep the ball and steady the ship? Call it professionalism or seeing a game out but I'd love it, just once or twice a year, if a side really went for the jugular with double figures and counting.

As I sit alongside my dad, we are as frozen as either of us remembers being at a game this side of the Millennium. In fact the last memory of being this cold was the first season that the brand new Derek Pavis Stand was built. We both recall a game where we sat high up towards the top of the stand and physically lost all feeling in our fingers and toes due to the chill in the air which made it so painful. Even more so because Notts failed miserably on that winters day back in the mid-nineties.

Today our cold feet are consoled by the three early goals and the positive nature of the play on offer though. Darlington, struggling down at the wrong end of the table, offer very little in terms of resilience and we look as though we could push on for more. But it's what I'd consider an economic display after Davies nets the third. Playing very much within themselves but conserving more for further down the line, with a busy Christmas period ahead, perhaps it's a sensible approach.

On the Saturday just gone, a 2-1 victory over Bournemouth in the FA Cup Second Round has ensured that there is to be some busy months ahead for the players and staff. Despite going behind to a Brett Pitman goal, Hughes and Westcarr scored after the break to ensure our safe passage through to the next round and, in turn, a meeting with Forest Green Rovers at home.

Tonight though, Jade is sat in with Julie, my dad's wife, having a bottle of wine leaving me and my old man to have a beer and watch the game. They were given the option of coming down with us but neither fancied meeting the elements in the fresh December sky.

As half time finds us, I tell my dad of my intentions.

"I'm going to propose to Jade."

"Nice one" he says with a smile.

My dad has never liked any of my serious girlfriends. For serious, see potential fiancés or actual fiancées (I've had a couple). He likes Jade though and has a lot of time for her.

"Does she know she's a lucky girl?" he says with a wink and the serious talk then starts with an analysis of the first half and the shape of the squad.

Despite an eventual 4-0 win, the game itself was quite forgettable in many ways. Hughes added a fourth and his second on 79 minutes in a game that could and should have seen eight or nine but the job was done all the same and when we return back to my dad's, we are both extremely grateful for the warmth of the house, the warmth of a cup of tea and the warmth of our partners.

My dad keeps tight lipped about the engagement fortunately. You never know with him.

Just Another Day

Today is what you may call a real mix of emotions all round. Where to start? I am not sure. Accrington Stanley are the visitors at Meadow Lane for our eleventh league game at home this season. The story so far is six wins and four draws but Meadow Lane has become a place to fear for the opposition. We give very little away and the only defeat we've tasted here was back on August 11th when Championship side Doncaster visited us in the League Cup.

Today is a totally different atmosphere down Meadow Lane though and understandably so. Two days ago, it was announced that Munto Finance were putting us up for sale. You know the guys I mean? Well actually you don't do you? Nor do the fans, the players or seemingly the Football League.

Munto Finance has decided that *'The Project'* is no longer on the cards for reasons unknown and potential investors are already being earmarked and negotiations, we are told, may have already begun. If nothing else, we are left feeling like we have only had part of the story but this is the Munto way, or so it appears.

It was quite apparent on Thursday that our new Manager Hans Backe was not overly concerned by the latest twist in this unravelling story when it became public knowledge.

"Nothing surprises me in football" said the Swede when asked if the latest news changed his perspective on his job and the reason he was brought in. *"I just focus on the football and leave the other things to Peter Trembling. What can you do about it? I just take it easy"* he added. I refused to share his calm approach.

To be perfectly blunt, his whole approach has begun to worry me in recent weeks and his comments on Thursday only strengthened my concerns.

"I don't know why I have no problems. Perhaps I am too laid back. I'll take it easy though" is not what you want to hear from your manager. Let us remember that this is the same guy who is supposed to be there to instruct and inspire the team.

Since his arrival, we have won two from two cup games which is all well and good but where it matters in the league we have two wins, two draws and that defeat away at Rochdale in the torrential rain. Not exactly proving his worth with flying colours considering what our expectations are right now.

This morning I awoke early and heard rumours on the world wide web that Trembling and Sven were indeed hoping to secure a takeover from Munto, which would be our second one in sixth months. I must say it was as good a piece of news as we were likely to get and it meant two things from what I could see:

1. Sven would still be around and working at the club. In turn, this meant that Notts County still had an attraction to the outside world. And by outside world I mean investors.
2. It means we were not left with a long, drawn out saga, by which we have owners who want out of a club that they cannot flog.

The initial thoughts that went through my mind on Thursday were ones of panic and concern but, having had two days to mull it over, good riddance. If Munto want out so early in the day, then they are not the right people to run/invest/hide behind/own a football club (I'd say delete where applicable but you'd end up doing no deleting from the aforementioned options).

Pretty soon it seems to be common knowledge what exactly is happening at Notts. Trembling is set to sign a deal with Munto to take full ownership of the club. For a nominal fee, Trembling will take over the club with immediate effect and maybe, just maybe, we can put the whole saga of the past six months behind us and move onwards with new investments and success on the pitch. Just why Trembling suddenly feels the need to move up in the world from being someone else's mouthpiece to the actual owner himself, we are not sure but for now, we will wait and see.

Today my pre-match drink is in The Globe, a pub which has really strange memories for me. It was the pub I sat with my old man the night before his old man was set to be laid to rest. Just a stone's throw from my grandma's house, The Globe was the obvious choice on that evening during a time that I more-or-less moved in with my gran to look after her after my grandad passed away. From memory, it was the only time I'd ever ventured there for a drink and on that night, it was a pointless exercise. Neither of us was really in the mood for a drink and more than anything I just wanted to have an hour or so away from the house to clear my head.

Today it is different and it is obviously a packed match-day. I cannot link the two occasions in my head. It feels like a different place altogether. Perhaps for my own reasons, this is not a bad thing. I meet up with an old mate for a quick pint or three and we discuss the recent weeks and the change of expectations given the latest news at the club.

"I'm worried" he says, *"I just hope we can keep hold of Kasper and Hughes."*

But after a couple of pints, the outlook is much rosier. Isn't it always? In fact, this whole takeover could be a good thing. Everyone was getting too carried away with Munto Finance and the missing millions. It has become an albatross on our shoulder and there was too much pressure on the management to spend cash and the players to steamroll each opponent laid out in front of them. We can do all but kid ourselves the future is fine.

I drink up and then take a mad dash across the road and over the small bridge towards the ground. The Navi is heaving as usual and I arrive just in time to meet with my old man and his mate Andy walking into the pub.

Andy Day is one of them. You know. From over there. Over the water and that. Andy was my dad's best man when he re-married the day before Greece beat Portugal in the Euro 2004 Final. Despite his choice of football team, he is a top bloke and the type that you'd refer to by saying *"you couldn't wish to meet a nicer guy."*

From experience, it is a phrase that is often over used. They say it by way of over compensating the person's faults or annoying traits. I have many mates who are some of the *'nicest guys you could ever wish to meet'* but ultimately, they can be a bit of an idiot on occasion. What I'd class as a good-idiot if that makes sense. Today Seany Ward is absent but he is a prime example of a good idiot. Likeable, supportive, loyal and always there for you, you cannot take Sean too serious however and he is always acting the clown. Andy however genuinely is the type of bloke who is as good and honest as they come.

My dad and I first met Andy on the day we moved up in the world back in the mid-nineties. Having managed to upgrade from our house in the Meadows in the late eighties to a nice semi-detached in West Bridgford, my mum was delighted and would never want for anything else again. The main reason for the move was an increased crime rate in the Meadows along with the fact that in order to get me into the schools she wanted, we had to move catchment area.

Fast forward a further six years and we left the house I'd consider my childhood home and moved to a bigger, much more plush semi-detached on Wilford Lane just minutes away from Trent Bridge and in turn, my gran's and the two football grounds our River Trent has along its banks. The day we moved in, a smiling and friendly neighbour made himself known and he and my Dad have been mates ever since.

Due to the nature of my parents split prior to Euro 96 (I cannot stop linking times in my life with tournaments – it's a bad habit), I saw very little of Andy after 1998. We (me, my mum and my younger brother Kieran) eventually moved back towards West Bridgford town centre as both my parents downgraded and with it, my regular contact with Andy ended after several years of football in the garden and watching Sky Sports on the box with him joining my dad and I.

Unfortunately, since then time has not been very kind to Andy. He has suffered badly with illnesses and had several major operations to try and remove tumours on his brain. At the same time, and more importantly he will tell you, he has suffered with his football club's downward spiral although at least now, for his sake, they are back in the Championship after a spell in League One.

Today, Andy looks like a shadow of his former self. A loss of weight, loss of colour and a loss of breath at times, Andy is not well and it is not a nice thing to have dawn upon you. We have a very quick pint as Andy and I catch-up after not seeing him since he came to one of my gigs back in 2008.

Much of the talk soon turns to piss taking though with football clubs, my hair style and his lack of hair style being the main talking points. My dad returns from the pisser, surely the smallest in any pub next to a Football League ground in the country, and we sup up and are on our way.

It feels like repetition when I say that it is cold this afternoon but the cold is something that is synonymous with this time of year and in turn, freezing cold football fans on the terraces. I would not swap it for anything, however cold we are or will be in the coming months. And to think my grandma actually used to offer me the chance to stay at hers whilst my dad and uncle Danny went down the ground. She was a right joker in her day.

As we eventually get into the ground, my Dad as an OAP, me failing as an under sixteen, we arrive just in time to hear the announcer welcome onto the pitch the new owner of Notts County Football Club, Mr Peter Trembling. He steps out onto the park and gives a wave to the fans. The fans to our far left in the Kop raise a song for the saviour of the moment whilst fans around me mumble and grumble. They are clearly yet to be won over. For now, in Trembling we have to trust.

The next 90 minutes are to be forgettable and painful for Notts fans. At first we were patient. We had to be. Patience can soon run out though and when Michael Symes put Accrington 1-0 up on 60 minutes, we began to fear the worst. We had feared for the wheels coming off the

Notts County steam train (or wheelbarrow) of late. Now the worries turn to a frank and possible reality.

On 74 minutes things became worse still when we fell behind further as James Ryan volleyed home amid a scrambling and confused penalty box. On the sideline Hans Backe seemed unfazed and unmoved. Matty Hamshaw, Matt Ritchie and Karl Hawley all came on in changes that seemed to make little difference and despite the false hope we received on 82 minutes when Hughes converted from the penalty spot, and further more when Kasper saved a penalty at the other end, it could not hide the disappointment we felt in losing our unbeaten home record in the league when the final whistle sounded around the ground.

Fans booed, sighed and complained as we exited the ground in a somewhat muted and orderly fashion.

"Not good enough son" said one old chap as I waited for my dad at the bottom of the stairs. "

"Bloody same as Charlie" he muttered as we walked on by with his head down.

On the way out, Andy gave his verdict, what with him being used to a slightly higher level of football on a weekly basis. Normally, I'd not take someone's opinion seriously when his all time England team featured Des Lytle, Steve Chettle and Steve Stone amongst other players from the other side of the Trent. However, jokes aside, he does know his stuff. The full force of his verdict was directed at the man in the dugout.

"I don't like his style. Doesn't seem too bothered on the whole" he says when describing Backe and I can't help but echo his sentiments.

We don't know it yet but in three days time Hans Backe will quit the club as Notts trail the leaders by ten points.

Coca Cola League Two Table:

	Pld	+/-	Pts
1. Rochdale	21	23	44
2. Bournemouth	21	4	40
3. Rotherham United	21	12	39
---	---	---	---
4. Dagenham & Redbridge	21	10	37
5. Chesterfield	21	5	35
6. Notts County	**21**	**23**	**34**
7. Morecambe	21	9	33

"It's Just A Game..."

I ready myself by the corner flag and await the forward runs from my centre-backs. It is freezing cold stood out here all on my own and the sooner my centre backs, Lee and Brice, get their bodies in the box, the sooner I can whip this corner in and get on the move once more.

Behind me a lad I work with is running the line for his team that happen to be playing on the neighbouring pitch and as he turns around to watch our game momentarily, our ref blows his whistle and waves his hand at me to take the corner.

As the old saying goes 'if you don't buy a ticket you won't win the raffle', so I give it plenty of whip and every chance of causing a problem in the crowded box as I deliver the cross in the opening minute of this Stokes Cup tie.

"You jammy bastard!" I hear from behind me as off I run off in celebration having opened the scoring direct from a corner. And this, against Trinderbox, the runaway leaders in our division without a loss to their name all season.

Perfectly struck, the keeper initially came for it then back peddled as my team mates tried to make contact. The ball needed no assistance or encouragement however and within a split second of it leaving my right boot, we have a 1-0 lead against the odds.

My ninth goal of the season is welcomed as I am mobbed by team mates and straight away we shout at one another for focus and discipline. We have the perfect start and we know it.

"Let's not blow this!" yells Lee, my skipper, as Trinderbox recommence and put us on the back foot.

With twelve games behind us in the league to date, we currently sit in third place on 21 points whilst today's opposition have a maximum 36 points from a possible 36. They've already netted over a hundred goals in league and cup games compared to our meagre 38 so if ever you needed to predict an outcome without seeing the sides perform, those stats would give you ample ammunition to have a £5 punt.

They instantly test us with a strike from distance but Lee blocks well before playing the ball out from the back. Suddenly we are in full-motion and brimming with confidence. The ball breaks quickly down the right flank and before I know it, I am finding myself on the shoulder of their last men and with a neatly threaded ball being played into my feet; I am bearing down on goal.

I pull away from my marker with no more than four minutes on the clock. I am at an angle but far from impossible, there is only one thought in my mind as I pull the trigger and drill an effort at goal.

"Unlucky Luke, good effort" is the rallying call moments later as the keeper tips my shot around the post and the Trinderbox defence begin an enquiry as to how they've given any player from this division the time and space to nearly score twice against them.

They are close to coming to blows in their own box as I trot across to take the second corner of the game but I cannot help but feel it should now be 2-0 as I once again await Lee and Brice to drift into the box.

Lightning does not strike twice however and as the ball is claimed by their keeper and spread out of defence quickly, I'd do well to have a good look at the ball as it is the closest I will get to it for some time.

Within minutes of my chance to make it two, Trinderbox pull the game all square when some slack marking gives their star man, already with 25 goals to his name this season, time and space to ghost into the box and convert from close range.

Our boys look disheartened, if not beaten, as we trudge towards the half way line with our shock lead erased as though it never happened.

"That second chance pissed them off" says Jay my strike partner. Unfortunately he is right.

Within a mere 30 seconds of the re-start we lose our heads again. No character or defiance against a superior opponent, we seemingly give up all fight and are trailing 2-1 after their play-maker dances his way through our entire side, or so it seemed. He laughs with team mates as they jog back to their own half and with ten minutes not even elapsed, they have turned the game around and look to be in control.

If we are not careful, this could become an impossible, uphill task. Unfortunately for my boys, careful is the last thing we are and by the break we trail 6-1 and have to watch Trinderbox skip off the park as we wallow in self-pity and despondency.

The frustrating thing is, on our day, we are a fantastic footballing side. Today we are so far off the mark though we are unrecognisable. The mud caked on my boots feels much heavier than it did after my goal and the pitch, having drained much of our energy for the first 45 minutes, looks like the last place we want to spend the next 45 minutes either.

I try and give words of encouragement but from the looks on their faces, it's a lost cause. Some talented lads stand beside me, shoulder-to-shoulder. Though now, we have certainly come up against a side that are far more than just a match for my CSKA lads.

As we drag the lads back out for the second half, I reiterate the need for character, effort and pride. The rain begins to beat down upon us and our white shirts became soaked through to the bone as the referee draws the whistle to his lips and signals for the half to begin.

In an honest assessment we'd say that for the first ten minutes of the second half we have our best spell in the game. Unfortunately for us, this means we simply go ten minutes without conceding as we chase the ball, chase shadows and chase like headless chickens. When we win possession we lose it instantly but we put ten men behind the ball and we demand more work rate from one another which I for one cannot fault.

Trinderbox are far too good for our division though. Today may be a cup game and therefore our targets and priorities for the season have not been affected but it is a timely reminder that with twelve games gone in the league and fourteen left to go, we still have to play this lot both home and away. Not exactly a game to eagerly anticipate now is it?

On 60 minutes they find a breakthrough when our entire side is ripped open with a procession of perfectly placed passes and some bewildering movement. I make two changes in the hope that fresh legs can try and counter the fact they are better than us in every department but we are only having our agony prolonged.

Shortly after, six becomes seven; seven becomes eight and then eight is joined by nine and ten. We lose our right back to what appears to be an innocuous but excruciatingly painful knee injury and our day continues to get worse as the downpour continues and our white shirts become a filthy shade of brown.

It's an eye opener of the harshest kind when balls are drilled from 30 and 40 yards at their forward who's able to control on his chest at pace and with ease before turning and hitting a first time volley on target from out near the touchline. The gulf in quality is not obvious. It's blatant.

Ok. So my lads continue to run around and they don't just roll over and die in front of Trinderbox. But it's a soul destroying exercise even though against the run of play we grab a goal of our own through Seany Ward before they finish the game off and make it 11-2.

Our heads are held low and inside, mine is as low as any of my team mates as this follows a Notts defeat at Aldershot yesterday. As the manager however, this is not allowed to show and I have to keep my chin up and give something positive to the lads as they make their way to the kit bags on the far side.

"We don't have to play them again till March lads. Think of it that way" I point out with a smile as I try to lift spirits and tell them that we have to put this down as a one off.

I go round, one-by-one, thanking them for their efforts and telling them to not be too downbeat whilst my assistant manager Matt helps our right back over to his car to give him a lift to the hospital to have it confirmed that he will not play again for the remainder of the season.

Driving back home after a game such as this, everyone has the feeling that the journey cannot end quickly enough. There are none of us wishing to dissect the game or talk about a goal. No one can come away with much credit from such a defeat and for me, 11-2 is hard to stomach when I know my side is capable of at least giving the best side in our division a hard fought game.

The car journey is predictably silent. Nothing other than the noise of traffic and Alan Green on Five Live registers in our minds as the downpour turns to steady drizzle and our soaked kit allows the chill to set in.

From memory I have only ever suffered a result of this magnitude once before today and that was an identical score line to last season's runaway champions in our division at their place. I was never on the receiving end of such results in the sides I played in as a youngster so understandably, I find it hard to take.

So upon arriving home, you can imagine my delight when I walk in, soaked, cold, covered in mud and downbeat. Jade, sat on the sofa, simply looks up at me.

"Oh well. It's just a game" she says. Never before were stupider words spoken.

Get Backe To Where You Once Belonged

I could not resist a second pun on the name that will go down in Notts County history as one of the most forgettable characters to have ever graced our club. As Hans Backe departs we are left with no real emptiness inside or fond memories to look back on to tell our kids about in years to come. He was here one minute, gone the next.

He was in charge for a total of nine games (two of which were FA Cup ties) and left with a record of four wins, three draws and two defeats. If you take out the two victories he enjoyed in the FA Cup, the overall league record looks pretty bleak for a side with promotion aspirations. More importantly, when he took over we were just six points from the top. Now we trail by fourteen as a busy schedule with a small squad lies ahead.

If the continuing story of the managerial merry-go-round was not enough to keep our nerves on the edge of late, matters off the pitch ensured us fans have had many a sleepless night. They say that weddings, house moves and having children are the three most stressful times in a person's life. Clearly such experts have never lived as a Notts fan between the months of August and May.

For starters, the loss at home to Accrington had so much lacking; it appeared inevitable pretty quickly that the day was going to bring little joy to our weekend despite Peter Trembling confirming his takeover of the club prior to kick-off. Although we had won seven days earlier on the road at Hereford (goals from Craig Westcarr and Mike Edwards), we had the more concerning fact that Sven had felt the need to go down to the changing room prior to the match to reassure players that any issues off the pitch were in hand.

Earlier in the month there had been reports in the Times that the Professional Footballers' Association had had to step in after some Notts players had complained they had not received their bonuses on time. In an article published by the Times, PFA chief executive Gordon Taylor commented:

> *I hope that this is not a case of all that glitters is not gold. Not all Notts County players were paid in full on time. There has been contact with the rep and I hope that it will be sorted. It's a big worry if players are not paid on time.*

Such reports were beginning to put serious doubts on the way Notts County Football Club was being run behind the scenes. After Sol Campbell's departure due to *"broken promises"*, suddenly there appeared to be a great deal of ammunition with which to attack Notts in the press.

To add insult to injury, it was then announced on 10th December that Munto Finance were putting the club up for sale (just six months after purchasing it) and now myself and fellow fans were more than just concerned.

BBC Sport's Pat Murphy explained:

> *[Sven-Goran] Eriksson and Peter Trembling are using their worldwide contacts to attract investors now that Munto Finance have lost interest. Eriksson would put money into the proposed takeover if it got County over the line. It would cost between £2m-3m to seal it. But if Eriksson and Trembling can't pull it off, their positions at Meadow Lane would surely become untenable.*

Surprisingly, just two days after it was announced Munto wished to sell the club, Peter Trembling would complete a takeover for a nominal fee of just £1 with a view to finding further investment. Trembling went on to release a statement saying:

> *I would like to thank Munto Finance for the way they have conducted the sale of the club. They have been responsible for the changing outlook of the club. Now we cherish ambitions to secure promotion this year and deliver sustainable progress into the Championship and beyond. This is clearly an important day for the club and one which will hopefully draw a line under several weeks of speculation.*

However, drawing a line under the whole situation was the last thing it was doing for passionate fans. Now more than ever, fans had questions that required answers. Could the club continue functioning in the way it had been for the past few months? Could the club afford to keep paying the likes of Kasper Schmeichel and Lee Hughes? Why did Sven want to stick around and what was in it for him? Who was going to be the new Manager?

For every question, we appeared to be left with empty answers as Trembling continually spoke of *"seeking further investments"* and *"continuing the project"*. There was now a divide forming amongst fans of those that were supporting Trembling and those that were suspicious. Whilst it was true that supporters finally knew exactly who owned the club, many were left confused to exactly what the past six months had delivered and we were none-the-wiser to who on earth Munto Finance really was.

Rather cool, calm and collected however, our then manager Hans Backe told the BBC how *"Nowadays I don't think anything surprises me about football. I'm rather calm and have no problems."*

However unfazed he led us to believe he was, within three days of the takeover the Swede had resigned following our first league defeat of the season on home turf and once more we appeared to be in turmoil.

Peter Trembling, speaking after Backe's decision to resign, told Sky Sports News:

> *Sven and I are working round the clock [on finding new investors]. Come the middle of January we could be in an extremely healthy position and not only back on track but maybe further down the line from where we expected to be, so I am disappointed that Hans has not waited around for that to happen.*

Furthermore, the latest departure appeared to fuel suggestion that Sven too would be set to leave the club in the coming weeks with various sections of the national press hinting that the catalyst for this very revolution was about to jump ship. Trembling attempted to dampen such speculation however stating *"How can I say he's going to be here for the long term? Sven has got ambitions and we have got ambitions and as long as they are aligned then yes, absolutely he will be here."*

Regardless of whether or not Sven-Goran Eriksson wishes to remain with the club, fans have to now come to terms with the fact that all our hopes, dreams and ambitions need re-assessing. Notts County is no longer the footballing magnet it had become in the summer and it appears the second half of the season is going to be just as dramatic and tense as the first half.

Seeing Out 2009

Burton Albion v Notts County
The Pirelli Stadium / League Two / 28.12.09

Despite the best efforts of the weather, the game at Burton is on. The biggest game in their club's history at their home and it is us Pies who are the lucky guests. As Sean and I arrive in Burton the streets are crisp and cold and we are searching for a pub in which to whet our lips and appetite for the day ahead. We bundle into The Great Northern just over the bridge from where we are dropped off and in we go to a mainly home-fan, dominated pub. We are fortunate too as we manage to get served before greater numbers pile in. No two ways about it. Notts have to win this one.

Waiting and anticipating, we sink a couple of pints and listen respectfully to the hoards of Albion fans around us discussing how they are going to do Notts. We, however, are anonymous, in both colours and accent. Fortunately, such local games give very little away when it comes to lingo. It's much harder for Manchester United fans to hide their cockney twang when they play the biggest team in Manchester.

Today could be the last day we are treated to Matt Ritchie and Brendan Moloney. With the duo set to return to their parent clubs and with future finances somewhat unknown at present, we are unfortunately going to have to just sit tight on this one and hope the duo return sooner rather than later...or more painfully never.

As West Ham struggle on the big screen away at Spurs we care very little for the in's and out's of the game. Some Burton fan in front tries to make conversation with us and fails to realise after three attempts that his over friendly manner is not really going to get me and Sean talking. The pair of us discuss Christmas with the families, football, my engagement to the Jade, football, his work on his new house, football and a little bit more football before and after but this Burton fan keeps butting in and trying to talk about West Ham. Eventually, we have to move. Fans can be weird.

At 2.30pm we start to make our way to the ground. It's colder now than an hour previous. However, the sun is shining giving false hope of rising temperatures and the atmosphere around the ground is feverish. A Notts fan nearly gets his car smashed into on the round-about when some copper gives a bad hand signal and before we know it, we're passing through the turnstiles having avoiding the numerous folk outside the ground trying to swap their seating tickets for our standing ones.

We're starving now but we appear to have very few options. The queues are huge and the prices are...well football ground sort of prices. We judge the end result is not worthy of the wait and Sean goes to buy us both a beer. By the time we've drank-up and have heard the team news (no Matt Ricthie which annoys us) it is time to make our way up the small number of steps onto the terracing.

Fun and bloody games here it is too. I am not a numbers man. Well that is something of a lie actually. I love statistics and facts and numbers but my point is I do not know how many tickets were sold although I'd guess at somewhere around too-bloody-many. We go to the middle entrance and are told it is full by the round bellied steward in bright yellow.

"Sorry lads. No room. Try t'other end" he says in an ignorant, could-not-give-a-shit, sort of a manner.

At t'other end, we're told the same. Eventually, after trying three difference entrances, we stand at the top of one of the gang ways and wait for the numerous fans behind us to force us into the crowds by pushing. It seems like the best way as we become packed in like sardines. Old men, women, little kids and us all crammed in together. It's all for one and one for all. Fortunately, we're Notts County and on assessment, the fans are a good bunch today. One chap tells us not to knock his dearest mother over.

"If you fall, fall on me 'cos if you fall on her, you'll wish you hadn't."

Thanks a fucking lot, we think. Fortunately, for both of us and his mum, we're not the types to push and shove but pretty soon, any movement becomes null and void. It is so full that movements become a whole one as a group, a crowd and a stand.

Numerous fans, it is reported and later verified, are under the stand waiting for the game to start as there is simply no more space on the terrace. There is a lesson there for all those wishing to drink right up until kick off.

The sides walk out, the atmosphere lifts and the Notts end is suddenly electric. I manage to get the Wheelbarrow song going early doors and as the players clap towards us, we've all high expectations today.

Schmeichel, Moloney, Jackson, Lee and Thompson. Davies, Westcarr, Ravenhill and Bishop. Hawley and Hughes. It is a decent side albeit with Ritchie on the bench. Westcarr is perhaps a lucky lad to be starting.

The tempo is up as are the fans. For the opening ten minutes we do not stop singing and it feels like the old days when I'd stand at Notts in the Kop behind the goal on the concrete steps. All the memories come flooding back. On thirteen minutes we win a corner and when it's flicked on and cleared to the edge of the box, Ricky Ravenhill stands well positioned before crashing home a thunderous volley.

My feet lift off the floor going with the sea of fans swaying from side to side as we celebrate, hug and embrace one another. Good old Ricky.

Up top, Hughes is a live wire as ever, getting in behind, creating chances and linking up play. Burton fight, scrap and slowly ease their way into the game. The momentum is all our own though and we are the big side today. They fear us and they fear it could be a big score line.

As they find their feet chances come for the home side. Pearson sends our hearts into our mouths when he hits the bar with a volley but moments later, he misses an absolute sitter and suddenly these Notts lads appear to need a kick up the rear. Lee and Thompson are beginning to look shaky at the back and the game is now open.

Shortly before the break a header is won outside the Notts box by a Burton head. Static and dumbstruck, the Notts defence watch on as Kabba remains alert and he nips in to slot past Schmeichel who becomes loud, animated and angry in the only way a Schmeichel family member knows how.

Notts start to look complacent and the game becomes scrappy with balls bobbling around and neither side seemingly able to control the game. It's all the more frustrating as for 30 minutes, Notts looked in total control.

Injury time arrives and the ball is still bobbling about in the middle of the park. However, that man Ricky Ravenhill is switched-on and he wins a header that sends Lee Hughes clear on goal with the fourth official already indicating we have seconds left. He takes one touch out of his feet and away from his marker and then with a firm strike....bang! It's there and its 2-1 to Notts! We all do the Hughesy as the far end of the ground is treated to the second Notts goal of the game. The home end does not seem to appreciate it as we do though.

As the break arrives there is a tap on my shoulder. It's an old friend and work colleague Mark. His old man, Oliver Beeby, played for Notts and made his debut back in 1959 after signing from Leicester City. Mark and I worked together coaching in Leicestershire so we spend much of the break pulling apart Notts' game and catching up on the past year or so. We agree that we could do with a centre half ("*or two*", adds a stranger given a sudden shakiness that is apparent) and when the second half is set to start, we lose one another in the large crowds that re-emerge from the gangways.

Sean and I rub our hands, stamp our feet and ready ourselves. Three minutes after the restart and Hughes is clear again. This time Westcarr is the provider and it is 3-1 as the top scorer in League Two slots home in front of our travelling support. We do the Hughesy dance, jump up and down and try to keep warm. Goals always warm you up at this time of year.

Just five minutes later Ricky sends a long range pass over the top towards our main man once more. If the term 'field day' was invented for a particular footballing performance, this was it. Lee Hughes rounds the Burton keeper Artur Krysiak before being brought down inside the box by his outstretched arms. We rise instantly, to our tiptoes and higher than we were already stood, and then we pause. Screams and cheers emanate from the stand as the referee points to the spot and calls the keeper over. Although he only see's yellow, we are in fine spirits now as we watch Hughes hit his third of the game into the roof of the net and with it, all three, much needed points are heading back with us to Meadow Lane.

Kasper Schmeichel earns the final plaudits of the day when he saves a Burton spot kick after some foolish defending but even this cannot mask our delight today. We came to small, cold, Burton. We came, we saw and we outclassed them.

It's the best atmosphere I remember at a game for many, many years. All the emotions mixed with the performance, the vocal support and passion has left me buzzing as we leave the ground. The fact that, despite things starting to go wrong off the pitch, the fans are still here and still showing their support makes you feel warm inside. Warm enough to fight off the low temperatures on such away day visits.

By the time we file out of the Pirelli Stadium, it is pitch black in the night time sky. We listen out for other results and head towards the pub we started our day in. Notts fans mingle in and amongst the Burton lot but most of the home fans seem to be heading homewards, glum, despondent and rather down in the dumps. For us though, the contrast could not be any clearer.

We needed today's result and display more than ever. After sixteen days without a game due to the weather, it was a welcome break from the news reels and doom and gloom merchants in the press telling us our club are still on a rocky road financially.

It was also a nice day for the understated, temporary era, under Dave Kevan to begin. Minimal fuss was made by the players or Kevan himself with regards to the events of late. He just got on with the job at hand and did the best he could as the sole caretaker. Hans Backe imposed very little impression on us with his time at Notts. That, in part, was the issue we had with him. He was so reserved it felt like he was not overly bothered. When he resigned, we fans felt this was confirmation of those beliefs.

From the rumours coming from within the club it appears Kevan will not be offered, and perhaps does not want the job full-time. Notts will continue their search for not only a new manager but new investors. Whilst Trembling works behind the scenes with Sven, Kevan will be tasked with keeping the ship steady. In Dave Kevan, I believe we have someone who can do just that for as long as needed on the pitch. I pray Trembling can do the same off the pitch though.

After a few more drinks that now sees me feeling worse for wear, Jade calls to tell us she is parked up in a car park just around the corner. She's been working in Burton of late so luckily for us, she offered to stay behind after her shift for a few hours in order to be able to take us home.

Within minutes of getting into the car Sean is dead to the world and snoring away on the back seat as I try and keep my focus and head and keep Jade company telling her about the game, the goals and my latest wedding plan idea's. By the time we pull out of the town centre, I am fast asleep.

Coca Cola League Two Table:

	Pld	+/-	Pts
1. Rochdale	24	30	51
2. Bournemouth	23	6	46
3. Rotherham United	21	12	39
--			
4. Notts County	**22**	**26**	**37**
5. Dagenham & Redbridge	23	7	37
6. Aldershot Town	22	10	36
7. Chesterfield	22	4	35

"...And A Happy New Year"

So welcome to 2010. Back at work and back in the all-too-real world where Notts are in a mess, I am broke and Jade is working the hours away in order to save for the wedding. Jade loved overtime before we had something to save for so now I imagine she'll go into over-overtime.

Despite the cracking win at Burton on December 28th, the Christmas footballing calendar was the biggest washout I can remember in my lifetime. I use the phrase washout but really it was just a big freeze. Burton Albion was our first sniff of football in the sixteen days since we lost on home soil to Accrington so by the time it arrived, it had been long overdue.

As with everywhere else in Britain, the festive period was hit severely. Our date on Sky Sports away at Bournemouth fell foul to the frozen pitches first off on December 21st. Subsequent cancellations followed with Grimsby at home on Boxing Day, Forest Green (twice) at home on January 3rd and January 12th in the FA Cup and Macclesfield Town at home on January 9th.

Notts were not the only ones hit by the weather though. Even Manchester United with all their top-end facilities and under soil technology saw games called off as snow caused havoc and Britain came to a standstill.

On the weekend of 9th and 10th January, seven Premier League games were postponed due to the snow fall and frozen temperatures whilst seven games in the Championship were called off and only two games survived in League One. League Two became a lost cause altogether.

If ever there were supporters of the winter break, now was their moment to gloat.

My winter had been quite good if truth be told though. On Christmas Eve I had proposed to Jade, telling her that I thought it was best for both of us if she agreed to look after me and tolerate me for the rest of our days. Fortunately, she said yes. In addition, my office job also sees me fortunate enough to have a prolonged break at Christmas so I had plenty of time to relax and unwind which, based upon seeing many friends and family members working over the festive period, left me in an enviable position.

As I await Notts' next game with Forest Green, the snow has given Jade and I time to relax, take a step back and try and right a few wrongs that had been ongoing of late.

I admitted that we needed to make more of an effort to spend time with one another and, given the fact I had recently proposed, I was let off with the usual remarks about me giving Notts County too much of my time.

All's well in camp so to speak. I gently suggested we enquire about booking Meadow Lane for the wedding but this was ignored. That said, perhaps a more laid back (and somewhat cheaper) option would be for the best anyhow.

The Christmas period was also good for the fact that for the first time in forever, I actually seemed to get on with Jade's mum and her fella. Don't get me wrong, they are lovely. But for whatever reason, we never seemed to click. It'd help if I could understand the Scottish accent for starters but the festive period brought out the best in all of us and I enjoyed spending time at theirs and even suggested to Jade that we travel up, north of the border and give her gran and grandad a visit in the New Year.

Strangely, I think I can now accept that I was in the wrong on occasions in the past. I probably did sometimes come across as someone who did not wish to make the effort. Some of my opinions had been formed on Jade's past and my views on whether or not she'd had enough support from certain sections of her family at varying points in her life but if they are trying to make amends now, I guess the least I can do is make more of an effort. Perhaps I am going soft? Who knows?

Because of no football (also being the case for CSKA Carnabys), I feel rather relaxed heading into the latter stages of January, probably proving that football causes my stress levels to rise.

I've missed it though. As I say, Burton was a great day out and had we not had that this Christmas, we'd have ended up going five weeks without a game of football. It does not bear thinking about. It was good to get out at a time when most people spend far too many hours of their Christmas week with extended families they'd rather not be with. It was also good to spend some time out with Sean and a welcome surprise to bump into Mark Beeby at the Pirelli Stadium.

Down at Meadow Lane there were regular broadcasts with BBC East Midlands Today looking at the pitch, talking with the ground staff and analysing the chances of football ever being played again.

For the club it has had much more serious consequences though. With problems of the financial variety now all too clear, the lack of money coming through the club's tills on match days has hit the club where it hurts. It is all well and good saying the games will still be played and the tickets will still be sold, albeit further down the line, but it just is not the case.

Football is an expensive game nowadays. Families cannot afford three of four games in quick succession and the beauty of the game is that in any given month, you are likely to have no more than three home games, dependent on cup runs.

Last night Paul and I said as much down the pub. Would we watch as many games when they are rescheduled in the closing months? Hopefully, yes. But money would be an issue. Games will come thick and fast once the pitches thaw and the sun threatens to shine down once again.

By this point, families will be paying for the holiday season they have just had, whether it be credit card bills or savings to re-save. For your average family that goes down to Meadow Lane, four home games in a couple of weeks will break the bank. Add to that the fact that many rescheduled games end up on a midweek night when people have to hurry home from work or perhaps long distance travellers struggle to get down in time and it becomes obvious as to why attendances drop a little compared to a game between the same two sides on a Saturday.

Unfortunately for Notts, the last week or so has brought further worries. Once again it is stories off the pitch that have dominated our thoughts and concerns after we were dealt the double blow of a winding-up order and a transfer embargo. The two, so it seems, have come hand-in-hand.

It came to light on January 5th that a second winding-up petition from HM Revenues and Customs had been served on 27th November 2009, just two weeks after disputes with HMRC were said to have been resolved by Trembling, then acting on behalf of Munto Finance.

Trembling told The Telegraph:

> *I appreciate the petition will come as a source of concern to supporters, I can assure them that we are doing everything possible following the management buy-out of the club to ensure that clubs finances are put on a stable footing.*

On the same day, The Nottingham Evening Post reported online:

> *The Football League has imposed a transfer embargo on Notts County. It means the Magpies will not be able to sign any new players during the January transfer window.*

The club's parent company Blenheim 1862 has been served with a second winding up petition from HM Revenue and Customs. A date has been set at the Royal Courts of Justice, in London, on January 27, for the petition to be heard.

To cap off what was a truly turbulent week, I was asked into a meeting at work to discuss why I was off sick during the first week back after Christmas. Confused, tired and with my head all over the place, I struggled to explain to them what the problem was. Do people not realise I have more pressing things on my mind?

Mixing It With The Big Boys

I had mixed emotions last night prior to this weekend starting. It was understandable really given the fact that the afternoon was spent at Andy Day's funeral. Family, friends and work colleagues turned out in force for what was an amazing tribute to a guy who was quite simply my old man's best mate. It was a sad day but also one in which we had a few drinks and shared a memory or two about Andy. I guess the emotions felt were slightly different for all involved. Different relationships conjure different memories and feelings.

To me, he was the bloke who lived next door, who let me run amuck in his garden letting me fetch my footballs and trample on his flowers. He was the guy who'd occasionally be given my brothers room for the night as our Kieran was ousted to share a bed with my mum and dad after Andy had been locked out after one too many drinks following a match down at the City Ground.

More than anything, I saw him as a big part of my dad's life and someone who helped my dad through his own troubles during the late nineties. Andy was also there in full support for the family when my grandma and grandad passed away in the early parts of the new millennium and for that alone I will always hold the uppermost respect.

At the funeral, the vicar read out various pieces about Andy and his love for the game and then a piece, written by my dad, that he was unable to stand up and read himself. Afterwards, I said to my dad that I'd have happily read it out for him and he said he was going to ask but didn't at the last minute. For the first time ever, I saw my dad as vulnerable yesterday.

He was upset when his folks passed on of course. He shed a fair few tears for his mum whilst staying strong. Andy's passing is something much more poignant though. Sons and daughters generally outlive their elders. That much is true. But when it's a close friend? A close friend who is younger than yourself, it's a defining moment. At 27, I've not lost a close friend of my own generation. I'm lucky in that respect. Andy was far too young to die though and seeing my dad upset and mourning, it made him suddenly appear mortal.

I don't like to think of my dad in such a way. He pointed out over the course of the evening that *"Life goes on"* and that *"These things happen"* but I could tell it had affected him and it hurt to see it. So as I left him, Julie, and his brothers last night and Kieran and I returned to

Loughborough, I couldn't help but feel a bit deflated about the game against Wigan. What did it really matter in the grand scheme of things? I think it is the first time I have had such a thought and it's quite scary. I was basically questioning the very thing that motivated me on a day-to-day basis.

Today is another day though. Rather like a crowd adhering to a minute's silence, I woke up this morning as though a referee had blown his whistle to end the very silence that proclaims respect. My awakening felt good. A new dawn, a new day and as my old man said, *"Life goes on."*

I know yesterday was a sad occasion and I know my dad will still reflect on it for longer than he'd maybe admit. Andy was a family man and a football man. They were the two things that had defined him. If he was to be looking down, he'd think people were daft for not enjoying the FA Cup this weekend even if it is watching a side of which is not his personal tipple from the opposite banks of the River Trent.

Today feels like a big day. It is a day that we cannot expect too much but a day that we dare to dream. I wrap my black and white scarf around my neck and I check myself out in the mirror. Freshly shaven and grinning from ear-to-ear, I can tell today is going to be magic. The arrival of Sean and our Kieran at the front door prompts the short walk to the train station as we meet up with our Kieran's mate Danny (don't you just hate it when two characters have the same name) who is a big Notts fan. The football talk, the butties, the cups of tea and the morning papers all make it a great start to the weekend. All of this is happening thanks to a slender 2-1 victory over non-league Forest Green just four days previous in the game that was eventually played at the third time of asking. Fine margins once again mean we have a big day ahead of us.

The journey comes and it soon it goes. We hit Nottingham and already the place is busier than usual. The northern accents and the blue and white shirts are on show and there is an aura of a bigger club being in town. After all, Wigan's climb to the top flight is the blue print of what we want to achieve. We head into the Fellows Morton & Clayton pub, order a pint and we watch Chelsea v Preston on the box. A few beers in and my old man shows up with my uncle's, Danny and Lance. The banter, the laughter and the early start, you can tell it's FA Cup Fourth Round day. It's the biggest for some time.

The last time me and my uncle Lance went to a Notts game together was over fifteen years ago. It was a small matter of Wembley Stadium to see Notts win 2-0. That is just a memory now. We need those times again. Midday and the pub is full. Notts fans dominate the place with the northern voices standing out a mile.

We drink up and take a walk, past the station and down London Road. FA Cup day and Notts are at home. It feels magic. The pavements are fuller than last time we were down. Accrington Stanley were not exactly the crowd pullers of Wigan Athletic's magnitude. They did us though, right, good and proper. Because of this, Notts owe the home crowd a display today with some real gutsy performance to get the club back on track.

A last drink in The Navi before kick-off and the fans are milling around in every nook and cranny. An old chap flogs his old badges outside and programme sellers cannot be seen. Team news filters through and we're up for this one today. Sat in the Pavis Stand, there is a good group of us for the first time in never, or so it seems.

This game will be pure adrenaline right from the off and we feel it sat up in the stands. Kasper, Thommo, Jackson, Hunt and Lee. Westcarr and Davies on the flanks. Clapham, Bishop and Ricky Ravenhill in the middle. Hughes up top alone.

"Come on you Pies!"

Notts start well, looking both motivated and alive. We jump on the ref's back from the off. We demand action after an innocuous tackle. It is exaggerated but the whole stadium is at it. The atmosphere, as they say, is electric. An early chance falls when Westcarr plays in Hughes. He looks up, ventures into the box then drags his effort narrowly wide. It's enough to tell us we have a chance today though. It tells us we can compete with this lot from the Premier League.

Moments later Hugo Rodallega is found in space at the opposite end. He, like Hughes, drags his effort but his shot is marginally better, if somewhat tamer. Schmeichel's hand tips it onto the post and, as the Wigan fans sigh, we are grateful. The game is tight but not too tight to call. We're the better side and we're fighting all over the park.

Ben Davies picks the ball up inside his own half and holds up play well. He has nowhere to go however and seemingly no options on the cards. Then he turns his man and curls a long, low ball forwards and within seconds Hughes lifts our hopes once more. He gets in behind Amaya and uses his body well against the defender. His experience and know-how comes together all at once and now is his chance. Our chance! One-on-one with the keeper Stojkovic and with Amaya trailing, he glances up and....Get in!!!!

We are 1-0 up and the stadium is rocking. Instinctive. Poacher-like. Invaluable. All these sum up Lee Hughes as he does his jig and has the whole home support is up on their feet. Schmeichel turns to the fans and celebrates at his end whilst the players crowd the scorer. Dave

Kevan smiles on the sideline and we cannot stop jumping up and down in the stands.

As the Wheelbarrow song breaks out throughout the ground, we have a good feeling. Dreams are now realistic ambitions. Moments later a deep through-ball by Jackson is misplaced by Amaya and that man Hughes again is on the mark to try and make the most of it. He collects possession some thirty five yards from goal and the whole stand rises to its feet as our top scorer looks to add to his collection.

Pulling away from the defenders however, Titus Bramble cuts across Hughes and brings him down. The former Newcastle man looks both slow and clumsy despite being up against a veteran in Hughes. Notts fans bay for blood. They want to see a red card issued to Bramble and so does Westcarr who goes sprinting in to remonstrate with the referee Mark Clattenburg.

Bramble is let off though and there are more digs aimed at the dugout from around us as fans make it clear what they think.

"Disgusting Martinez. Fucking disgusting!" shout supporters towards the Wigan manager. Roberto Martinez turns with a wry smile, fully aware of the somewhat over-the-top tone of the fans voices.

Now we compose ourselves and await a Ben Davies free-kick. Clattenburg speaks with the defenders, he checks the wall and Davies stands, still and ready. Totally focused on the ball and the goal he waits for the whistle to be blown. There is a short pause.

Within a split second we are jumping up and down on one another's backs. Super Ben Davies whipped it low and firm into the bottom corner and suddenly we are dreaming of the next round. Jubilant and delirious, this is pure, raw, emotion. Davies sprints towards the Kop to celebrate and the fans welcome him, open armed and raucous in volume.

Wigan players stroll back towards the half way line, dejected and with their heads hung low. They look distraught as Martinez demands focus. He demands they regain their heads whilst his opposite number Dave Kevan is screaming instructions. Whilst Wigan search for their heads, Kevan stresses Notts must keep theirs.

Unfortunately, very little time passes before we find ourselves holding on at the other end. Wigan break forward and they win a 50-50 when Jackson is out-jumped near the bye-line. Suddenly, youngster James McCarthy has found space in the box and we are anxious but relieved when we see his left footed strike hit the foot of Kasper's post. Kasper instantly bemoans his backline, yelling at them until he looks blue in the face. His passion is clear for all to see. He is a natural winner.

Martinez and Kevan stand just yards apart on the touchline, almost copying one another's static stance as the sides look to play out the half.

Then Clattenburg blows and we look around at each other satisfied with the 45 minutes we have witnessed. Notts trot off with much more of a spring in their step than their Premier League opponents. Wigan may not be at full strength but it is still a side with plenty of class within its ranks so it is a case of so far so good.

We make our way underneath the stands and talk amongst the crowds. We all chip in a quid to predict the minute of the next goal whilst one of the lads tries to get some beers in. FA Cup days are a welcome release at present from the demanding league games that we have had and the never ending story of ownership and finances.

We are all in good spirit, having a laugh, sharing a joke and drinking a beer, albeit quickly. We are 45 minutes away from making the Fifth Round of the FA Cup for the first time in some eighteen years. It's a massive day for the club and on the form of the first half we are favourites now.

As the sides get the second half underway, it is Notts who make the early pressing count. Davies whips in an inviting cross into the Wigan area and when Lee Hughes sneaks a toe on the end of the ball, we jump, arms open wide, only to see Stojkovic pull off a impressive save and leave Notts with a mere corner.

"*County, County, County, County*" sing the youngsters behind the goal at the far end in the Family Stand. Again we anticipate and expect. Davies trots along to take the set piece and fans in all corners of the ground, except for the travelling Wigan contingent, hope for the best. The chance comes and goes though and Wigan snuff out the danger and live to fight the rest of the half.

Some fans continue to wander back-up the steps and to their seats. The mad rush for drinks at the break means that many missed the early Hughes chance and some are still under the stands when Jordi Gomes combines well with Jason Scotland on 52 minutes before Rodellega finds Scotland with a neat pass and the forward fires past Kasper Schmeichel to put the Premier League club back in the game.

The Notts fans momentarily go silent and it's as though with one strike, the whole home section has realised that this is going to be a massively difficult 40 minutes. Now Wigan look to assert themselves on the game and with it, the away following start to give some vocal support. The Pavis Stand is more nervous than raucous and we're clock watching with far too long left on the clock to be doing so.

The orange shirts of Wigan are the ones now creating spaces and openings as their movement becomes increasingly impressive and vibrant. They've shifted up a gear that's for sure and now all seem to want the ball into feet. My dad glances across and I can read his mind.

Scotland finds himself in the thick of it again and this time Wigan are held back by Kasper at the front post who parries the ball out for a corner. Luke Rodgers is introduced to the scene to add a bit of bite. Perhaps a spark of pace that is now needed. Ricky Ravenhill is the man making way after an incredible display of fight and determination from the central midfielder but fresh impetus is required.

Within moments of Rodgers introduction Notts come alive once more. Kasper launches the ball long and a loose ball falls to Hughes. Neat and intricate, he feeds the ball through to Rodgers and suddenly, as he bears down on goal at a tight angle, we have an opportunity to win the tie. The whole ground stands for what seems like an age as the pacey front man reaches the edge of the box. He strikes the ball firm and direct but Stojkovic parries well. It's a frantic few seconds and the fans agony is heard all around before the ball falls in the box. Westcarr reacts quickest but is denied a clear rebound with defensive bodies laid out on the line to cut off his view of goal. Then it falls to Lee Hughes. He readies himself, he swings and his foot is caught on the back swing and he falls. As he crashes to the ground, we jump in the opposite direction to appeal.

"*PENALTY!!!*" we demand and Clattenburg nonchalantly waves away the protests as Wigan hack it clear.

We are not asked to wait long for further opportunities though as moments later Hughes is sent clear on the right only to spot that Rodgers is in more space centrally. He squares the ball at pace and we rise once more in the hope we can finish off this giant killing upset. Rodgers readjusts his body in order to get a strike at goal but Stojkovic is more than equal to it again and with that said, the chance is gone.

A little less than ten minutes left now though and the risks are starting to seem unnecessary. In the FA Cup, teams go with the flow however. The home support smells the scalp of a big club and the fans excitement funnels down to the touchline and in turn onto the park. The noise levels are as loud as we remember in this stand but we have to continue to keep things tight now.

Now it is Wigan's turn to break and create. Watson plays a long ball down the right flank and Wigan are satisfied when a blocked cross from Rodellega goes out for a corner. Adding to the tension and drama, Wigan send the big men forward as the atmosphere builds.

I glance up at the scoreboard and we have just seven minutes left to hold out. There are just seven minutes until we book our place in the next round of the FA Cup. Who knows what big tie could await us.

Wigan substitute Charles N'Zogbia jogs across to take the corner for the visitors as the Notts supporters in the Kop are loud and encouraging to the defenders. Almost willing the side to keep the ball out of the end they usually draw it into. The cross comes in deep, both high and over-hit. At least it was over hit until Bramble stretches his neck and directs it back in the direction it came from and thus saving it from going out of play. Just when we were starting to believe we were close enough to see our numbered ball in the bag for the next round, Ben Watson nips in at the back post and nods home Wigan's equaliser and now the only noise we hear is from the away support as it is their turn to jump deliriously, shout, cheer and scream. It's 2-2!!! Fuck!!!

Now we must regroup. Now we must make sure we don't throw it all away and see ourselves exiting the cup after flying at the break. Notts are positive though. Hughes again is found in space on the right and again he looks towards Rodgers with a low, whipped in cross. Rodgers is waiting to poach. Poaching for that all important, winning goal. He is positioned well and we can't help but rise once more to our feet only to see orange shirts, with desperation in their legs, stretch themselves to block the cross and narrowly put the ball past their own post to deny Rodgers the winner. His hands go to his head. That must have been close.

Surely this is the last chance as the clock ticks to 90 minutes. The volume increase one last time though. Maybe from the corner. Maybe, just maybe. Davies sprints across showing himself to be eager and with one thing on his mind. Numerous bodies jostle for position as the winger delivers the set-piece. Hughes, Hunt, Bishop and Lee are all bypassed as the ball enters the box at pace however. The pace sees it hit Titus Bramble full-on, on the leg and suddenly we dare to dream again as it heads towards his own goal with purpose and pace. Stojkovic denies us once more as he tips over and fans stamp their feet, clap their hands and beg for one last match-winning moment.

But that was the last chance. The last opportunity for an upset goes as does the chance for the players to send us home with smiles bigger than those we now portray. For today now feels like a defeat. A defeat snatched from the jaws of victory. The players have earned their pay-packets today though. Dave Kevan applauds each one off the field as do the fans. Each player has given every ounce of energy out there on the park today. No one was carried. No one gave less than the required 100% and for that we show our appreciation.

The magic of the cup was so close to springing a surprise but in doing so has left us feeling glum. For on Tuesday week, a few of us will make the trip up north to Wigan. Wigan on a Tuesday night would have been a derogatory chant a decade or so back. Now, it's a trip to a Premier League outfit. The odds are now stacked against us more so than they were 90 minutes ago though.

Chances to win these games usually only come once. Usually on home soil with the support and atmosphere behind the players. I cannot fault the player's effort today mind.

As we traipse away from the ground, my dad and I briefly talk about yesterday and the funeral. We comment on the usual things people comment on. How it was a nice service, a good turn out and a fitting tribute. All of it is true though. Even though I am only 27, I doubt I will ever witness a funeral first hand with so many people present to pay their respects as I did yesterday. It was like the old days on the terraces. Standing room only as many people were asked to filter down into aisles and stand in front of the windows that flanked the room so as everyone could get in.

As emotionally draining weekends go, this one would win by a country mile.

FA Cup Fifth Round Draw:
Fulham will play.......Notts County or Wigan Athletic.

Jungle Training

Your heart is pumping. It beats like a boxer's gloves on the punch bag. Over and over and over and over. Thud, thud, thud. The cold winter air still present and filling the lungs. A deep breath and you look both ways. An eagle eye just waiting for the opportunity to make the move. You cannot beat this feeling. Adrenaline. Pure, determined adrenaline. A break in the traffic and my dad grabs me by the arm and then he yells..."*GO!!!*"

We dart across the road, arms entwined. A father's firm grip, dragging his son along the way. Guiding and ushering across a busy main road with cars racing around the corners of the side streets that lead on to Meadows Way.

I turn my head back and glance at my grandparent's house and stumble as we hit the abrupt curb on the other side of the road. Cars glance past us but my dad and I, along with my uncle Danny, are safely across the first stage of our deadly journey. It's like going over the top or running the gauntlet. And it is where my weekend begins for I am nine years old and excited by this grown-up tradition I am invited to become a part of.

Most of my mates don't go to watch their team. Their dad's (or probably their mum's) don't let them. They'll continue not to let them for a couple of years too.

"*It's a bit busy*" or "*We'll wait until you are a year older*" my friends are told. Not me. I am one of the guys. No reserve games for me with a few hundred fans. No empty stands or quiet walks towards the stadium with my family. I am in the thick of it.

Now comes the more exciting but more daunting moment. The heart begins to beat that little bit quicker. The blood pumps around the body and the cold feet are now warming up. We are prepared for the task in hand and determined to do it well. We want to do it quicker and smoother than last time around.

"*Ready?*" asks my Dad. Arms still entwined. Firmly gripped and side by side. "*GO!!!*" and so begins the second leg of our dangerous, demanding mission. Weaving in and out of the trees we go. Up, up and away we shoot aiming for the top of the hill in the distance. Slipping in the mud and trying to steady the feet, we begin to lose grip from beneath ourselves. My uncle Danny lags behind but only by a few feet.

Closely following us, he uses the path we create for ourselves as one of his own.

Branches appear as we duck and dive. We grab a tree trunk to pull ourselves onwards in our endeavours. Like an explorer holding on for dear life, the top of the hill is within sight. The noises from the other side increase in volume. From high up here, I look down to the sides. I use my vantage point and pity those that chose the longer, but easier, route around this great mound.

"Nearly there" calls Danny as he joins us as the top and away we go heading down the other side, nipping between the trees and avoiding the fallen branches that block our path. We jump when needed but now pray our feet won't runaway with us. The steep hill would defeat a lesser person but I've been trained well.

"Watch your feet....careful!!!" says my Dad as we are momentarily parted and I slip from his grasp. We split as not to hit a tree full on and then, just as the body is in full motion and ready for more, we halt. We reach the bottom and the 'Jungle Training', for now, is over. We pause. My dad's arm rests on my shoulder and we pant for breath as we compose ourselves.

"You alright?" he asks me and I give him a wink.

We wait for our moment to complete the final leg of our glorious effort. One more main road remains between us and our destination. One more opening is required for us to dart across the four lanes and make it safely to the other side. And then, without warning or demand, I am dragged once again and we sprint across the road halting for a split second in the middle before continuing our run and hitting the pavement on the other side. All three of us are in one piece although trainers are slightly muddied. Our hearts race but satisfaction is there in body and mind.

"Good lad" I am told by my uncle Danny as he ruffles my hair and the three of us begin the somewhat slower walk over the bridge as we stroll towards Meadow Lane.

Fast forward nineteen years and it is still those memories that stand the test of time. It is still those feelings and emotions that are instilled in the mind. I pass my dad a beer as we continue to reminisce. He can't remember why 'Jungle Training' ever began on match-days and nor can I. It just did. It became part of the ritual and part of the tradition of going down Notts.

Tonight we are sat down at his kitchen table in Woodthorpe in Nottingham. In very much the same way we used to sit at the kitchen table in West Bridgford back in the early nineties we are sat waiting for

Notts County's away game at Wigan to kick-off. More through hope than expectation, we have a drink and await the team news.

Having drew 2-2 at home just over a week ago, you could be forgiven for assuming our chance has passed against the top flight opposition from the North West but having seen off both Dagenham and Barnet with a 3-0 and 2-0 win respectively since we last met Wigan, we are a side in form. We continue to talk about the past. Some sort of comfort is found in doing so. People rarely reminisce about the bad times though do they? We prefer to forget those. So what if the memories are something of a glorified version of the real thing? The pre-match rituals were the very thing that I looked forward to each fortnight and I am delighted that my old man shares the enthusiasm for discussing it.

The journey from my grandparents to Meadow Lane was a short one. In fact so short was the trip, we could leave their place just before 2.50pm and still make the ground in time for kick-off. But as the crow flies, the quickest route to Meadow Lane was directly over the two main roads that split the two sides of the Meadows. The residential side and the more industrial, cattle market side of the Meadows is divided by the busiest route into the town centre. Add to that the grass verge which, at the age of nine, felt like a mammoth ascent beyond the realms of possibility, and we were able to have some fun getting to the ground each time we were at home.

We began this little ritual at some point during the 1990/91 season but unfortunately, that is as precise as one can be. We know as much because we both remember a specific, memorable game which saw us 'Jungle Train' it to and from the encounter at Meadow Lane.

Before games we drank copious cups of tea (hot chocolate for me) as my gran played host and fed me biscuit upon biscuit. We'd watch Football Focus, take off our coats (in order to feel the benefit when we went back outside according to my gran) and settle down for a few hours. It became the norm, especially when the colder afternoons began to set in, for us to delay leaving for the ground until fairly late in the afternoon at which point someone would often point out we needed to hurry along.

I can only imagine that from here, we pushed our luck further until one day we were required to run to the ground to arrive on time and in turn, 'Jungle Training' was born.

For the life of me I will never be able to explain what we did towards the end of games though. Despite our close proximity to my grandparents and despite the fact we never shot off straight after the game to return home, we used to leave Notts games after around 89 minutes week after week. The idea was to beat the crowd and avoid the rush. But what rush? We were only walking a few hundred yards to watch Final Score so why we were so desperate to get away? I still cannot fathom it to this day.

The first real memory of this exciting, fast-paced journey between my grandparents and Meadow Lane goes back to February 16th 1991. The game was Notts County v Manchester City in the FA Cup Fifth Round.

Notts were the underdogs, very much like tonight with our tie away at Wigan. Notts were up against it, again like tonight's game at Wigan. It was Notts County v top flight Manchester City. The similarities continue.

On that cold, nerve wracking afternoon, Notts knocked at the door and threatened to do the job on their illustrious opponents. Notts battled as we cheered. Notts created openings and we began to dream. But as time wore on, it became more and more apparent that Notts may have to settle for the draw and to go and try their luck at Maine Road in a replay, the same situation we find ourselves in this evening as my dad and I open another beer.

It was back in the day when there was no such thing as a fourth officials holding up a board to indicate the amount of injury time set to be played. In fact if there were any officials on the day other than the referee and his two linesmen, we were not aware of them.

I remember it all so well even now...

My dad glances at his watch. Across the way, their fans are penned in the away enclosure and whistling for the end of the game. One or two fans sit up from their bench seats and make their way down the wooden stairs towards the exits as Notts push on and press for a winner whilst Manchester City, in their pale, sky blue shirts and tiny shorts, stand defiant before me.

I watch on in amazement. Mouth wide aghast. Then I feel a tugging on my coat.

"Come on" he says to me as I turn my head and I see we are set to leave. Danny is already up and walking along the row whilst my dad grabs me and tells me again to get moving. *"Come on Luke. Let's get away before the crowd"* and before I know it we are out of the ground and jogging back to my grandparents in a brisk, eager fashion.

Week on week we left early. Often hearing faint cries and sighs from the stands but rarely anything that changed a game would be missed. Sometimes you'd be trying to guess what the noises were for. Had Notts gone close? Had we nearly given a goal away? Was Draper creating one last chance for Johnson or had Craig Short put in a last ditch tackle to deny our opponents?

More often than not, we burst through the front door at my grandparents with Colin Slater talking us through the dying seconds.

"They just had a chance" my Granddad would tell us, explaining what the despondent cries from the Kop were as we made our way out of the ground.

It was that day - February 16th 1991. We were in fine form heading back to the safety, comfort and warmth of Final Score and cups of tea. We shot off up the hill. Fearless now of the trees that stood in our way, we already knew our path and had our journey mapped out over the treacherous terrain. There would be no slips this time, just pure speed. Up we went without hesitation before we hit the top and bombed over the summit and down the other side. Determined and focused on the task in hand, the target was to be indoors before the whistle. Keep it going. Keep on running.

"Straight over..." instructs Danny as he glances up and down the stretch of road that lay either side. We lay our trust in his call and without a pause for thought we run straight across the road. My arms once more in my dad's grip. Over we go, away from the danger of the busy cars and we're nearly home and dry. Nearly hitting our destination as we'd intended when out of nowhere, like a bolt of lightning, a car pulls out around the cul-de-sac we are entering at full speed and we momentarily pause. Feet firmly planted by ourselves. Breaks firmly hit by the driver. The bonnet is just inches from our bodies and everyone takes a deep breath as our hearts skip a beat and grinds to a sudden halt.

Danny raises his apologetic hand. My dad looks at me with assuring glance as he pulls me from in front of the car and onto the pavement. We're no longer running and certainly in no mad rush. We've just had 'a moment' I guess. At the age of nine, it's not a nice moment to have.

"You alright?" is again the question aimed at me but now the question is posed under different circumstances. *"Don't tell Mama"* (the name for which I'd always used for my gran) I'm told with a wink and a serious face.

In our wake the car has not restarted or moved.

"Oi!!!" shouts the stranger's voice. *"Oi!!!"*

"Sorry mate" my Dad shouts back but the guy is not having any of it.

"Oi!!! Oi lads, we've just scored" and instantly we all turn. The guy has his window down and is stuck firmly where he had halted but now it is apparent he is donning a Notts shirt.

"First week I leave early and we've scored" and he starts to pip his horn and cheer as my dad, Danny and I look at each other and then sprint as though our lives depend on it, through the cul-de-sac to my grandparents.

I'm first in, almost bypassing the handle on the front door and steamrolling my way into the house.

"Yeahhhhhhhhh" I shout as I celebrate under strange circumstances.

"You've gone and bloody well missed it?" asks my grandma. Cool as you like, she is so composed.   Seconds later my dad and Danny pile in to discover Gary Lund has netted a late goal against the odds.

"Get in!!!" and with another wink, my dad gives me the confidence that we've done it. Moments later, Colin Slater announces the full-time whistle and Notts are through to the next round.

Had the goal not have been scored? Had we drawn 0-0? Well a trip up north for a replay like the one we face tonight would have been the outcome. The other consequence of Lund not finding the back of the net however may have seen a random driver not putting his foot down on the breaks to listen to the late drama at Meadow Lane. Who knows what may have happened? We snatched it at the eleventh hour though that day and we lived to tell the tale.

Even now, as my dad and I sit to listen to Colin Slater nineteen years on, we can remember that day. It's perhaps testimony to this great game that, despite the fact we missed the goal, it still stands as one of our greatest footballing memories. It was a once in a lifetime moment. The adrenaline of our run, the pace from which we broke from the ground to the house and the moment we saw our lives flash before us led to the moment we experienced pure elation. It was and never will be rivalled.

Each moment is unique in itself and for that, football is fantastic. We left the stadium just over a week ago fearing our chance of further FA Cup success had all but gone. Replays away at bigger clubs rarely produce the desired result for the minnows.

Two hours later my dad and I are hugging in the kitchen as two late goals, one from Stephen Hunt and a Stephen Caldwell own goal, ensure we can dream once more of FA Cup success and have a date with Fulham to look forward to.

Such is football.

As Long As Sven Is Here

Thinking back, I forget the amount of times I uttered these words. I forget the number of occasions I heard a fellow fan down the Navi or Meadow Lane dare speak the phrase. But not today. *"As long as Sven is here, there is hope"* we used to say. Investment was possible! The dream still on!

Well today, for the time being, our dreams and hopes have died. Notts County are yet again subject to a takeover. Takeovers in football are not as common as you would think from reading this book. A new comer to the game reading this would presume that it would happen at least once in a season to such a club. But as we are set to welcome new owners, we do so with trepidation and concern.

Sven-Goran Eriksson has resigned whilst Mr Trembling has sold up for £1. The very reason we all still held out some hope for the future has now gone. But who can blame Sven?

For his time with Notts, Sven has acted in such a way that will forever endear him to the hearts of the black and white half of this city. Upon arriving at the club, he was slaughtered as some sort of a mercenary. What would his role be? What would he do? Why is he being paid handsomely to be involved?

Ultimately, Sven has eradicated all doubts step-by-step. Matt Hamshaw today told the press how he *"never missed a day's training even in the snow and rain. He has stuck through it all. He was a real gentleman and was always there to help players out."*

Sven, the guy who has been there and done pretty much everything, had a vision. Like me and many other fans, he brought into this dream we were sold by Munto Finance and probably in much the same way many of us lapped it up, so did he. It's a sad day if truth be told but, with Trembling now gone, all links with the takeover during the summer have well and truly evaporated. Perhaps this is not the worst thing for Notts County Football Club.

Peter Trembling's statement read as follows:

> *I am delighted to announce that the search for investment into this football club has concluded and last night I signed over my 90% shareholding in the club and hence the ownership to a new consortium. This consortium will reveal themselves and their plans for the club at a press conference on Monday.*

We have been on a relentless search over the last couple of months for parties intent on of investing £25m - £50m into Notts County. I have said all along that for relatively little investment and the capability to build thereafter, this opportunity represents one of the best, pound for pound deals in football. Proposed investors have concurred with that statement and have shown intent and proof of funds in their respective quests for getting involved with Notts County.

However, the biggest challenge all along has been time and it has proved impossible to secure the major investment in the tight timeframes we have. The new owners of the club are not of the £25m+ ilk but they do know the football business and most importantly have sufficient funds available to ensure the immediate survival of this football club and not least in view of our court case in less than two weeks time. In addition they are intent and focused on promotion from this division this season which has been the major objective from day one.

Accordingly, I am satisfied with our due diligence and that I am passing the baton over to people who can take this football club forward. Furthermore I have passed over the details of the bigger, longer term investors and with the additional time there should still be an opportunity for significant funding into the club. It is a great club, it will and has attracted enormous interest and I anticipate that will continue from here on.

The new owners will bring their own senior management team into the club and accordingly Gary Townsend and I leave the club with immediate effect.

I would like to take the opportunity of thanking the staff, the players and the supporters for the magnificent support I have received over the last few months. This club was left in a desperate situation courtesy of Munto Finance and at the appropriate time I will reveal more information as to what happened there.

It is a sad day for me to be leaving such a great club but I am pleased to be leaving it in such capable hands and from afar I look forward to watching the progress of Notts County FC. I will be at the Fulham game on Sunday and can think of no better stage than an FA Cup Fifth Round tie against Premier League opposition to say my farewells.

Thank you again for your support.

Upon reading the statement, if feels like something of a cop out. We're left wondering just what has happened. It also leaves us with so many questions still unanswered. When Trembling came in (initially with Munto), we were fed such big tales of success, ambition and dreams. We were not just sold the hopes of top flight football. We were told we would get it. We were told we'd see Champions League football here at Meadow Lane.

As recent as this month, Trembling managed to delay the winding up order with HMRC because it was viewed that he had secured the necessary funds to secure the clubs future. We were led to believe the club were simply *"Dotting the I's and crossing the T's."*

With each day that passed however further delays came with regards to investments, identity and monies available.

I think what has hurt most of us is the fact that whilst we were waiting to see what the fate was of our old club, we were led down a garden path and shown fruits that would get us dreaming once again. Ok, so Munto had gone (whoever Munto were) but now Peter Trembling promised that he would guide us. He and Sven would seek out investments and ensure the dream remained alive. They were pursuing several promising leads of *"£25million ilk"* according to Trembling himself.

Well suddenly it appears all such leads have vanished. Trembling has sold the club to a Mr Ray Trew, Sven has resigned and the financial plight of the club seems no better than it was prior to the whole Munto takeover. In fact, it appears much worse.

Businessman Ray Trew, former Chairman of Lincoln City, has purchased our club for the princely sum of £1. The same £1 Trembling paid not so long ago to the previous owners. For his £1, Trew gets the Oldest Football League Club in the World but he also gets the clubs debts, estimated at being around £2.5million at the time of takeover. To try and second guess any incentives to buy our club would be just pure madness at this point though. The one overriding factor of this season's story is that at Notts County, there is plenty of speculation and rumours.

Speculation, in my eyes, is all a bit pointless. After all, it was speculated that Figo, Roberto Carlos and David Beckham would join Notts and we all know this didn't happen. Mr Trew? Well I know very little about him. However, I have promised myself to remain positive. I don't think I could take much more negative vibes at present.

I have optimistically e-mailed Trew in the hope I can meet-up with him for a chat. One thing I have learnt so far this season is that unless you press for an opportunity, you'll be fobbed off continuously. Previous regimes proved this much.

If it was not for the fact we'd seen a decent amount of success on the pitch so far this season, I think my qualms and moans about Munto Finance would have been much more bitter and intense at this stage. The short of it is, they could have seriously endangered the very existence of our football club. Who has the right to do such a thing to a community, a region and an institution?

Some seven months or so after the takeover was completed just what has happened? Well there has been the biggest turnover of players we've ever seen. The squad has drastically improved and the wage bill has drastically increased. In came the likes of Hughes, Davies, Kasper and Sol along with Sven as a Director of Football. Then out went Sol and later our manager Charlie McParland after we flopped on Sky.

Hans Backe came in, Munto sold up, Trembling took over and Hans then left. We beat Premier League Wigan, we played better football than many of us can remember seeing down Meadow Lane and we were in the papers every day with transfer gossip and winding-up orders galore. It has been hectic, action-packed, dramatic and stressful but maybe, just maybe, this latest news may be a sign of us coming out at the other end still intact. To cap off the last seven months or so, we are now seeing the third takeover since the summer, Sven departing and new owners coming in to hopefully steady the ship. Regardless of who is running this football club however, we still have taxing issues (taxing quite literally) on the financial front. Last week, with Notts County in the high court to face the second winding-up order of the season, the club was given what appeared to be a temporary stay of execution. Despite the club not being anywhere close to a stable, financial footing at the time of the hearing, HM Revenues & Customs agreed to give Notts a 28-day deferment on outstanding monies owed.

The alternative was administration and so, understandably, we were relieved at the additional time our club was given to bring our arrears up-to-date. The Guardian wrote:

County have repaid almost half of the £600,000 owing to HM Revenues & Customs but, with Trembling, their Chief Executive, refusing to reveal the identity of his "investor", even that was not enough to placate the taxman. The court registrar has marked the 24th February repayment deadline as 'final'.

HMRC was not the only creditor at the winding-up hearing yesterday and Marston's PLC, the brewer owed £95,000 by County, yesterday dismissed Trembling's talk as mere 'rumour'.

So the news of a new arrival at Meadow Lane in the form of Ray Trew means several things. Firstly, Trew will need to reassess the club, the structures within it and mark out areas where money can be saved. Over the next few weeks Trew will have to ultimately decide whether or not Notts County are in a position to be saved from administration. He'll ask himself is the club in a position to continue with its assault on promotion as it currently operates or are the internal affairs so bad that administration is the only way to go knowing that as a result, a points deduction would come?

The fans view at this stage appears to be that we all knew a change was needed. After broken promises and dashed dreams, Trembling appeared to be unable to deliver just as much as the previous 'regime' (in inverted commas as he was also part of that one too).

So the latest development must be viewed with optimism albeit with a dose of caution. Hopefully Trew and his Chief Executive Jim Rodwell can take the club forwards into the future without the need for administration but for now, we just need to take it a day at a time I guess.

All we need to do on the pitch is attempt to address the gap between us and the automatic spots and perhaps we can sleep a little easier at night. Farewell Sven.

Coca-Cola League Two Table:

	Pld	+/-	Pts
1. Rochdale	29	34	59
2. Bournemouth	30	6	56
3. Bury	29	5	54
4. Rotherham United	27	11	48
5. Shrewsbury Town	30	8	48
6. Chesterfield	29	6	48
7. Notts County	**26**	**31**	**46**

Meeting The Even Bigger Boys

Fulham v Notts County
Craven Cottage / FA Cup Fifth Round Proper / 14.02.10

So much has happened and so much has changed that it seems this ever-confusing saga of a Football Club is all about off-the-pitch issues. Ok, perhaps the majority of it is. After all, we've had takeovers, players walking out, managers coming and then going, money troubles, money assurances, further money troubles, more clouded assurances and that is before you go into the debt details and winding up orders.

So as I arrive in London for today's games, I do so with some relief on my shoulders. I never envisaged that this book would be so tiring and hard to maintain. I simply wanted to document a season of a League Two club. No more than that. It helped that it was my club and it made it somewhat exciting that it was set to be one of the most historic campaigns in our long, rich history.

Frankly, this story has been impossible to fully understand, follow and grasp though. We play today in the capital knowing we are possibly just 180 minutes away from a Wembley trip, albeit in an FA Cup Semi-Final. The scene of my greatest footballing memories was in London so today I am excited. Craven Cottage is a ground that many fans have a soft spot for. It is steeped in tradition and atmosphere. It helps that it is not a round bowl such as The Walkers, Pride Park, Stadium MK, The Stadium of Light etc.

Old grounds feel more homely than the modern day, less iconic variations that are popping up all over the country. At Fulham, perhaps they have even more of that old ground magic with the Johnny Haynes stand (a grade II listed building) being the oldest football stand in the world.

As me and my old man mill around outside the ground, we cannot help but get carried away with the anticipation of it all. When we spoke the other week, we touted this as merely a day out with no expectations. Not now.

The club's fortunes may have turned but it is still the same players out on the park that can do a job. The likes of Schmeichel, Hughes and Davies may not be around for much longer given the change of circumstances but for now they'll be donning the black and white shirts and doing us proud.

As we make our way to the ground, the atmosphere around the place with the Notts fans is superb. We're with a group of twelve who've made the extra effort for this day out. A few songs brew around the ground as buoyant, optimistic, Notts fans enjoy the London surroundings. I am soaking it up and extremely excited.

As we get into the ground, it feels like there are 20,000 of us as opposed to the 5,000 reported. Everyone is stood up and songs are sung. Fans bounce about and we're buzzing. The Fulham stands sit, silent and lifeless. It is certainly far from in-keeping with what I have heard about this lot.

As eager as anyone, I cannot help but have some jangling nerves inside me on days such as this. It feels like that cup run that ended too prematurely at Spurs all those years ago. I never screamed as loud as I did when Don O'Riordan scored a scorcher at White Hart Lane to give us a 1-0 lead in the Quarter Final of the '91 FA Cup. But if we can just see off Fulham today, then who knows? We dare dream for a bit longer. The season can still be a massive success.

Suddenly the players emerge and the whole stand roars.

"Come on you Pies!" we sing loud and clear. The home fans are now more apparent and present but still rather muted in comparison to our following. As the players stroll out from the corner of Craven Cottage, I feel a sense of pride in the club I support. We've had some shit to put up with in recent weeks, let alone the years that preceded it. Today though, we are here for our club giving it everything we have and showing Premier League Fulham and anyone else who cares to take a look, that we are very much still behind our club. The time between the players walking out and the actual kick off feels like a lifetime. Songs continue and we let our opponents know exactly where we are from. We line up with a strong side. Not one that would be fazed and certainly not one that would feel threatened.

Schmeichel, Thompson, Edwards, Hunt and Jackson make up the rearguard. Davies and Westcarr providing the width with Ricky Ravenhill in the middle of the park with Bishop and Clapham. Hughesy up top alone.

There is not time for nerves now though. It is just passion and raw emotion as the game kicks off. Neal Bishop sticks an early foot in on Danny Murphy much to our delight and the away support celebrate it by way of approval. We press and push and do not give our high profile opposition time on the ball. Hughes roams up top alone and set to be over-worked. But he'll do it for the cause.

We settle well, they let us have the ball and we look at ease sharing the park with top flight Fulham. We chant, we sing and we enjoy the banter. We mock the cockneys for their quiet, subdued, support and we're enjoying our day out.

Then they turn on the class with a drop of a shoulder. Simon Davies (no relation to Super Ben) finds the rejuvenated Bobby Zamora who within an instant creates his own space. He blasts wide and we breathe a sigh of relief. It is a warning shot and shortly after a second one comes when Chris Baird finds David Elm who turns John Thompson inside out before bearing down on goal. However, he hadn't banked on Kasper Schmeichel who spreads his body, makes himself big and blocks well from close range.

What doesn't kill us and all that. We sing louder.

"I HAD A WHEELBARROW, AND THE WHEEL FELL OFF...." rings out as the whole stand rises. We've come for a party and we're not allowing the hosts to set the tone. Then the ball falls in Notts' favour for the first time. Craig Westcarr receives the ball some twenty-yards from goal, opens his body but fires wide. Our first real chance and it was over within a split second.

We continue to try and force the issue. We sing and stand as Davies picks up the ball, looks up, drops a shoulder and from nothing fires the Magpies second attempt on goal. We jump on our feet. When Ben Davies is on the ball, we have expectations. The ball swerves as he strikes with venom but Mark Schwarzer is equal to it tipping over for a Notts corner and we step it up a decibel.

The corner is poor but we get a second bite at the cherry. It falls inside the box to the one man you want it to fall too. Lee Hughes tries to re-adjust himself. He tries to dig the ball out from under his feet and then pokes it goalwards but the effort is tame.

"You'd not know who the Premier League side are" I suggest to my old man. He agrees.

"Oh when the Notts, go marching in, oh when the Notts go marching in..." sings the entire away end. There may not be much between the two sets of players but the gulf in support is there for all to hear.

Danny Murphy picks the ball up deep in the Fulham half and he looks for that searching, probing ball. He pauses then suddenly switches on as if flicking a switch. It is a delicate, intricate ball that finds Simon Davies. His back to goal he turns, penetrates the box and then fires on the turn across the face of goal and into the bottom corner of Schmeichel's net. Momentarily we pause as Fulham celebrate and we're hit in the guts. If we could have kept it tight, there'd always be a chance to grab a goal.

Now we must compose ourselves and not panic. We must find our feet. Ricky and Bish both see enough of the ball in the centre of the park and neither looks lost or in the wrong company. Chances are few and far between though. We wait. We hold on.

"If we can go in at the break just 1-0" we say.

We get hold of the ball and remain vocal as we sing our songs. We chant eternal gratitude to the now-departed Sven-Goran Eriksson. We bob up and down and then, suddenly from nothing, we jump up. Westcarr finds himself with a sight at goal once more. He steadies himself as we gasp and then we sigh as his effort is thwarted by the ever-green Schwarzer who's now having a fine game. The moment is gone as we look to one another with despair.

Those looks etched on our faces as we raised our hopes for a split second and then, without warning and without chance to prepare, we go 2-0 down. Bobby Zamora, talked of as a potential England man of late, strikes well from the edge of the box on the break and Fulham have a flattering lead to take into the break.

As much as I like to hold onto hope and as much as I try and keep my faith, I am now fully aware that for now, this chapter of the fairytale is over. We continue to stand, sing, clap and encourage. It is, from all my memories of following Notts, the best away support I can ever remember. We don't let up even though we're two goals down.

Half time comes and we're subjected to some Viva la Fulham song over the tannoy but even this doesn't dampen our spirits. The black and white half of Nottingham is certainly giving it their all today. Damien Duff makes it three on 73 minutes but by now, we're in full swing and the party atmosphere is certainly present in the away end despite the home side romping to victory.

On the way home, it is hard not to reflect on the cup run as something of a diversion from all the off-pitch problems. Although it finished 4-0 (Stefano Okaka netting on 79 minutes to complete the score line), defeat away at Fulham is far from something we should feel disgraced about. We matched them for the early stages and played well. That distraction is now gone though. Now we have no choice but to face reality.

A threatening administration, winding-up orders, take-overs and unhappy fans aplenty, now the important stuff really begins.

On a personal front, today will also have come at a cost as for those eagle eyed readers will note that it is Valentine's Day. That great old marketing tool. At least Easter and Christmas we have action packed Football schedules (weather permitting).

Neither Jade nor my dad's wife Julie will be mightily impressed with today as an event. At one stage we had invited them along but it was an empty offer. I knew Jade would say no but in offering I brought myself a free pass to London for the day.

Perhaps I will feel the full front of that later but for now, I've enjoyed the day out despite the outcome.

Compromising Situations

I've fucked up. In fact I have royally fucked up. Many, many weeks ago I promised Jade that tonight we could head over to see her friends or go out for a meal or just do something special. Given the fact that we knew Notts were playing on Valentine's Day, the fact I have training on Monday's and the fact she was down to work Tuesday, I agreed that on the Wednesday we could do whatever she wanted. I left it as her choice and her decision. It would be entirely her call.

It appears that for women, this is not enough. It is not a grand enough gesture to say *"Yes I will be free that evening"* as now, I am needed to be proactive and make a decision as to what we are doing. For me this is tough.

Why have I royally screwed this one up? Well tonight is Notts County v Grimsby Town. Struggling Grimsby who I imagine we could rack up a few goals against. They are poor at present. In fact they've been poor for much of the season. We came away with a 1-0 win at their place just eleven days ago in the league as they attempted to kick lumps out of our boys and now we meet again due to a fixture pile up after a decade's worth of snow fell back in December and January.

Prior to Fulham away, Grimsby and Bournemouth on the road proved rather fruitless as three expected points against The Mariners was followed by defeat away at The Cherries. Now Notts are out of the cup, there is only one item on the agenda and that is league success.

"But Notts don't play on Wednesday's you said" states Jade reminding me all too clearly when I happen to point out that Notts are at home. She is irate. She is also correct. Usually Notts don't play at home on Wednesday's but this winter has caused for more games in quick succession than ever before in my lifetime. Add to the mix a cup run and you can see why the fixtures machine has struggled to pen Notts' schedule of late.

All being well, Notts will travel to Aldershot this Saturday for what will be the clubs seventh game in just 21 days which is no mean feat. A game every three days for three whole weeks is as demanding as it gets in this game.

It is great for the fans that can afford it, the players who are fit and in their prime and the armchair supporter who listens on the radio. It is a nightmare however for football-widows, cash-strapped fans, veteran players, injured stars and concerned management.

So when Jade's tone became one that I'd classify as *majorly* pissed off, I react quickly and say I will not go tonight. It pleases her. She smiles and she appreciates the gesture. What women also do is then turn it around but I am sure you are all aware of this. With 30 minutes left until kick-off, she points out I can still go if I really want to. It's a lovely offer, especially as it is too fucking late.

We've just finished eating and I go to turn the radio on and she now poses a new question.

"Why bother staying in and not going to the match if you are then going to spend time just listening to the game?"

I must say I agree entirely. Why bother indeed? I should have just gone given the fact the alternative is a night catching up on soaps and Come Dine With Me. I am happy to have a night in and watch rubbish television once in a while. It's all about give and take and compromising to keep one another happy. Not whilst Notts are on though surely to God. It just makes no sense to me so we have it out.

We spend the next hour or so 'talking' about it in the kitchen and mulling over what we need to do in order to stop this pattern. It's all about priorities according to her and I understand this but, at the same time, there does not need to be a pecking order. If there is a pecking order, someone is always going to feel disappointed with their ranking. Ask a Welshman if the FIFA World Rankings are needed? Course they aren't. Not when you are much closer to being 100th in the list than first. So pecking orders rarely appease all involved.

The conversation gets better and we can laugh at it all. She knows I am frustrating and I apologise for being so and as we wash-up and listen to Notts, I am happy that we have crossed this particular obstacle as Lee Hughes nets his 22nd goal of the season to give Notts the lead on eighteen minutes. Uncle Colin is soothing tonight. In fact if I were to be taking the credit for smoothing things with Jade this evening, Colin Slater would be claiming an assist as his calming, warm voice was a joy to listen to for much of the first half as we agreed on some fundamentals and joked about some of our faults of late (Jade and I that is. Not Colin).

I am not naive though. As Colin takes his assist I am smiling but it is not the last of it from any stretch of the imagination. There are still issues bubbling away. There are still things that we need to address in the coming weeks. This particular saga is far from over. Just as I accept this to be the case in my own mind and just as we finish doing the pots in the kitchen and I tell her I am sorry, Colin delivers a blow and tells us of Devitt's equaliser for lowly Grimsby.

It's the stroke of half time and it is widely accepted as the worst time to concede but concede we have. Colin gives the verdict at the break and whilst it is not the end of the world, it is perhaps a dampened verdict. Dampened by the goal, by the atmosphere and perhaps dampened by the fact that, apart from the Darlington game on a cold Tuesday night prior to Christmas, it is the lowest turn-out at Meadow Lane for a league game this season. Take away one more for my own absence too.

It appears where I have to learn to compromise (and indeed I have this evening), Notts are doing the same. As the second half passes me by, Notts don't seem to have enough to step it up a gear and kill off Grimsby Town.

This, the result of all those extra games packed into the busy schedule. This is also perhaps the price for a cup run that took in the sights of Wigan's DW Stadium and Fulham's Craven Cottage in South West London. Players can't keep going forever. They can't produce game-after-game without a let up at some point.

The fans have to accept that tonight's poor showing is partly down to the success we've had of late. Despite the supposed millions that were going to be invested Notts have never, at any point during the season, had a huge squad and now Colin suggests they are paying the price.

Luxuries such as Kasper Schmeichel, Lee Hughes and Ben Davies come at a cost. A smaller squad, an FA Cup run and frozen pitches have all played their part in this and now, tonight, we watch (or in my case listen) as Notts stutter to a 1-1 draw with lowly Grimsby Town.

Grimsby, the side that struggle to score, that leak goals and were dirty at their place and tried to kick Notts off the park.

To make matters much worse, I listen on as Lee Hughes sees red late in the game. He followed through for a ball that, according to the commentary team, was there to go for. The ref clearly has not agreed with the Notts men in the gantry and so tonight, both Notts and I have had to give some ground.

Maybe this is a case of taking one step backwards in order to progress. Let's just hope it is followed by two steps forward.

Coca Cola League Two Table:

	Pld	+/-	Pts
1. Rochdale	29	34	59
2. Bournemouth	31	5	56
3. Bury	30	4	54
---------------------	---	---	---
4. Rotherham United	28	12	51
5. Shrewsbury Town	31	10	51
6. Chesterfield	30	7	51
7. Notts County	**27**	**31**	**47**

Relationship Status:

Strained.

"Am I Miserable Because of Notts?"

Aldershot Town v Notts County
My Front Room / League Two / 20.02.10

Today I woke with a thick head. Last night was a late night and the late night involved a few drinks and much talking. I used to rate myself as a talker. Not anymore.

I think it is imperative that when things are not going well, you should sit down, talk about it and try and work out how, as a team, you can put things right. My late night discussion proved I am no longer this person. I have had that particular characteristic drained from within and for whatever reason it is, I could not summon it last night to put in enough effort.

Mine and Jade's late night talk about us, the future and the way things have been of late happens to have coincided with the worst run in Notts County's season so far and because of it, my mood is dark, subdued and showing a distinct lack of motivation.

Since deciding to get married on Christmas Eve, it has gone pretty much downhill rapidly. Ok, it was not an instant thing. Christmas morning was quite nice and the lunch was enjoyable. It got a bit much after lunch when everyone had had too much to drink and was pointing out what a miserable git I was being (this is an annual event I find). We escaped the family Xmas mid-afternoon and spent a nice evening together however.

After the holidays were over, it was back to normality for us both though. Jade was working six or seven days a week and coincidentally, I seemed to be training or with the band on most of her nights off. In turn, I was travelling home and away to watch Notts whilst she was putting her name down for extra shifts. The short of it was that one of us was trying to save money and one of us was doing a fairly good job at spending it.

So last night was strange because she suddenly decided she wanted to talk about it. I was not pressing the issue and nor was I in the mood to discuss why we were hardly ever both in the house at the same time or why we were at one another's throats when we were. I was just prepared for a curry, a couple of drinks and a quiet night in. I think she was too, initially.

It started off as a remark. Was it a remark or an observation? Either way you look at it, she pointed out that I spent more time and effort on things that, for her, were not as important as perhaps things that were in the bigger picture for her. My job, my driving lessons (yes at the age of 27 I still do not drive), my savings (or lack of them), my interest in sorting out things for the wedding. The list could have gone on.

I reacted and I pointed out that I had made plans for the wedding. I had pencilled us in to have the bash at the local pub (which she seems to think I spend too much time in according to the chat), I had spoken to a mate, Sam The Toffee (an Evertonian), about having his Beatles cover band play and I had found the sixties style suits that both I and my best man Paul would wear.

She pointed out that she had not been consulted on any of this. She was right.

By the time it was dark, last night had turned into a discussion about why I am no longer happy and why she no longer makes me happy. I upset her, hurt her and made her angry but each question was answered with an honest response to which I stand by always being the correct one. Better to tell the truth than to lie and lead someone on after all.

We have been growing apart if truth be told. Until last night, neither of us chose to talk about it though. In the early hours of the morning she drove off to go and stay at her dad's in Melton and I had the house to myself. I sat up a little longer, drank a few bottles of beer, watched a VHS of Notts County v Tranmere Rovers at Wembley from 1990 and blasted out The Kinks till the end of the day when my eyes shut for the last time.

I heard nothing from Jade this morning when I woke up but I felt shit both emotionally and physically. I was not sure why last night happened if truth be told.

Two weeks back, Notts lost on the road to Bournemouth after beating Premier League Wigan Athletic 2-0. It was a firm reminder of just how far we had to go. Five days later we were beaten 4-0 away at Fulham in the Cup, although as performances go Notts could be proud. Throw in the fact that Peter Trembling's promised investment of the £25m ilk had gone tits up, Sven left and we drew 1-1 with relegation bound Grimsby at home and it perhaps paints a picture as to why my mood going into the weekend was so bad.

When I eventually heard from Jade this lunch time at just after 2pm, I was not best pleased that more talking was on the cards just an hour before we kicked off at Aldershot. My intention was to lay on the sofa with a beer, put Sky Sports News on mute and listen to Uncle Colin. Instead, another two hours of talking was on the cards.

At just gone 5pm, after a more heated discussion and with Jade asking me if I want her to go and stay with her dad for a few days and give me space, I had been given my space and I was met with the news that Notts had drew 1-1 with Aldershot.

Now in fairness, a point away at Aldershot given our current run of form was not a bad result but given the fact my current run of form meant I was in a foul mood, a mere point just heightened my frustrations. I didn't look at the scorer or when the goals went in. I didn't check who'd played and what chances we had had. I simply saw the score, swore at the TV and Radio (a real hard man when I want to be) and slammed the door behind me as I went for a walk, and as a result, another beer with the aforementioned Toffee man named Sam down The Boat Inn round the corner.

Had I chose to be reflective, I'd have perhaps been quite happy that we had stolen a point late in the day with a Ben Davies free-kick. I'd have been equally pleased that we had not really deserved anything from the match yet had still taken something. I did not stop to learn these facts though. All I knew was we'd lost out on a much needed three points and now we were sat fourteen points behind League Two leaders Rochdale and I was all on my fucking own.

To make matters worse (oh yes, that was possible), I was advised at 7pm that CSKA's league game tomorrow morning was called off due to severe weather conditions (surprise, surprise) and despite having won four league games on the bounce, we were now going into our third weekend without football due to this shit winter we are having.

So I am sat watching Match of The Day. I am not talking tonight and I am not even reflective. I am just not thinking in general. If I think too much, I'll just realise how shit my life has become. I already think I think too much as it is.

I remember someone once saying that the music they listened to was a direct reflection of their own mood at any given time. The point was raised as to whether the music was a result of the moods or the moods were a result of the music. I never really gave it much thought at the time.

At present, that is how I feel about football. A win for Notts and CSKA in the same weekend and I am bouncing my way into Monday morning. Defeat for one, or even worse both, and the Monday is that little bit harder to contemplate. Not very comforting when your own happiness is in the hands of eleven blokes knocking about on a Saturday afternoon is it?

Even less comforting when those eleven blokes may do their job but your club goes under regardless because it is still potless and owing money left, right and centre. Strange days indeed.

188

Coca Cola League Two Table:

	Pld	+/-	Pts
1. Rochdale	30	36	62
2. Bury	31	5	57
3. Bournemouth	32	5	57
4. Chesterfield	31	8	54
5. Rotherham United	29	12	52
6. Shrewsbury Town	32	9	51
7. Notts County	**28**	**31**	**48**
8. Accrington Stanley	29	2	46

Relationship Status:

Going down.

Counting Costs

After a depressingly dour weekend, I failed to realise that there were some blunt consequences of the recent months set to impose upon my day-to-day life. Speaking on Saturday after the game with Aldershot, new chief executive Jim Rodwell told the BBC how administration was very much on the cards despite the most recent takeover:

> *I would say [administration] at the moment is probably 50-50. A decision will clearly have to be made at the beginning of next with week with the winding-up petition on Wednesday.*

As further debts were unearthed following Ray Trew and Jim Rodwell's arrival at Meadow Lane, the likelihood of taking the club into administration appeared to increase on a daily basis.

The BBC reported that *"The new owners have now uncovered debts totalling around £6m since taking over. Rodwell admitted there could be another winding up order served on the club."*

Fans were left staggered at the figures being suggested having been told by Peter Trembling that Notts County had relatively small debts, believed to be around the £2.5m marker.

Prior to the Aldershot game, The Nottingham Evening Post confirmed as much, reporting:

> *Notts County chairman Ray Trew has confirmed no decision has yet been made on whether to place the club into administration. Mr Trew's accountants are compiling an appraisal of the club's financial positions, so decisions can be made on how best to move the club forwards.*

As you might imagine, with a painful few weeks behind the club and with my personal life appearing to stutter to equal magnitudes, more bad news was certainly not what was needed at this point.

In his interview with the BBC, Jim Rodwell went on to say:

> *The problem is not just that winding-up order, which in the grand scheme of things is for a relatively small amount. The problem is that you pay that and I think we'll find we'll have another winding-up order within 24 hours of paying that one.*

Things happen on a daily basis, and people present you with bits and pieces for astronomical sums of money, for services you wouldn't necessarily associate with a League Two football club. It's staggering what we've found, there are even chauffeur bills and we don't expect that type of invoice but we've got plenty.

£6m is an astronomical amount of money for a football club to owe, but you would be amazed at the goodwill from a lot of the creditors. A lot of people will wait for their money, people who are realistic and who want to see the football club survive.

You have got to understand that a lot of the people who have given their services to Notts County Football Club are supporters as well, they don't want to see the football club fail.

That night, I spoke on the phone to a friend who went on to suggest that fruit and veg shops were amongst the long list of companies waiting to be paid. It was suggested that the previous regime had simply used a supplier until their patience ran out for payment demands and produce was refused. The club then moved on to a new supplier, each time failing to do the right thing and pay for the produce it was using (This was never confirmed but given the state of affairs, it was not a story I was about to refuse as a myth).

At home, Jade is still at her dad's. To be fair, we'd have seen very little of each other the past few days regardless of where she placed her head at night but after a short conversation over the phone today, it was agreed that she'll come back after work tomorrow.

Most worryingly for me, I don't feel myself of late. I'm not sure what the catalyst has been for this but on a day-to-day basis I feel that I am merely existing and each day is fading into the next. Because of this, my reaction to Jade coming back is perhaps not as positive as she'd have hoped when she called.

The house looks like a bomb has hit it, there are beer bottles littered all over the place and the washing is piling up. She has only been gone a couple days.

Relationship Status:

Postponed.

It's Looking Good

Yet another massive day in the football clubs history and another deep sigh of relief comes from Notts fans the world over. As things stand today, we could have had a heavy point's deduction with further repercussions to follow.

With Rochdale topping League Two with 62 points and the third and final automatic spot filled by Bournemouth on 57 at present, we knew that if we were to have any hope of promotion this season we had to come out of today with our current tally of 46 points still intact. An eleven point gap between us and third is just about an achievable feat. Lengthen that with a deduction though and our season would be all but over.

As it was confirmed today, Notts County Football Club would not be taken into administration by new club owner Ray Trew despite fears that the hierarchy may have no choice.

Trew told the BBC:

> *With my business hat on, administration was the right thing to do. But the people who suffer in administration are the local businesses and we couldn't do that to the local business community.*

> *We got all the staff in at midday. They were very subdued and shocked. I think everyone, including the supporters, thought administration was a certainty. I'm happy to announce that's not the case.*

If the fans ever needed a lift, this was it. Trew would later reveal that his wife played a massive role in talking him into not going into administration late in the day on Monday 22nd February. It appears she persuaded him to go with his heart rather than his head and for that, we are eternally grateful. With debts spiralling out of control since the season began, Trew now has the unenviable task of making this club financially sound after years of uncertainty. However, he also has a target to achieve promotion and League One stability beyond that.

As soon as the news filters through to me, I am instantly sending messages to my old man, Mark, Danny, Sean, Paul and anyone else who wants to know or will show an interest. It's only when I call my old man during my lunch break however that I learn of the second piece of news.

"[Steve] Cotterill has been named the new Manager" he tells me.

After a somewhat short playing career which spun eight years from 1988, Steve Cotterill has enjoyed two particular spells in management, first with Cheltenham Town and then Burnley, prior to arriving at Meadow Lane.

Having initially started off his managerial career with Sligo Rovers, Cotterill joined Cheltenham in 1997 when the club were still very much a non-league outfit playing in the Southern Football League Premier Division. He enjoyed five years with the club achieving Football League status and then promotion to the old Second Division as well as FA Trophy success.

Cotterill then had spells with Stoke City, and as Howard Wilkinson's assistant at Sunderland, before a three year stint with Burnley saw Cotterill become the longest serving manager in the Football League (outside the Premier League) prior to his departure, having been with the club for three years and seven months by the time he left Burnley by mutual consent in November 2007. Cotterill subsequently turned down a spell in the MLS (America's Major League Soccer) in 2008 having only been offered a short term deal with Minnesota Thunder.

Despite not managing for a few seasons, his appointment appears to be a positive one though. With some testing fixtures in the coming months ahead, simply getting by with our coach Dave Kevan, who'd since categorically stated he did not want the manager's job, would not have been the correct approach.

Upon his arrival, Cotterill told the BBC:

It came out of the blue but I'm looking forward to the challenge. It's been very much a whirlwind - I've met a lot of good people in a short amount of time.

I don't know whether there's a vision at the moment - that's probably a bit longer-term. If the club had gone into administration, I would have still come here because I think we can reach the play-offs.

Meanwhile, Chairman Ray Trew added *"We had two managers in mind when we first took ownership. We were not going to appoint one until the summer but we felt the place needed a lift. We wanted to make sure that promotion was a certainty and not a possibility."*

Upon returning home from work this evening, I am excited to watch the local news and once more I can feel a sense of optimism about the football club. It appears the fans, on the whole, are a happy bunch at present and I am straight on the phone and talking at length with my old man.

The talk coming out from the club all appears to be upbeat and positive and suddenly all the focus appears to be on a serious push for promotion rather than holding off the tax man and additional creditors.

Steve Cotterill has eighteen games to hopefully turn this season into a success after it all appeared to be destined for a doom and gloom ending.

As East Midlands Today comes to an end, Jade walks in. I have forgotten that she was due back this evening and I have also forgotten that the house needed a good tidy up prior to her return. She does not appear too bothered however and we spend the evening talking about relatively little of importance and watching some average television.

Considering how I felt yesterday evening; today has turned out relatively well.

The Gaffer Arrives

Sat somewhat despairingly, I cannot help but think that with Hughes missing, we are really showing a real lack of cutting edge in attack. Despite it being Steve Cotterill's first game at the helm, Notts appear to be lacking drive and desire. To be frank, it's a poor start.

For today's encounter, I'm sat in a new area of the ground for me. Down at the bottom corner of the Kop, right next to the big Magpie flag and close to the away support. After ten minutes the bloke in front of me pointed out *"this is a shit game"* and he wasn't wrong. Some games just go that way at the end of the day. Whether you follow Arsenal or Accrington, we're all accustomed to watching some bad games. Perhaps more so for those of us in the lower realms of the Football League but we are all subjected to some of it none-the-less.

Of all the football I have seen so far this season, only Rotherham away at the Don-fucking-Valley matches this opening 30 minutes for, well, nothingness. We may have found the back of the net when Karl Hawley nodded across goal for Luke Rodgers to poach at the back post but it was judged to have been offside. Credit to Hereford, it has been a tightly contested game with neither side warranting a lead.

The past few weeks have been something of an energy draining few weeks for the fans. Today I need a release however. We've finally got back to a Saturday afternoon down Meadow Lane (this being only the second league game on a Saturday down here since December 12th 2009) but part of me will be glad when the 90 minutes are over. Just as long as we can sneak a 1-0 win.

Songs in the Kop are more muted and diluted today. With Johnnie Jackson sent out on loan to Charlton due to both personal reasons (his partner is expecting) as well as the board trying to tighten the financial belts and deals to extend loans for Matt Ritchie and Brendan Moloney never materialising, we are certainly short of depth compared to where we were prior to Christmas.

Due to the financial irregularities brought upon us by the previous regimes, the Football League's transfer embargo imposed upon us does little to help the situation we are in but ultimately, the club brought it on itself even if it was prior to Trew's reign.

Ray Trew commented during the week that Notts overspent on wages by some 290% more than they were allowed. Football League regulations stipulate that a club may only spend 60% of their total income on wages when plying their trade in League Two. It is thought that, what with the way the game has spun out of control in recent years with money, clubs need to be brought in line with one another.

Another big question mark must surely be placed next to those who regulate the game though. The men who sign off the contracts that are agreed and the guys who give the seal of approval to those who buy the clubs in the first place should surely be held responsible for a club being so far outside the boundaries of the spending caps. I know I have been here before and I probably gave the Football League some stick for not pushing things through quicker at the time but then I was speaking as an impatient fan. I realise now that pushing the deal through was in nobodies interest and if doubts were there then why were Munto Finance allowed control of the World's Oldest Football League Club.

Prior to today's game, I spent some time with an old work colleague and staunch Notts fans Mark Beeby before joining him in the Kop. We drank in The Navi and spoke of the good old days with Tommy Johnson and Mark Draper under Neil Warnock. He spoke of even older days with the likes of Don Masson, Les Bradd and Jimmy Sirrel and we enjoyed the hassle free memories it brought with it.

"I'm just grateful we still have a club" he reluctantly says. *"We could have been gone by now. I feel much more comfortable now than I did when we thought we had millions"* and I agree.

It is a credit to the new regime and how they have taken steps to communicate with the fans from day one. The general feeling is positive, not just with me and Mark, but throughout the Notts following. Ok, there is always going to be some doubters and we'd be naive to think otherwise given the recent lessons. Lest we forget, Trembling was hailed as some sort of saviour a few months back. Saviour? More like failure if truth be told but everything Trew has said to date has been promising so we have reasons to at least try and be optimistic.

Ultimately, games are still there to be won and without the points in the bag, Trew's words will not matter. However, as Westcarr and Rodgers press the Hereford backline deep in their own half, finally a moment of joy is brought upon us. McGynne slips inside his own box, deep in the danger area of the penalty box and with predators around. The sliced clearance could not fall any better as Westcarr pounces on it like a hunter. A raised head, an ounce of composure and he slides the ball past the helpless Adamson in the Hereford goal and we all come to life.

Finally something to celebrate as we feel the relief and the tension alleviate from our heavy hearts. Notts are in the lead and back on song.

"Come on you Pies, come on you Pies!" sing the Kop, full of heart and soul, energy and passion. Wanting more and expecting no-less. Hereford's small following remain optimistic but we have seen plenty of sides crumble under the pressure of Notts so far this season down at Meadow Lane. Why not another?

Heading into the break, we are lively once again. Mark and I talk about the importance as if to reiterate to one another that three points are needed. We reassure one another. We raise each other's spirits. Elsewhere? Rochdale, Bury, Chesterfield, Dagenham, Bournemouth, Rotherham and Accrington are all being held. All currently sitting tight at 0-0, we could not wish for a better set of half-time scores. Not only could it be a massive three points for us but two or three gained on others around us.

The second half is soon underway and Notts are on the attack. They work the ball left and then switch to the right. Westcarr is wanting the ball and demanding it to be given to him. He shows more hunger today than he has for some time. He has critics. I, at times, have joined them. Lazy and laid back. Lack of hunger and no desire. For all of Westcarr's frustrating characteristics, we must also see his strengths though. The boy has ability and the boy can cross a ball. For all his doubters, he has his fair share of goals so far this campaign and now he looks very much up for it.

He has a chance to increase his tally but is denied at the last second. The stand erupts but not to appreciate any efforts. At the top, high in the Kop, trouble has arisen. Fans from all four corners of the stand look to the top. There appears to be an incident up in the heavens and a Hereford fan, in the middle of all those Magpies thought it wise to start trouble and now the stewards are on the march. Up they run, step after step, higher and higher. The game continues and I turn back. Seemingly the only one before Mark turns too.

"Corner ball" he says nudging me and we decide to stay focused on the real entertainment. A chance comes, and then it goes. We glance back and some big lad is having his marching orders and rumour has it that the Notts County drum and drummer has taken a knock. Peace and quiet for his neighbours up there then.

We turn again as Notts turn on the style. A quick break with Rodgers involved. A neat shimmy and a burst away from his marker, Rodgers and Hawley now have Hereford stretched. Westcarr is found by a great Hawley spot and as the winger beats his man, we ready ourselves. We hope. We pray. And then bang! Top drawer stuff from Notts County's number 20 as Craig Westcarr uses his pace and guise to beat his man before firing into the far top corner with a great finish. Game, set and match surely?

Notts now in cruise control and the ground is loud and euphoric. The disappointment of drawing at home to Grimsby and the stalemate at Aldershot are slowly fading away. Sharp and alert, Notts want more. This time Rodgers wants in on the act. A fine ball into the striker's path and a reckless goalkeeping challenge later, Rodgers scrubs himself down to see Adamson being shown red and making his way to the dugout. Rodgers wants the spot kick himself but Westcarr isn't having any of it. Emphatic and assured he makes it 3-0 and 'lazy' Craig Westcarr has the loudest laugh today as he makes way to a standing ovation whilst Hamshaw replaces the hero of the hour and moments later long-time servant Mike Edwards replaces Neale Bishop.

Notts maintain their mindset. Attack, attack, attack. Hereford, with all their discipline and focus now lost, struggle to contain their hosts. Notts are now moving freely. Roaming around the park and creating space for one another. Hamshaw does well in the dying moments. He turns provider and he crosses into the corridor of uncertainty for Luke Rodgers to finally grab his goal as he pounces in mid-air from close range and makes it 4-0. Results elsewhere have been kind too, if not as kind as they were at the break.

Steve Cotterill is applauded from all four stands. He could not have asked for a better debut. It's cold. In fact scratch that. It is freezing. Through the eyes of a Notts fan though, the skies could not be more blue and clear if it were mid-summer.

We go in search of some icing to pop on top of the cake. Hamshaw follows up a half-cleared effort on the edge of the box and guides it goalwards. Well placed and steadily hit, we rise and fall with some cries of despair as the ball seemingly drifts wide of the mark. The referee sees it otherwise. From this end of the ground, we fail to see the man handling the ball on the line. Paul Downing is given his marching orders and with no Westcarr on stand-by in Hughes' absence, Luke Rodgers grabs his second of the game to make it Notts County 5-0 Hereford from the spot.

To our right, Hereford's numbers have dwindled in the away enclosure. Their fan base diminished. Elsewhere Bury, Chestefield and Bournemouth have all seen points dropped whilst Rochdale have maintained their march towards a seemingly inevitable title.

At Meadow Lane we are back in business and back on the hunt for promotion though. With games in hand, there is much work to do but to not finish in the top seven from here? It'd be catastrophic.

Days like this feel perfect. Everything goes right in the end and the ground is buzzing as hoards of fans make their way down the steps of the Kop to the streets of Nottingham.

"The new gaffer must be delighted" declares an exuberant mate of Mark's on the way out.

Later that evening Steve Cotterill will talk of how it was a good job well done. He speaks at pace and without pause. He talks with passion but not complacency. He is here to do a job and that job is ensuring that the club are not in League Two come next season.

He sounds like a proper, down-to-earth, Gaffer.

Coca Cola League Two Table:

	Pld	+/-	Pts
1. Rochdale	32	35	65
2. Bournemouth	34	7	60
3. Bury	33	5	59
---	---	---	---
4. Chesterfield	33	8	57
5. Rotherham United	31	13	56
6. Shrewsbury Town	34	10	55
7. Notts County	**29**	**36**	**51**
---	---	---	---
8. Northampton	34	5	49

Rice Pudding Brigade

Stood in silence except for the clink of a glass as the barman pours a drink. I'm waiting, rather nervously, for Mr Ray Trew and the rest of the Notts County board members and invited guests. I walk around the room, trying to calm my nerves as I glance out over the Meadow Lane pitch at the empty stadium. Around me, staff busy themselves, readying the cloak room and polishing cutlery.

Within weeks of taking over the club, Ray Trew has invited me behind the scenes; something Trembling and Co' were clearly reluctant to do. Looking back now, maybe it was the fact that all was not smooth in the boardroom. Maybe they simply did not want an outsider sharing their company who was writing a book about them and the club.

Either way, I am much more positive now. Up on the wall are photographs of some Notts County legends. Raddy Avramovic, Don Masson, Dean Yates and John Chiedozie. I stare and read the small side notes taking longer than I normally would as to pass the time and not to appear too uncomfortable.

It's not every day you are invited into such a place and as a result, I do not feel as comfortable as one might have thought. As one or two guests are brought up to the boardroom though, I feel more at ease. I speak with the chap behind the bar.

"I'm not really a football fan to be honest" he tells me rather embarrassingly. *"I'm at University here and needed some work. I look out for the Nottingham clubs though."*

I point out to him with a laugh and a smile that the less said about the other lot the better and he goes on to tell me how he joins his housemates down at the City Ground from time to time.

"No really, the less said the better."

He doesn't quite get my humour.

For the next ten minutes, we discuss my reasons for being here tonight. For the first time in my life I am asked *"What line of business are you in?"* and he is happy to talk and tell me the changes he has seen since Ray Trew took over the club.

"It was all silver service beforehand. Very posh. Mr Trew has changed that to a buffet sort of thing now. It's more relaxed now" he explains.

At this very moment Trew walks into the room and straight towards the cloakroom. I wait, quietly and patiently until eventually, he returns to the room and motions towards me. I offer a hand and introduce myself.

"So, you're writing a book?" he asks whilst standing alongside me but looking across the room.

"That is the hope" I respond.

At 6ft plus, Ray is of a slender build. His smart suit and tie and straight posture beams authority. His eyes, sat behind a small pair of glasses, rarely wander from a spot, instead focusing, composing and engaging before moving on slowly. He strokes his beard momentarily before pausing for thought. He turns towards me and makes eye contact before slowly returning to his original stance.

"You should read the book we did at Lincoln" he suggests.

"Oh right, who wrote that?" I enquire. He pauses again. As though he is picking his way through the sentence before speaking it out aloud.

"We did. The club, the chairman, the board. Lots of different people had input" and with that said, my moment ends. Two gentlemen approach me and Ray and he politely excuses himself from our conversation and begins to talk with them.

Now though, I am stood in a busier, livelier room. As the two men make conversation with Ray, two more groups walk in and make themselves at home, pulling up a chair, putting their coats away and ordering drinks.

I stand alone, sipping my drink and watching those around me. More than anything, I am trying to soak up the moment. Take it all in. Perhaps my chance to speak with Ray has passed now. I am not sure. I have little time to ponder as a host of people are introduced to me by a charming and radiant lady called Daphne.

Daphne, I soon learn, is the wife John Mounteney, former vice-chairman of the club and fan for 63 years and counting.

"So you're writing a book?" she quizzes. Within seconds she is nudging John to come and meet me properly and have a chat.

"We must have a proper talk" he says. John motions towards me and places his hand on my arm and pauses. *"I've been conned out of £600,000 so I am only too happy to tell you what they did."*

John Mounteney is a well presented gentleman, many years my senior. He has seen it all down Notts but despite this, he is fresh faced and looking vibrant as his loving wife encourages him to talk with me.

For the next 30 minutes, the couple talk endearingly to me about the club and about their history with it. John, as it turns out, was born and bred in the old Meadows much like me and my old man before me. Those same terraced streets where I first kicked a ball.

"The club means everything to John" Daphne tells me as she talks with love and a comforting smile.

201

We talk about all things Notts County, from previous managers to the current side and whilst this is not how I envisaged my evening going, I am grateful for their hospitality and putting me at ease. Daphne tells me of how she remembers a young Tommy Johnson at just fourteen years of age arriving at the club and how fantastic he was during his days at Meadow Lane. She has paralleled fondness for the likes of Mark Draper and Neil Warnock, instantly realising the era from which I'd recall my favourite memories from.

Occasionally she slips a name in before adding *"he was before your time"* and apologising but it is fantastic to be greeted by two people who despite being pulled through the mill of late, have all the optimism and hope of young children.

As we continue to chat, John becomes more prominent, asking questions and giving me snippets of information. He introduces me to Derek Pavis, the former Chairman and the man that the stand we are about to watch the game from is named after and Derek treats me with equal warmth as Mr and Mrs Mounteney.

"This guy! Make sure you put him in good light for this book of yours" Pavis tells me tapping John on the shoulder. Pavis laughs, winks and then shakes my hand before promising we can have a chat at a later point and he makes his way to get a drink using his walking stick to assist him.

"They treated him terribly" John tells me as we move on from Derek's own comments about John. *"Derek took the Munto guys to take a look at a possible training ground and they showed little gratitude. He showed them the land, spoke of what could be done with it and they treated him like a fool. Said the land was far too inferior to anything they would be considering. It's sad."*

As they continue to discuss the last few months with me, I sense an over-riding feeling of hurt from John and Daphne. I don't see any anger in their eyes or hear it in their voice. I think, given their experience, they have dealt with the anger in their own way. Several times they use the words *"conned"* and from the depths of their hearts, they appear shocked even now that someone could have done this to them and the football club they love, especially in this day and age.

I briefly meet with Glenn Rolley, the man who chaired the supporters trust prior to the Munto takeover, and again I am met by a man who wants to talk. He tells me all too briefly that he has many stories about the takeover and Munto. He speaks quietly however and within moments of meeting, he makes his excuses and leaves me with Daphne until Ray Trew returns and interrupts us.

Ray invites me to eat with him and the rest of the board over in the far corner. Again my opportunity with Ray seems very limited as he sits quietly eating whilst outside the atmosphere for the game builds. Alongside me, I talk to a John Wheeler, an associate of Ray's who is originally from Stockport way. He tells me how one day, he'd like to be able to invest into a Football Club with his own riches and how he had hoped Ray would invest in his home club Stockport County for some time.

We move onto how clubs run by fans rarely work out, with the exception of FC Barcelona, and he feels this is mainly because football fans don't have business minds. I also pose to him that perhaps it is also because they tend to rule with their hearts rather than their heads but the business brain inside of him insists it is because they just cannot run businesses. He has a point. Fortunately for us, Ray went with his heart over head when he chose to keep the club out of administration though.

By now, Ray has left the table. He has gone for a quick chat with one or two of the other board members whilst John Wheeler and I continue to talk football about the Notts squad. He is not familiar with the squad on the whole so I offer what wisdom I have and before we know it, it is time for kick-off.

I step through the doors and the chill I receive is immense. Some two hours since I ventured into the warmth, the temperature has dropped and it is a real eye opener of the night. Rubbing my hands together and pulling my coat up tight, I look out over what is now a fairly busy Meadow Lane given it is a midweek match.

I feel as though I am up in the heavens in comparison to my usual vantage point in the Derek Pavis Stand.

"Enjoy the game young'un" says one stranger as I pass him on my way up to the Directors box. I pass Glenn Rolley and two of his colleagues and they shake my hand sternly.

"So you are the one writing a book eh? Take a seat here with us. Plenty of room" and I oblige. My allocated seat is a little further up the row and as it turns out, positioned alone. So I welcome the company of these two elders who want to have me join them for this evening's entertainment.

It is a scrappy start. Long balls are driven from each side and Notts, in similar fashion to Saturday's game with Hereford, are not dwelling on the ball in defence. With Hawley unavailable, Steve Cotterill has opted for Craig Westcarr in a more advanced role and brought in the experience of Jamie Clapham into midfield allowing for Mike Edwards to return into the back four. Other than that, it is the same team that did well at the weekend so I am in high spirits as the game begins to settle.

On the touchline, managers bark orders and demand more. In the Kop, fans sing, jeer, rise and fall back down. The game has little to offer in the opening periods though. Behind me, several representatives from the Macclesfield board watch on, more vocal and obvious than the Notts contingent.

"Go on big'un..." they repeat each time the ball in driven high and long for their powerful centre forward Ricky Sappleton. More often than not he fails to hold play up and Notts' big back four combat the threat well.

After fifteen minutes however, Notts finally start to play. Westcarr is found through the middle with an exquisite ball from Clapham. He pulls away from two men, creates space and finds an opening but he snatches at the ball and it goes low to the keeper's right hand post. Still, we applaud.

It showed promise and hope. Moments later Notts break again and this time Luke Rodgers latches onto a ball from Westcarr. Rodgers, always direct when the ball is at his feet, looks up to the space in front of him and makes a beeline for goal. As he enters the penalty area, and with a man on his back, he unleashes a ferocious effort that crashes against the underside of the bar before bouncing back out against the ground and Macclesfield clear their lines.

I am now more vocal in my encouragement and why not? The Macclesfield board behind me are keen to complain about every little niggle and each decision that goes against them. Ray, two seats in front, is animated but quiet. He seems to be willing the team forward with every move yet hardly speaking a word to anyone during the opening stages.

Notts continue to press. The ball is worked well down the right this time and John Thompson finds himself with time to deliver a cross on eighteen minutes. It is floated high and deep into The Silkmen's box and there, arriving at the back post, is Jamie Clapham who nods home from close range for his first goal of the season. Now my nerves can rest.

"Once they get the ball down..." says the gentleman to my left, suggesting they look a much better side for it. He's correct of course.

Behind me the Macclesfield guys are now demanding more and the visitors give them just this. They break forward as the half continues and have occasional glimpses of goal with *"the big'un"* seeing their best chance fizz wide midway through the half.

Not long till the break now though. Notts with a firm foothold on the game but, at 1-0, the game is far from over. Macclesfield break, this time creating space down the right, and deliver a telling cross. Former Notts man Richard Butcher arrives at the back post where he has space, time and the goal gaping. Somehow he pulls his shot wide and his hands, along with Keith Alexander's on the touchline, cover his face as they rue the missed opportunity.

With the referee now keeping one eye on his watch, Notts have the final moments of the half. A direct ball from Kasper finds Westcarr down the middle before a neat touch away from his marker and suddenly we can see 2-0 on the cards. I gradually rise from my seat and then thud back down onto the soft leather cushioning as Westcarr blasts over from close range finding nothing other than a fan in the Kop.

"Good chance" I say. I receive a disappointed smile back.

With that chance gone, the half is over. We return to the warmth of the boardroom to find Rochdale leading Rotherham. Now looking unlikely to be caught, Rochdale will surely secure their first season outside of this division since 1974 come May?

For all the strange and new experiences this evening, it is now I feel it most, stood at the break in the warmth waiting for a drink at the bar. No plastic cups or queues for the toilets. No cold concrete floors or dodgy tannoy announcements. Daphne walks over.

"Not a bad half. They like to hit it long don't they?" she remarks.

"They do. I'd take 1-0 now. Shame we couldn't have stolen another before the break though."

She eagerly pours herself a tea from the table and tries to warm herself up as her husband John joins the likes of Derek Pavis and Glenn Rolley for a bowl of rice pudding. I cannot help but think back to the statements made by Roy Keane about those in the boardrooms who like their prawn sandwiches. Not quite that down at Meadow Lane is it?

Back in the late-nineties, I used to occasionally venture up to these parts at the break with my old man and my uncle Danny. Rather cheekily, we'd walk up towards the VIP lounge behind my uncle who had an air of confidence about him that meant he'd never be turned away. Numerous times, when asked, I'd simply point and say *"I'm with him"* and it worked. It was not the Directors box or board room of course. But it was the bar further down the corridor that we'd often find ourselves in.

Tonight is very different though yet I still cannot help but feel like I am blagging my way up here at the same time. Ray is suddenly stood next to me, solemn and calm.

"Not bad" he states as he looks towards the TV with Sky Sports News on. He says no more but needs not to, for he is right. It isn't bad and, if in an hour's time, we have three points in the bag, it'll be another step towards League One.

As the second half begins, the atmosphere and volume in the ground lifts a notch. For all my years watching Notts at Meadow Lane, I feel an overriding sense that the stands are all supporting together now.

"I had a Wheelbarrow, and the wheel fell off" rings around the ground as Notts kick from left to right and make the early impressions. Ray returns to his seat some ten minutes into the half and momentarily stands to look around the whole ground before taking to his seat.

In the middle of the park, Neale Bishop and Ricky Ravenhill battle harder than I have seen them battle to date whilst Graeme Lee and Mike Edwards are exemplary at the back. Ok, there are still calls for the *"big'un"* of Macclesfield to produce the goods but on the whole, we are troubled very little. The visitors pose threats from set-pieces but Notts stand strong and look good value for three points. Just so long as we can hold on.

With 63 minutes on the clock, Steve Cotterill appears positive as he searches for the second goal. Delroy Facey comes on for Clapham and both players receive a standing ovation. Macceslfield's probing is limited however and shortly after Delroy's introduction, Ben Davies finds Stephen Hunt in the box with a delicate cross but the header doesn't test Brain in the Macclesfield goal and the pattern returns to kick and rush for the team in blue.

Former Notts man Paul Bolland is introduced to the fray by the visitors boss Keith Alexander but Cotterill is just as eager to mix things up with Ade Akinbiyi and then Matty Hamshaw introduced. As the clock ticks down, we see Akinbiyi and Facey press for the elusive second goal before a strong handball claim is waved away in the Macclesfield box.

Cold, bitter and chilled to the bone, the whistle is finally blown as Ray smiles wholeheartedly for the first time.

"I'd have preferred it if Aldershot hadn't won" he says as we stand looking at the other scores back inside.

"We'd have taken those results at 7.45 though. I don't think we need worry about Aldershot" and he again smiles but says very little.

I make my way to the bar, much more confident and at ease than I was pre-match. The Macclesfield board walk in and walk to the corner of the room, quiet and subdued. Ray and Jim Rodwell offer their hands to the Macclesfield guys and console them by suggesting it was tight but on reflection, there was only one football side out there tonight. I can imagine such meetings being quite difficult when there has been bad blood between clubs, managers, fans and players but tonight there are just winners and deserved losers.

As pleasantries are exchanged, Jim makes his way over to the bar where he begins to entertain a group of guests from Lincoln City Ladies team. I stand to one side, half listening in on the conversation, when Jim asks two young American girls if they liked the songs the Notts fans were singing.

Within seconds the whole group are engaged and discussing football chants, terminologies and reasons.

"They sing, I had a wheelbarrow and the wheel fell off..." laughs Jim enthusiastically. He admits he knows no reason as to why as he swigs a bottle and the group begin to speculate.

I have spotted my opportunity and I take it well. I tell the group, as I interrupt and step into the circle, that Notts were away at Shrewsbury in the early nineties and misheard the home fans singing a song as they led 2-0.

"Notts fans interpreted what they heard. No more than Chinese whispers really" I proudly say.

"That's fantastic" says Jim with a broad smile. *"They just carried on did they?"*

Jim Rodwell, formerly a player with the likes of Rushden & Diamonds and Boston United, was a no-nonsense centre half and his stature makes it clear as to why he was good for such a role. With broad shoulders and an imposing figure, Jim is much more outspoken than Ray and seemingly willing to talk to everyone in the room. His views are loud and his laughs are louder but he too comes across as a warm hearted character of who is only too happy to entertain and engage with people around him.

After telling the story of the song sticking and being sung under the Twin Towers of Wembley, Jim enquires about the book and asks about the progress and my background. He stands proudly, chest out and chin up as he tells me how he'd be a great subject for a whole chapter and I laugh telling him that we could certainly discuss the idea at length.

"So why did you get involved at this level?" I ask. *"I remember you as a player. Where did the transition come?"*

"Well Ray just bullied me" he laughs taking another swig from his bottle. *"Ray said come and get involved so I did".*

He missed my point somewhat as I was enquiring as to how a player moves up to the boardroom level but with days as a caretaker manager at Boston turning into being Chairman, it is obvious that Notts is not the thing that forced his hand at such a role.

I comment on the apparent honesty at the club and the seemingly frank interviews that have come from both himself and Ray since the takeover was completed and he is quick to add to this.

"We're honest blokes. We'll always tell the truth" and he raises his eyebrows as if to say it is my choice and ultimately the fans choice as to whether we believe him.

"I've said it before. But the club is literally snookered [financially]" and at this point a smile turns to a gentle, consoling frown. He knows the task ahead is set to be a long arduous one. But if he is walking into it open minded, then perhaps he and Ray can pull it off.

"Some fans initially felt there was lack of ambition. They've had so much promised to them that suddenly realistic aims do not sound too exciting" I point out.

"There is no lack of ambition here" he says frankly.

Like with my conversations with Ray earlier in the night, everything suddenly ends.

"Excuse me" he says tapping me on the shoulder. *"Keith the Chief"* he yells as I turn to see Macclesfield Town boss Keith Alexander enter the boardroom via the stand.

Certainly taller than anyone else I've met so far this evening, Alexander is just as imposing as Jim but in a different way. Dressed in a tracksuit, football socks and Macclesfield sports cap, Alexander looks comfortable walking amongst the shirts and ties to meet his old mate Jim. It takes a man of extreme confidence to stand in such company in this manner and as he and Jim catch-up, Ray Trew also exchanges handshakes with the man who managed the Lincoln side during his tenure there as chairman.

There are smiles for all three gentlemen whilst Derek Pavis also says hello to Keith and offers the man a drink.

For me time is flying. It is passing by as though all my surroundings are in fast forward. Tonight has opened my eyes to a different side to both the club and the game of football on the whole. No prawn sandwiches or pretentious characters. No upper-class snobbery or pre-conceptions of what I am here for. Perhaps it is me who has misjudged people at this level.

I check my watch and then look towards Ray. I will not leave before thanking him for his hospitality and kindness but at present he is busy. Another beer maybe? Probably best. I chat for the rest of the night with the American girls and their manager Rod Wilson. Daphne, John and Derek all come and greet me farewell and goodnight and as I ready myself to leave, in walks Steve Cotterill.

Steve is a happy man and rightfully so. Very different in appearance to Alexander, Steve is looking smart and content although perhaps a little on the tired side. He is introduced to the Lincoln contingent and speaks politely but with short answers before spotting myself on the edge of the group. He wanders over, introduces himself, shakes my hand and I simply tell him my name as he smiles and returns to play a bit part in a conversation. I decide that for tonight, I have done enough. I will be patient and speak with Steve another time when he is perhaps fresher and much more relaxed.

"Excuse me all, I need a word with Ray" and off darts Steve to find the Chairman saying goodbye to the Macclesfield guys.

As the night draws in and the floodlights are turned off Ray wanders over and we each in turn thank one another. I step out of the boardroom with Ray, Jim and Steve whilst Daphne and John, still making their way our through the foyer, talk with staff tidying around them. Up on the wall, clear as moonlit sky, a portrait of Jimmy Sirrel looks down over us all. I smile politely as we all say goodnight and I walk out into the cold, frost bitten night.

Now that was surreal.

Coca Cola League Two Table:

	Pld	+/-	Pts
1. Rochdale	33	39	68
2. Bournemouth	34	7	60
3. Bury	33	5	59
4. Chesterfield	33	8	57
5. Rotherham United	32	9	56
6. Shrewsbury Town	34	10	55
7. Notts County	**30**	**37**	**54**
8. Aldershot Town	33	9	51

Keith the Chief

03.03.10

Comfortable, happy, laid back and polite, Keith Alexander last night made conversation and evaluated his teams defeat at Notts in League Two. Born in Nottingham, at 53 years of age, Keith has enjoyed indifferent success down the years in both non-league and lower league football.

Jim Rodwell referred to him as *"Keith the Chief"*, a name that stuck since the pairs paths first crossed many years ago on the Sunday League park pitches. Others fondly see him as a man who inspired black players up and down the country to move into management after he became the first black man to be permanently appointed in the English Football League in the summer of 1993 with Lincoln City.

This morning, the football community mourned his death as he passed away in the early hours following his return to his Lincolnshire home from the Notts County boardroom.

Just like that, life can be taken and everything goes into perspective.

As I returned home this afternoon, I saw news reports and tributes to Keith who last night managed Macclesfield for his 99th game in charge. At Lincoln City, fans placed flowers, shirts and scarves in the dugout for the man that led them to four Play-Off campaigns.

On the news, Notts County's youth team coach Michael Johnson talks about the advice he asked for the night previous whilst Richard Butcher of Macclesfield speaks openly of how he was given a lift home last night by Keith just hours before his passing.

It's a sad day for League Two and football in general and even more painful for the family and friends of Keith Alexander. A football man through and through, he will undoubtedly be missed.

A Battle With The Locals

Notts County v Chesterfield
Meadow Lane / League Tow / 09.03.10

By far and away, the biggest game so far. Tonight, just a small handful of League Two sides are in action and for Notts it is a chance to make up lost ground with one of our games in hand. Glancing across to my right, rows upon rows of expectant fans all sit facing one way. They all face a tense 90 minutes of football here at Meadow Lane. Chesterfield, despite my early season predictions, are very much in the running and as John Sheridan leads his side out at Meadow Lane, we know that three points tonight could make or break our season.

It is dark and cold but lively and atmospheric. The bright lights above the stands point down casting the stars of the show into the forefront of our attention. Three wins in three and Cotterill is a manager in form. Following wins over Hereford and Macclesfield, we sought some sort of revenge on Saturday when we beat Accrington Stanley 3-0 away from home. Ben Davies, Lee Hughes and Luke Rodgers were the men with the goals just three days ago and now the Gaffer will hope they can reproduce tonight.

The Chesterfield allocation is full and bouncing. A local derby and all quarters are out in force tonight. 7.40pm and the Spirerites are ready for the game ahead too. The Wheelbarrow song echoes around the stadium whilst the blue shirts that traipse out onto the field of play applaud their following for simply turning up. As with us, they are only too aware of the importance of tonight's encounter as they press for a potential Play-Off place.

Schmeichel, Thompson, Hunt, Edwards and Lee. Davies and Westcarr with Ricky Ravenhill and Bishop in the middle. Rodgers and Hughes up top. Attack minded and strong all round. This is our strongest eleven at present and it appears Cotterill knows it.

"Come on you Pies, come on you Pies!"

We clap, encourage and roar as the game kicks off and the ball bobbles along the patchy surface. Play interchanges quickly and first Notts press before Chesterfield respond. Possession changes hands all too often and the game is 100mph. Fast and furious, passionate and heartfelt.

Sat here in the Pavis Stand, I am joined by my old man and my uncle Danny. The Kop to our left is in glorious, full voice. The seats that surround me are filled to the brim and oozing with optimism. It may appear a normal thing for most fans but here, at Notts, viewing the glass as half full is not the norm. History has not been kind enough to us I guess.

Notts break early doors with Craig Westcarr running at pace and with increased confidence given his form of late. A low whipped cross looks good and we watch on with hope more than expectancy as Ben Davies attempts to make up ground in the middle. The chance goes begging and now it is our turn to defend. The visitors break with energy and vibrancy down the left. Neat play and clever footwork creates an opening and we are grateful when the evergreen Davies finds himself covering at the back post to nod to safety.

The game does not stop there though. Five minutes are still not on the clock and Notts break courtesy of a quick release from Kasper in goal. Westcarr, Rodgers and Hughes all motion forwards with pace before Bishop is found in space at the back post to nod towards goal. Keith Stroud, the referee for the evening, signals to his linesman that he has spotted the offside and play halts. The pace however is relentless.

Moments later and Davies is again the key figure as he whips in a dangerous ball towards the front post and Chesterfield survive by scrambling away for a corner. We are looking good.

"Fantastic start" says my dad. I'd take a dull start and a goal though.

Inside ten minutes Chesterfield receive the first yellow card and the tension rises somewhat. The tackles are flying in, the pace is nothing short of breathtaking and both sides are out to try and win the game. Chesterfield are mixing their direct balls with some clever football in the final third but it is Notts who make the most telling opportunities. They press and hound and search for the opening.

There are nineteen minutes gone and Chesterfield are on the back foot. Notts pressure and close-down all over the park. Lee Hughes causes problems and forces the visitors onto the back foot at every given opportunity. A poor clearance does not meet its intended target and suddenly Notts smell an opening as Davies wins the ball some 25-yards from goal. He waits for the ball to settle and, as it bounces in front of him, he readies himself and looks up. We ready ourselves too and I grasp my old man's shoulder as we slowly begin to itch to our feet. We pause momentarily with bended knees then leap as a sublime volley and a lethal strike is unleashed by a creative spark. It's 1-0 to the Magpies and Davies sprints off to receive his adulation.

I turn to my right and we jump and cheer. No doubt about it, it is a big goal for us. The moment is even bigger though and Notts are firmly on top. There are smiles all around in the Pavis Stand as the Kop raises the roof.

"Super, super Ben, Super, super Ben, Super, super Ben, Super Ben Davies" we all sing joyously.

Stroud blows his whistle demanding the players return to their own half for the restart but we want more now. The ball finds Westcarr on the far touchline as he jockeys for position, sells his marker and then hits the line. The cross is telling and dangerous but we think of what may have been as the ball is blocked and Hughes is denied from close range.

The ball continues to bobble in the middle of the park and Ricky Ravenhill, competitive as ever, receives an unjust yellow for his over-zealous nature.

"Get a grip referee" I yell as I fail to hold back in the heat of the moment. It was a well-timed tackle and Stroud was having none of it. Now he is seemingly stopping the game whenever the opportunity presents itself, breaking up play and ruining the match.

The boo's ring around Meadow Lane as Ricky walks away, disgusted with the decision and now walking a disciplinary tightrope for the remainder of the game. The ball drifts from end to end. With Kasper at one end and Chesterfield's Lee between the sticks at the other, both are kept busy and on their guard picking out crosses whilst remaining alert at the back.

Our own Lee, Graeme, gives away a free-kick midway through the half and Davies' attempted clearance sees him receive a yellow for kicking the ball away. The second Notts man of the game to be booked and we again feel aggrieved. When the ball is drifted in from the resulting free-kick, Lee and then Edwards, stand tall and win the ball with firm headers.

The sand, the bumps, the divots and the faults are all on view on this surface tonight as balls run heavy and we see legs being left in that split second too long. With each passing moment the stands become more animated.

"Fuck off ref" we roar as yet another call goes against us. It feels as though we are playing against twelve men. Sheridan is up and out of his technical area and we let him know exactly what we think of him and his sides approach.

"Get back ya twat" yells one bloke behind me. Sheridan turns. He smirks and takes it in good humour.

"Steve Cotterill's black and white army" sing the Kop. They bounce to the beat and vibrations are felt all around us. Feet are tapping hearts are beating. Notts break and have a half chance in front of the Kop but seconds later Kasper is called into action at the other end as play remains frantic. The game has opened up, too much for our liking given

the lead we have. Davies and Westcarr offer the outlets but Chesterfield, like Notts, have a good, steady shape to their side.

Then, seconds before the break, Bishop becomes the next name to be added into the referee's notebook. It is becoming a joke. A disgraceful decision from Stroud as his puppets on each flank do nothing, say nothing and simply back up his calls with a nod and a wave of the flag. In the dugout, Sheridan demands even more though. It is as though Shroud has not given him enough already. Every single 50-50 and each and every close call so far has gone their way. Literally every decision in the balance has gone to the team in blue. Chesterfield's fans are not as vocal now on the far side but still they raise the volume when a corner is awarded before the break in their favour. Lee again is the man to head clear and set Notts on their way.

Half time comes and we gladly take it. Bury are trailing, at least for a minute, until the announcer advises they score during first half injury time. 1-1 at home to Darlington fills us with promise though. A big second half ahead of us now, anything gained on Bury will be very much welcomed.

As the temperature drops, the importance rises. The next 45 minutes could really set us on our way to promotion. Prior to this evening Chesterfield have shown fine form winning seven from their last eight league games. They've began to produce form at the business end of the season with the weeks drawing in and the points seemingly more vital than those in autumn. We know the value remains the same however and three tonight would counter the three they took off us at their place back in August on the most frustrating night of my season so far.

The second half starts and we settle back into our seats, albeit momentarily. Stroud is at it again calling things from the perception of Sheridan. Cotterill turns to his bench bemused and dumbfounded. Notts' eleven men verse twelve for the next 45 minutes by the looks of it.

A few minutes in and now Bishop is on the receiving end of an unjust tackle. The tenacious midfielder was clearly thwarted by Chesterfield's Conlon but no card is shown and we are irate.

"Exactly the same as what Bishop was carded for" I point out to my old man.

My fellow match-goers are starting to show just as much frustration as myself. Man-for-man, we refuse to understand how the referee can be so one-sided. Notts remain strong though and they do not buckle or lose discipline. In fact, the reaction is the total opposite. Within seconds of each other, Ben Davies and John Thompson test our visitors resolve.

Davies sees his effort well blocked but the ricochet eventually finds Thompson who hits the foot of the post with a well placed effort. It is a let off for Chesterfield and they know it.

Finally, on 52 minutes, we roar and applause in appreciation. Conlon goes into the book for a late tackle of Mike Edwards. Edwards, dependable and determined at the back, is not shaken. He takes it, jumps up and continues to do his job.

Notts fail to show any weakness on the park. Cotterill is a livewire on the touchline always asking more of his players...demanding that little extra from his men. The players clearly respond to him as they lay their hearts down on the line. We break once more and we look the more-likely of the two sides to score. Hughes goes roaming, searching for an opportunity. The ball fails to fall his way however and the striker gives away a soft free-kick.

Just before the hour mark, Sheridan mixes things up a little. We see a double change to try and force Notts to think differently. Barry Conlon and Derek Niven both leave the field to be replaced by Scott Boden and Danny Boshell and we are now checking the clock more regularly. We wish for time to pass as it appears to slow down.

For all our early optimism, the game is tighter and too close to call. In attack, Chesterfield remain very much apparent without proving clinical. Up the other end, Hughes and Rodgers are finding it difficult to create openings against a tough, no-nonsense Chesterfield side.

At the heart of the Chesterfield defence, Robert Page is resilient in his presence against a Notts attack that is the most lethal in the country. Despite being in his veteran years, he shows all of his experience winning headers and snuffing out our attacks although in Davies and Westcarr, we possess that little extra for them to deal with. Westcarr presses, interchanges and looks hungry for the action. Whether it is the renewed belief after getting in amongst the goals or the apparent lift that Cotterill has brought to the club, I am not sure but he is appreciated by most in the Pavis Stand now and I will happily admit that he is proving me wrong.

Alongside Cotterill, former Sheffield Wednesday man John Sheridan is far from impressed despite the bigger decisions falling his way. Stroud wanders over. Sheridan, demanding and furious on the touchline, barks into the ear of the fourth official once too often. With one finger pointed firmly at the stands, Stroud makes his feelings known and their manager is sent-off with the biggest cheer since the goal bellowed out by the Notts faithful.

Notts win a free-kick deep in the opposition half. Keeper Tommy Lee positions himself nervously as set-piece wizard Ben Davies steps up. Beckham-esque in stance and approach, this time he falls short as the wall rises to head clear but we are still the stronger of the two sides and still the more likely to net.

"Come on you Pies, come on you Pies!" sings the whole ground. From the Kop Stand, to the Pavis and from Pavis to the Haydn Green Family Stand and Jimmy Sirrel, the noise is immense and then *"sssshhhhhh"* as we hit the away enclosure. They are quieter and something of a diluted version of their first-half-selves.

I'd take 1-0. We'd all take 1-0. All but the nerves would take 1-0 at this point. Rodgers, with 70 minutes on the clock, breaks down the right flank. He signals for the ball and shows for it. He wants it, demands it and then gets it. With some short, sharp footwork and a jinking movement, he looks steady in possession as he opens up and shifts the ball out of his feet. He does so just enough to have a sight at goal. He strikes with power, venom and impetus and the ball screams just over the bar as we sit back down and let out a deep breath.

Moments later we create another chance, this time with Lee Hughes looming large in attack. He is found just inside the box, still hungry for more and still likely to be the one to fire us onwards to three points. He too shifts the ball from his feet and he too hits the ball with intent. He is denied this time by the flailing legs of Robert Page however and Chesterfield hang on.

Not long left now though. A few travelling fans depart down the gangways with their heads down and accepting defeat although defeat is something that is far from confirmed. At the back, Thompson, Edwards and Lee combat an aerial bombardment we are in receipt of but still they hold Chesterfield off. On the touchline, Sheridan's assistant manager and his coach Mark Crossley (you know, the one that played for them over the river) looks back and forth, up to the stand, wishing for some enlightenment from Sheridan. Like an actor lost without a director or a student without their teacher. He looks onwards without any influence or hope to change the pattern of the game. But will they need it?

Notts give away a sloppy free-kick on Thompson's side of the park and Chesterfield throw Page and Co' forward into the attack. Now they surely view such a free-kick as their most likely source for a goal. The ball is angled well and delivered with ferocity but in our Kasper, we have the safest hands outside the Premier League. He grasps, clutches and falls to the turf, holding onto the ball for dear life. We rise, cheer and let out a deep sigh of relief as though we've just increased our lead.

We're now into the dangerous period of the game for a goal now, against the odds, would leave us with such little time to hit back. Such effort for just one point would feel like an empty reward for tonight's endeavours. The glowing lights and the cold, fresh, chilling air both point towards a victory now though. It feels like a night for success. Sometimes, you can just tell that everything is going to be alright.

Now there are 81 minutes on the clock and just nine long minutes left for us to hold on.

"*It'll feel like a good fifteen*" says my uncle. Talk about stating the bloody obvious. That was not what I needed to be reminded of.

Chesterfield continue to go in search of a goal to dampen our spirits. Whalley sends a fine cross into the Notts penalty area but, in much the same vein as the previous 80 minutes or so, Graeme Lee puts his head right back through the ball and ushers his men forward and out of the final third.

The play only comes back at us however. Danny Boshell receives the ball, some 35-yards from Kasper's goal. He looks up and with no options left, he tries his luck. We jeer and the Kop gratefully throws the ball back to the pitch side as Boshell looks on with disappointment.

"*Replacing Luke Rodgers, number 22, Delroy Facey*" we have it announced and we rise to our feet to applaud both the departing and incoming players. Delroy, a fan's favourite down at Meadow Lane, is the sort of player you cannot help but wish success on. His fitness and touch, at times, appear to let him down but we love him for his effort and desire.

For the later part of the 2009, we saw Delroy farmed out to Lincoln City on loan where the big man only hit the net once in ten outings. In recent weeks, with the squad depth seemingly depleted and the siege mentality instilled into our club from the transfer embargo, Delroy has had several cameo roles in the later stages of games though and showed plenty of endeavour. If there is one thing that football fans can appreciate, applaud and acknowledge, it is a player that gives his all.

Within seconds of his introduction Delroy is charging down the Spirerites backline, not giving them time to turn on the ball and compose themselves. The ball is sent into the channel and Delroy gets his body in line with the ball, holding up play and slowing the tempo right down. We encourage and push the side on and Westcarr responds. He breaks inside of Delroy and after receiving a perfectly weighted pass from the target man, Westcarr flashes the ball across goal only for Davies to have a strike blocked by Tommy Lee.

We exhale once again. Knees bent, elbows rested firmly on them and hands up against my cheeks, I know we need to hold out. There are just a few more minutes to go now. We have little time to relax or ponder though. Lee Hughes finds himself in space and with time. Surely now we can wrap things up? But the flag is up and the cheeky front man turns to disagree, telling Stroud that he and his assistant are wrong before working back to defend.

Thompson is booked in the closing minutes after going in late and the card tally continues to increase. Chesterfield continue to launch balls forward but in Edwards and Lee, we have a pair very much on their game. Westcarr's number is put up in lights and as he strolls off, we can feel the three points being notched onto the table already. Appreciative and respectful, we again clap for the departing and incoming, with the evergreen Jamie Clapham, scorer of the winner the last week against Macclesfield, coming on.

The fourth official returns to the touchline and the board is held up.

"It'll be four minutes" I say, nodding to my old man as my predictions are duly confirmed. *"It's always four minutes when we need a whistle"*.

We battle and fight. Fight and press. Steve Cotterill is on tenterhooks as he watches on unable to do any more. Matty Hamshaw warms up and readies himself for the final moments as Clapham swings a cross towards Hughes. Maybe now, with just seconds remaining, we can kill off the resilient Chesterfield side. Their fans continue to walk away, apologetic and quietly as Hughes jumps but, rather than powering home a header, he leaves a hand up to try and knock the ball at goal. A yellow card being the obvious outcome, I look and my old man and smile.

"Hughes will get booked tonight" I had told him earlier this evening. *"One more yellow for a suspension. We'd be better to lose him for Crewe and Bradford than Bury and Rotherham that will follow."*

Was it obviously going to happen? No. Likely? Yes. At that moment, Notts again show their gratitude for the shift just put in as Hughes is brought off with Hamshaw as his replacement.

The Kop Stand sings *"Let's all do the Hughesy, let's all do the Hughesy, la, la, la, la, la, la, la la"* as they dance and celebrate, pre-empting the three points.

Now Stroud is checking his watch. Pausing but checking. The free-kick is launched forwards by the Chesterfield keeper but no sooner does it cross the half way line, we jump to our feet and celebrate the biggest three points of our season to date. Cotterill shows just a slender sign of happiness and emotion as he moves across and shakes the hands of a Sheridan-less bench.

"Don't worry, about a thing, cos every little thing, is gonna be alright" blasts the tannoy system. Fans all around me join in. Some sing along

218

somewhat passively as others enjoying the moment, belting the words out. A small section in the Kop begin to sing *"Up the Football League"* we go.

For those that did not believe at the start of the night, now they must realise it is our destiny. Surely promotion is ours to lose now. We are one point off the automatic places and with games to spare. Suddenly it is all looking very promising.

"Come on you Pies, come on you Pies!"

Coca Cola League Two Table:

	Pld	+/-	Pts
1. Rochdale	34	39	69
2. Bournemouth	35	8	63
3. Bury	35	5	61
4. Notts County	**32**	**41**	**60**
5. Chesterfield	35	8	60
6. Rotherham United	33	8	56
7. Shrewsbury Town	35	7	55

Living The Dream

Smart, charming and, in-keeping with my experiences within the club so far, very welcoming. Just a few choice words that describe Ralph Shepherd as we sit in front of a Football League Charter from the 1890's that is behind a black and white striped sofa that yells Notts County.

We are below the main stand here at Meadow Lane after Ralph invited me down for a chat about the season, the future and his role at Meadow Lane. At 22 years of age, Ralph has grown up supporting Notts albeit from a very different background to me.

Although born in Amsterdam, Ralph's family originated from the West Bridgford and Wollaton areas of Nottingham and from a pretty young age he, along with his parents, moved over to the UK from Amsterdam and settled in Derby of all places. However, his footballing instincts ensured he was of the correct County variety and the rest of it, as they say, is history.

We exchange pleasantries and make our way up the carpeted staircase, passing the picture of Jimmy Sirrel, and taking a seat in the 1862 suite up within the stands. If my story for being in this place, at this time, seems somewhat random then Ralph's is even more special.

"I studied Media at Leeds University" he begins when I ask about his background and the paths that led him to his role at Notts. *"Back in October, I was just a regular fan. I still have my season ticket with my Dad and the rest of the family"* he says pointing out towards where the pitch is although, what with the walls and doors in the way, we have to use our imagination to see it.

"I just mailed the club. I thought the website was pretty poor. Me and my colleague (Dane Vincent) both got in touch with the club and sent in our CV's."

He sits smiling, and happy to tell his story but seemingly shy and embarrassed about the ease at which the role became his.

"I was invited down to the club and interviewed by Paul Ewen and Matt Lorenzo."

I question if this was 'the one day' that Lorenzo seemed to be at the club and Ralph laughs.

"Yeah" he responds glancing up towards the sky. *"It was surreal. There we were talking and suddenly the door opens and in walks Sven and a photographer from the Guardian. I remember thinking if nothing else comes of this, what a story I'd have to tell my mates."*

At this timely moment, the door opens and I instinctively turn. Although we both know it will not be Sven marching in today. A middle-aged chap with a screwdriver and pencil glances in. Previously seen in the corridor, he is simply a sparky doing some work in the suites so we return to our talk.

"It must feel like everything has calmed down now then?" I ask, suggesting that it would have once been someone much more well-known walking in randomly.

"Yeah. It was crazy. For the first few weeks all I did was reply to e-mails for Sven. I couldn't answer them quick enough to be fair."

Moving back for just a moment however, Ralph reminisces:

The evening after the interview I walked back to my grandparents in Bridgford. We had a Chippy tea and talked about Notts and the interview and that was that. I was not driving back then so my grandad gave me a lift to my flat in Derby and we thought that was that.

It was literally moments after I got home. I walked into my front room and my phone rang. As I picked up the voice said "Hello, this is Simon Cowell and you have the X-Factor". I just assumed it was a mate on a wind-up at first but suddenly realised it was Matt Lorenzo. He just told me I had the job, that my first day was on the Tuesday and we'd be travelling away to Notts' game with Bradford in the Johnstone's Paint Trophy. Then I hung up and started doing the Hughesy in my front room.

As Ralph tells his story, I cannot but admire the enthusiasm and passion he tells it with. In any other job, anywhere else in the world, I don't think such enthusiasm could be drawn. But for Football? Well it must have been the next best thing to being out on the pitch or managing the side?

"Yeah it was a dream come true for me" he confirms. *"Surreal."*

A typical week for Ralph sees him arrive at the ground at around 7.30am and leave around 5pm except when there are evening games.

"I have Wednesday mornings off and Sunday's are my free time. My only day off at the moment but I don't mind."

"So had this been the case since day one? There have been changes constantly after all?" I pose:

Not always. I got a phone call on my only day off, late on Sunday night one time from Peter Trembling asking for stats. I guess he was going to possible new owners with spreadsheets and power point presentations. I had to research the whole youth set-up. The likes of Michael Johnson and Mick Leonard. Their histories and careers with figures. I was then asked to then get stats for a list of ten players they wanted to sign, including David Beckham. It was pretty surreal. Absolutely crazy. David Beckham was just there, at the bottom of this list.

For a few seconds we share the moment. Is it a case of 'what could have been?' or just admiration for the outright ambition that was being shown at the time? I don't ask. I leave Ralph with his views and me with my own and then look to move the conversation on.

I question him on just how much the club has altered in the short time he has been part of the staff. After all, since October, Notts has seen more changes than many of us, including Ralph and I, care to remember. He tells it straight:

Within the first week working here, Charlie was sacked. He walked into the office and simply said "Everybody, I've been sacked" and that was that. I was shocked. But this is my first job in football. I knew it happened but it all seemed so quick and suddenly.

As it happens, Ralph was also the last guy to interview Charlie along with Dane Vincent on that fateful evening when his future (or rather lack of it at Notts) was sealed with a draw at home to strugglers Torquay. That same evening, Charlie McParland told Sky cameras that fans were fickle, and in fairness, he was partly correct. Ralph recalls Charlie being at ease that evening however saying *"There were no signs that he knew he'd be sacked. I just remember it being the last interview with him though. Strange feeling that."*

If this was not a baptism of fire into the world of media work in football, then I don't think there has ever been one. It was not all negative at the time for Ralph and the Notts squad:

For Bournemouth away in the Cup, Dane and I travelled with the players on the plane. We stayed in a swanky hotel and were looked after. It was a brilliant experience. In my role, we don't see any of the preferential treatment. I heat up the Pukka Pies in the press room pre-match on a Saturday for example so I'd not know what went off in the other rooms. But that was an occasion where we saw the benefits on the other side of the coin. Looking back now, it all seems a bit crazy.

As the never-ending story of Notts County Football Club continued forwards, changes were certainly set to be made. Even the most premier of crystal-ball readers could not have seen into the future and predicted what was set to unfold as Ralph and the rest of the staff experienced not only one, but two takeovers after the Munto flag began to waiver.

"Hans came and went pretty sharp-ish. Then Peter [Trembling] took over. At that point we were thinking something is seriously wrong with this" explains Ralph with a more sombre, concerned look etched across his face.

Suddenly there were rumours about these guys who were down the ground who were being referred to as the 'Lincoln lot'. Their cars were parked here for about two week's non-stop. They were walking around as though they already owned the place. Everyone was cautious and nervous about their jobs. In the first meeting we had with the new owners, we were told there would be redundancies and I was like (pulls a face as if to be worried). I thought it would be my dream job gone. I'm still here though. The mood and the spirits around the office are the best they've ever been since I joined. Everything feels stable. No longer do we get calls in the middle of the night asking for this and that. I can relax and also have a social life as well as a working life.

It is clear from talking to not only Ralph, but others in and around the club and on the terraces, that Notts under the guidance of Trew, is an altogether a more stable, happy ship and that in turn is also down to the success on the pitch under the new boss Steve Cotterill:

Out of all the managers we've had, the Gaffer is the first to have come and mixed with staff and talk to us guys. It is like a proper office. There was this girl downstairs...she had a blind date one day last week. The Gaffer was a right wind-up merchant about it. Sat there in the office just like another member of staff giving her stick about it constantly which is good for spirits. That sort of normality is nice and keeps everyone happy.

For all the money, or supposed money, Ralph insists that the connection with the fans was never strained during the Munto/Sven/Trembling days however. I pose the issue that since Ray Trew took the club over there appears more transparency at the club. Certainly more interaction with the fans who, after all, are the ones who are the reason the club exists:

I'm a fan at the end of the day. I don't think that was not the case before Ray Trew came in though. I don't think there was any disconnection from the fans. It was always the same except we had these massive stars at the club like Sol and Sven. I cannot speak for everyone however. I never used to go to the fans forums or anything like that because it wasn't my thing. But as a fan I didn't feel any differently.

At this point I listen to Ralph whilst thinking maybe I am bringing to much hindsight into my thought process. I for one cannot help but feel that those people running the club only told us what they thought we wanted to hear. Especially during those dark days when we went from being the richest club in the world to broke in one simple £1 takeover step.

What really happened? Who was really to blame? According to Ralph, certainly not Trembling:

I always thought Peter was open. I think he was honestly trying to help the club. Maybe he was duped by King and the Willett's. He was what I'd call merced (a phrase coined from Rio Ferdinand's wind-up TV show) by his supposed friends. I've always had a saying that "As long as Sven is here it'll be Ok". All the players were saying it in interviews and such. They'd be asked about recent form or rumours behind the scenes and they'd simple cite Sven as a reason to keep their belief.

It is clear by this point that Ralph, along with many Notts fans, still holds the man we call Sven in the highest of regards. Despite all the turmoil and bad press the club had in those winter months, it appears no one, including the guys who worked closest to him, can find a bad word to say about him. I ask Ralph about what the club meant to Sven and his response is clearly positive:

A connection with the club? Yeah, definitely. Every Thursday when I had to go and look after the press down at the training ground, he'd be there...he always was. We'd talk about Notts and League Two and all the latest ticket news. We'd talk about players and such. He knew them all by name or nickname. He said to me a few times about Hunty being a good player for this League and beyond. At Christmas he gave every full time member of staff a bottle of champagne. It was just the sort of guy he was. So I've got that in my flat now. It's a nice little memento. The day he left, we all went across to Hooters for drinks with him to say bye. But you won't find anyone with anything bad to say about him.

We continue to talk about the club and, as fans, what we believe is in store for Notts in the coming weeks, months and years. For Ralph Shepherd is simply that; a fan of the club. It just so happens that he is a fan with an inside role within the club he supports.

"I think we can go up. The games we have coming up, especially down here [at home], are huge games."

As we draw our talk to a close, Ralph remains relaxed and happy to share his experiences however:

It's all stable now. The programme sellers have gone and the Pies have gone. We're just cracking on. The girls (programme sellers) were on a crazy amount of money. £800 or something like that per game to hire them, I forget. They were just models. But stuff like that is now getting sorted. I never realised how much work went into a game. So much effort is put in behind the scenes. Proof reading the programmes, filling seats in the restaurant and such. It's never ending.

Effort is one thing but when singling out people for their efforts, Ralph is quick to hand out the praise:

Stuart in accounts. He's had the most stressful job in the world. At one point, I was not getting any media calls. Just people who were all wanting Stuart. Asking for money. Creditors and such. But of course, there was no money to pay them. He couldn't do anything. He took a lot of flack back then. Then when Ray bought the club, he brought some of his own men in who went through everything. He must have been so relieved though. Stuart kept it together through the really bad days.

As I walk away from Meadow Lane with a further date penned in the diary to meet with Ralph when Notts host Lincoln City later in the season, it is nice to know that a local club has people at the heart of the community working within it. Ralph may give the impression that he is a lucky chap who was in the right place at the right time but in terms of improvement and development, the media side of things at Notts has never been so good with himself and Dane Vincent busy behind the scenes.

The Magpie Player has become a successful tool from which fans can stay connected to the latest news, views and footage within the club whilst the club has its own, well maintained Facebook and Twitter feeds which appear to give 24 hour updates on club news and competitions.

I just cross my fingers as I leave Meadow Lane that he is right about promotion because without it, maybe some more redundancies that were forewarned will be on the horizon as well as another campaign down here in League Two and right now, that does not bare thinking about.

The Proverbial Six Pointer

Notts County v Bournemouth
Meadow Lane / League Two / 15.03.10

Well just six days ago, our meeting with Chesterfield was deemed the biggest game of the season so far. But six days is a long time in football and with those three points well and truly in the bank, the visit of Bournemouth tonight proves to be even more vital now given the standings and the results from the weekend.

At the weekend those sides just behind us both lost. Chesterfield capped an incredibly poor week falling victim to Port Vale at home in a 5-0 defeat whilst Bury lost on the road away at Macclesfield.

Unfortunately it could not be a hat-trick of results going Notts' way as both Rotherham and top-of-the-table Rochdale won against Dagenham and Shrewsbury respectively, both recording narrow 1-0 wins. Chesterfield's result in particular was a stern reminder that shocks were always possible in League Two.

We come into tonight's game knowing that destiny is firmly in our own hands. Victory tonight against second placed Bournemouth would see us leapfrog The Cherries into that second automatic spot and, with games still in hand, be near-to-certain favourites for promotion.

It is a different atmosphere once again down at Notts tonight though. Tense? Of course it is. Just as much as it was a week ago, if not more so. But now there is also an air of confidence about the club and in turn, the fans. Steve Cotterill has seen four wins from four so far. He has also seen something of a goal fest with Notts bagging ten without reply since his arrival. Notts have had something much different about them of late and now, going into the game with just one defeat from eleven, we are expecting to win games rather than waiting to slip up as with our early season form.

Down on the touchline, a nervous Ray Trew speaks to the Sky Sports cameras ahead of the game whilst under the stands, screens show the live images as bodies warm themselves, tapping their feet and rubbing their hands for extra warmth. Bournemouth have brought a small but die-hard following that look no more than 80 or so in numbers. But for a mid-week game on a cold March night, with the game on Sky and a round-trip of seven hours and some 400 miles, credit has to be given to those small few that have made the effort.

We are sat just behind the dugout as the stand fills quickly around me prior to the big kick-off. The Kop is in splendid voice, singing for the cameras and generating the atmosphere. Unfortunately, as with the

Torquay game earlier in the season, the middle park at the top of the Kop is closed off for the camera crews but looking from side-to-side, there appears to be very few seats spare despite the draw of the game being televised.

"Oh when the Notts....Go marching in......Oh when the Notts go marching in...." sing the fans. The stands have a rhythmic beat to them. Somewhat tribal as you see the Kop motioning up and down, clapping hands and speeding up as they reach their crescendo.

"In goal, Kasper Schmeichel" calls the announcer and a roar erupts in honour of his name. He is joined by Thompson, Hunt, Lee and Edwards at the back. In midfield Westcarr, Davies, Ricky Ravenhill and Bishop whilst Hughes and Rodgers are upfront to hopefully strike some fear into the heart of The Cherries backline.

It is arguably Notts' best side now. Some Hawley admirers would possibly pick him ahead of Luke Rodgers up top. But Rodgers, the tank, has proved his worth lately. Tireless running and pressing, he is always on the shoulder of the defenders and always giving reminders that he's ready to pounce.

Although they may lack in numbers, Bournemouth do not lack in volume. They cheer their players, sing their songs and make it clear they are here over in the corner of the Jimmy Sirrel Stand.

Despite the importance of tonight's game, you cannot help but feel a sense of fear amongst fans too. For both clubs are now firmly in two of the three driving seats in League Two and it's only theirs to lose. Throwing it away now would be the most painful end to what has felt like the longest of seasons.

To their credit Bournemouth have played much of the campaign with limited resources that makes our transfer embargo of late look like a minor footnote. With the Football League imposing similar sanctions on the South coast side since the start of the campaign, they have really shone under the guidance of Eddie Howe to the extent that regardless of who wins the division, Howe would be in with a shout for League Two Manager of The Season.

It may be March but the weather has not let up as of yet. We still feel the chill and the wind is still painful against our faces as both sides ready themselves for kick off. Whilst it is important to take three points tonight, it is vital that we don't lose. For our visitors, it's an identical scenario and defeat is something they cannot and will not wish to contemplate.

Notts start off the brightest, kicking from right to left from my vantage point and that of the viewers sat at home watching on Sky. Our

Gaffer is agitated on the touchline as is Howe for The Cherries but we do not have to wait long for our first moment of hope when Hughes finds himself getting on the end of a Ben Davies corner only for his tame effort to find the grasp of Jalal in the Bournemouth goal.

Despite the best of intentions early on, it is soon Notts on the back foot. Wiggins works well down the left flank and when he cuts past Westcarr and ventures infield, Notts are at panic stations as a misplaced ball falls on the edge of our penalty box. Three red shirts close-in on the ball with intent and purpose to have a strike at goal whilst Graeme Lee and Mike Edwards scramble across as though their lives depend on it to try and block any goal-bound effort. As Anton Robinson meets the ball with a firm right foot we pause momentarily, holding our breaths with pained expressions for an agonising wait which last all of a split second. Firm, low and on target, Kasper gets down well and makes a good save to keep things all square.

Now Bournemouth have their minds on the game and when Wiggins delivers a corner, we watch on as a catalogue of errors leads to a game of pinball within our own box. Bouncing around on the firm, hard surface, neither side can control the ball but Edwards blocks before Lee clears off the line with his feet. Still we cannot push out though and then, with time and space, Feeney pulls back into the box although his header is not enough to test our Great Dane who rises to claim the ball as it is headed towards his goal.

At this point, worried would be the wrong turn of phrase. Concerned is rather apt though as Notts do not appear to have much control and our opposition seem to be growing in stature and promise by the minute. Their small following are now becoming extremely vocal. Our own support is frustrated but hopeful. For all their possession and chances, they've yet to make it count. That is a good sign for us at least.

Bournemouth now break again. This time direct and down the middle as a ball is played into the path of Feeney. With little support, he closes in on goal from a slight angle and drives an effort at Kasper's goal only to see another parried save and another panicked clearance from our defenders following up.

"Come on Notts" ring the cries from those around me. The Kop lifts things a little but they are yet to see much action at their end. Cotterill is furious on the touchline and insistent and passionate in his mannerisms. His efforts come to no avail as moments later Bournemouth again enter the final third and this time we see Fletcher get a strike away on the turn only for our shot stopper to get across and save well once more.

Now the groans begin to come out from the stands. Fans are groaning about the side that is the in-form side in not only in the division but in the country. The groans appear a little strange at this point but the fans know the importance of tonight.

"Come on you Pies, come on you Pies..." sing the Kop whilst Bournemouth continue to keep the ball.

It has been a hectic start to proceedings and we know that our time will come in the encounter but things remain tight in the middle of the park. Things remain tense all around in fact and possession for both teams is all too sporadic and ever-changing.

Only twenty minutes on the clock though and Westcarr picks up the ball on the left touchline in front of us. He is like a new player under the Gaffer. Fresh impetus from the wide man is clear for all to see as he runs at his marker, twisting and turning as he then tries to play a ball into the box. Just like at the other end, the ball fails to fall too kindly, instead bobbling about and becoming another game of pinball for all those within close-range.

Hughes attempts an adventurous flick which is duly blocked and we sigh before Davies picks up possession. A neat touch, a sideways shimmy and then down he falls. He's tripped and we jump sharply to our feet. All in unison and all with anger etched across our faces and then, as the ref points to the spot, all with delight as Hughes heads over and grabs the ball to put on the spot.

Against the run of play and without any real opportunities of our own thus far, we now have the chance to take the lead and the Bournemouth attack will begin to rue their misses.

"Hughesy, Hughesy" chant the Notts faithful before he has even struck the ball. The ref stops and waits for the players to get out of the box. The fans sit, poised and motionless. Jalal bounces on his line and Hughes stares intently at the ball. He takes a stride back, begins his run up and we wait nervously.

As the ball is struck, we all begin to rise, expecting the net to move. We expect to take a one goal lead and we expect us to all begin the Hughesy dance. The strike is poor and into the ground though. It bobbles and stutters its way towards the goal and Jalal is not overly concerned, falling down to the left and blocking. But lesson one in shot stopping is lost on their keeper and instead of pushing the ball away from goal, the ball returns centrally and back at the welcoming feet of Lee Hughes who, with a second bite of the cherry (excuse the pun), lashes at the ball and sees it fly with true power into the roof of the net.

Our semi-complete jump becomes the finished article as we rise and embrace fellow fans. To my left, my old man and uncle Danny rejoice as we know we have not deserved the lead. We take it, as does Steve Cotterill, Tommy Johnson and Matty Hamshaw on the touchline, all of who celebrate with us.

Games turn on the smallest of moments and as a result of this one Notts are now hungry, in full-flow and playing with purpose. Rodgers is sent clear over the top with me and the fans in the stand still celebrating the goal. From a narrow angle he gets a shot away which is saved but it lifts us even further. Then we switch to the other side and Davies finds himself in acres of space on the right. As he delicately chips the ball over the on-coming keeper, we fail to see why the linesman's flag is held aloft ruling out his effort that crosses the line. We are not bothered now. It's just a matter of time for the next goal to come our way, surely?

Next up, Stephen Hunt ventures forward to give The Cherries more to be worried about. A neat one two with Rodgers and Hunt himself dares to dream as he strides into the box, away from his marker and slides an effort towards goal when perhaps Hughes was the better option square of him in the box. We applaud and welcome the positive play from the left back as there is only one side now in the game.

The break arrives and on reflection, it arrives at the wrong moment. We had chased and struggled for the first twenty minutes and been much the inferior of the two sides. However, once the lead was ours we had much more control of the game with the midfield duo of Ravenhill and Bishop really clicking once more.

Underneath the stands we do not warm-up. The chill spreads throughout the ground as fans grab a half time pie or cuppa from the kiosks. We are no longer on edge about losing, more fearful that we may throw three points away.

"Must not sit back" says my Dad. *"Should have a real go at them in the second half"* he adds.

Bournemouth, knowing their season may hinge on whatever happens here, will be pumped up for the second 45 minutes. They'll be ready to make a fight of it and take the game to Notts. The analysis on Sky Sports suggests Bournemouth shaded the first half and it's not far wrong. If anyone following the boys in black and white is expecting us to simply see this game out though, they need to have a rethink.

As the whistle blows for play to recommence, loud shouts of *"Come on Notts"* echo around the stadium as a rallying cry for the lads.

"The next goal is vital" I tell my Dad reeling off a carbon copy statement that I often give to my lads at the break on a cold, wet,

Sunday morning. It's all too true for Notts too though, so containing the opposition is vital in the early stages of this half.

Much like the first 45 however, Bournemouth start the livelier of the two sides and straight away they are the team showing intention. Rather clumsily, Neal Bishop put in a rash tackle on 49 minutes when Connell nods the ball past the midfielder and no sooner had the game found its stride once more, here we are gifting them a chance from a set-piece.

We sit leaning forwards, elbows on knees once again, hoping Kasper is ready and alert. Brett Pittman places the ball down as Notts players remonstrate with the referee but in truth, there is nothing to complain against. The wall retreats, Kasper stands on his post trying to get a clear view around the wall and Bournemouth's small following anticipate something from their top marksmen.

"It looks too far out" utters the chap behind us. He's bloody wrong though. Within a split second Pittman trots up, composes himself and slots a neatly placed and finely weighted effort around the wall and into the bottom corner where a second or two ago Kasper was stood. Off he runs as around me there is stunned silence. Pittman delighted as Kasper stands, hands on hips and frustrated. We've let them back in after such a valuable lead at the break.

A stadium sounds at its emptiest when a small following celebrate a goal and we are treated to that feeling now as Notts players turn and walk back towards the half way line and the referee whistles at Pittman and Co' to make their way back to their own half.

Once more the Notts support, to a man, tries to lift the lads and as the Wheelbarrow song resonates from the Kop, Notts get the game restarted and keep the ball just as they should have done at the start of the half.

Now back to square one and fans all around readjusting their 'ideal' and 'worst-case' scenario's in their mind. What if we lose? What if we fall further behind? Would we take a point as we stand?

Within minutes we stop asking ourselves such stupid questions as a further twist arises. Bournemouth break and now look like a side wanting more than just a solitary point. Both managers now agitated in the dugout, the game could threaten to become stretched. Notts snuff out the attack, regain possession and release Westcarr down the left flank. With energy and vigour, he runs at his man before slotting a ball to his left where Hughes hugs the touchline. Open bodied and aware of what options he has, he delivers a first time cross towards Rodgers which is well intercepted only for the header to return to Hughes in his wide berth.

A second cross is whipped in as bodies challenge and bravery is not questioned but once more it's a red shirt that connects and this time is cleared as far as Davies, the play-maker and architect of most things good down at Meadow Lane. Unopposed and able to look up, he gives the ball plenty of whip as he crosses back in, this time from the right with Rodgers as his target. The ball is slightly off the mark though and as it bounces in the corridor of uncertainty, both Rodgers and The Cherries centre-backs miss-time the flight before turning to see Hughes arriving late at the back post. Skipping up off the firm, cold turf, Hughes adjusts his own run and body and somehow, when all appears lost, manages a header which loops over Jalal and into the top corner.

No sooner had we lost our advantage, we have it restored and the Family Stand is subjected to a Hughesy dance after he gallops over to the small stand behind the goal.

My dad and I embrace once more. With each new goal we see netted down at Meadow Lane we feel that one step closer to the season's targets. Delight clearly fashioned across my old man's face, I'm not sure how much more of this rollercoaster ride any of us can take.

As the temperature drops, the atmosphere rises and minute-by-minute we watch our side marching onwards towards a much-desired victory. Bournemouth now appear lost in the middle of the park whilst Westcarr nearly finds Hughes in the box only for a defensive header to clear the danger. But we are in the ascendancy now.

At 2-1, we know we have a tight lead. Whilst there is a mere goal in it, anything can happen and we know the visitors have the players capable of turning it on. For this reason we are indebted to Stephen Hunt when later in proceedings he reaches out with his long legs to snatch a chance away and clear for a corner. Mike Edwards serves a timely reminder that they must stay focused, pointing at his head and shouting instructions at those around him and we in the stands do the same, checking our watches and shouting encouragement from afar.

Screams and yells emanate from Notts' dugout as the games draws to a close. Direct instructions from set-pieces of exactly what is wanted from each man. Each man with his tasks as the backline is probed and tested.

Schmeichel saves from a header after good work out wide on the left and we applaud the stop but out of nowhere Feeney appears at the back post. Our hearts in our mouths, our nightmares coming true and the equaliser inevitable as the Bournemouth man approaches a gaping net only to see his effort shake the side netting and all those on the touchline watch in shock and amazement but with varying emotions to the miss they have just seen.

Cotterill signals to his bench that it was a let off and here in stands we know as much. Surely now? Surely we have done enough. Time is on our side as though employed as a twelfth man. Bournemouth remain calm though and fail to be rushed.

A cross field ball, from left back to right wing, is drilled across the park as Notts need to hold off for a few more seconds. Edwards stretches, and manages, to part clear the danger with a header but, as the ball is floated back into the box, Notts' defenders are at a loss as Jeff Goulding turns, opens his body and smashes an effort past Kasper into the back of the net.

Once more we have to watch on as a small, select few celebrate on the far side. A clear contrast in the reactions from the dugout is shown whilst thousands of disappointed faces surround me in the stands. Suddenly the game has a different complexion altogether.

"*They sat back*" I hear my old man state. I wish he was wrong.

Coca Cola League Two Table:

	Pld	+/-	Pts
1. Rochdale	35	40	72
2. Bournemouth	36	8	64
3. Notts County	**33**	**41**	**61**
4. Bury	36	3	61
5. Chesterfield	36	3	60
6. Rotherham United	34	9	59
7. Northampton Town	36	9	55

"It's A Funny Old Game..."

Since we last met Trinderbox in the Stokes Cup, we've only managed five league games from a period that should have seen us play ten. We are more susceptible to the big freeze than the professionals so given the temperatures over the festive period and beyond, I am delighted having managed to win all five league encounters we've had.

We still sit second in the table but with 36 points to our name, we trail Trinderbox by fourteen as they sit pretty on 51. It's a similar gulf to that which faced Steve Cotterill upon his appointment at Notts but somehow, I envisage our chances of narrowing the gap much less likely than that of the Magpies.

Trinderbox have been a machine in the league. They have seventeen games under their belt and seventeen victories to their name to date. They are too good for this level and their form is remarkable. No blips or stuttering performances. No off-days or unlucky outings. Just win after win after win featuring goals, goals and more goals.

Today I am able to name my strongest line-up of the season. It is the eleven players that have performed most consistently despite one of two of those missing having had excellent spells in the first team. We warm-up gingerly as we take note of those up the other end stretching their groins and half heartedly knocking balls about.

I stress that we must play our game though. We must get the ball down and believe we can match Trinderbox in every department. For if you have no belief, you have no hope and I am a firm believer that a little self-belief can go a very long way.

We are as focussed as we've ever been this morning and with the injured Jake watching from the sidelines on crutches, that alone should be inspiration as well as a reminder of the state we left this pitch in back in December in an 11-2 defeat.

The referee is one we have had before and straight away I worry about what the next 90 minutes could have in stall for us. Trinderbox like everything their own way in much the same way top sides often do. They demand decisions. A strong willed ref is needed but certainly not what we have in front of us.

Lee shakes hands with their skipper, listens to the referee's instructions about decision making and respect and before we know it, Jay and I are ready to kick off proceedings.

"Let's not do this too often today" jokes Jay as we get the game underway and we instantly make a beeline for their left back area. We attack with good intentions and push forwards from the off and Trinderbox suddenly switch on into a game mode that was distinctly lacking prior to kick off.

Within minutes we are looking dangerous, as we did in our first game here in the early stages just a few months ago. This time we have an air of caution and an awareness of just how quick our opposition can hit us. Just how easy they can tear a side apart.

As the game settles, so do our in-form opponents. Pretty soon they strut their stuff and switch play from left to right but at the back, Lee and Brice regiment the defence well as those in front of them work hard in order to give little space away.

Then, on twenty minutes, after what felt like ten long minutes of constant pressure in and around our box, we break with Brice playing the ball out to Maggs on the left. Normally a full-back, Maggs is occupying a midfield role today in the hope that he'll give us more resilience and better work rate in the middle of the park.

With a determined energy and strength about him, he skips two tackles before venturing over the half way line and looking up. Admittedly, our options are limited given the system we've come with but it is a system we know may be the key to avoiding a drubbing such as we did in the Stokes Cup so when Maggs finds Jay in middle of the park, it is an appreciated and well thought out ball that allows us to continue our forward momentum.

Glancing up, options are now even more limited however. With only me and Irish Chris for support, Jay runs at his man before sliding a ball into Chris' feet and then moving into space for the return. Chris is a manager's worst nightmare and dream come true all rolled into one. He tries flicks and audacious passes when they are uncalled for but also manages to pop up with moments of brilliance when least expected. However, when his heel looks remotely close to coming into contact with the ball, I cannot help but sigh for we have seen this many times before.

This time is different though. He holds off his man with strength and his back to goal and as Jay runs beyond him, it appears Chris' moment to play Jay in has passed. Chris receives a call from a deep-lying midfielder and I hold my run as play looks to have stalled before suddenly, without warning, Chris back heels the ball through the legs of his marker and into the path of the advancing Jay.

Now, with their back line stretched, Jay ventures further forward as I make my move and the remaining nine CSKA players watch on with baited breath. For all their possession and for all their class, Trinderbox are under threat and desperate now. A lunging tackle nearly brings Jay to the ground as he breaks from his marker but he manages to keep his feet. As he reaches the edge of the box, a less-composed, greedier player would have wasted the opportunity and snatched at the moment. However, with finesse and style, Jay feigns a strike at goal before squaring the ball to me on the edge of the box.

Far from being the best goal I've ever netted, there was something much more satisfying about this goal as I stroke it into the far bottom corner with my first touch. We celebrate with grace and we fail to get carried away in the moment. We've been here before after all. We've learnt this lesson already. The look in the eyes of team mates as we trot back to our own half tells me that we won't allow it to happen again though. We know how resilient we must endeavour to be in the time that remains until the break.

"Come on CSKA. Play as though it's 0-0" is the rallying cry from Paul in the middle of the park as play is once more underway.

We battle harder and fight with more energy than ever before. We have a perseverance about us that tells Trinderbox they are going to have to perform better than ever if they want to keep their perfect run going into April. And then they score.

Call it undeserved or call it against the run of play. A goal is a goal and they are all worth the same. Despite our keeper Warner making some fine saves, his goal is finally penetrated just before the break when a counter attack down our right sees their star man (now well beyond 50 goals for the season) cut inside and slice an effort into our net.

There was an ounce of fortune in the strike itself but he'd argue he had done the hard work and with it, we are pegged back and left to lick our wounds as we depart for the break just seconds later.

"We've done it once" are the words I dare to use at the break. True and to the point, I know full well that Sir Alf Ramsey had said exactly the same to the England side of 1966. But what is management if it isn't learning from others, borrowing ideas and echoing sentiments?

"We can do this. They don't like the fact we are a match for them and the more we give them a game, the more frustrated they'll become. Don't shy away. Don't give them too much respect. Let's fucking well get stuck into them" and once more my players look to have an air of belief about them.

Matt, my assistant, walks around the lads geeing those up that need the encouragement and passing advice on as he makes his way around.

Matt and I have a brief chat and again reiterate the importance of keeping things tight and keeping people talking as Lee and Paul give another rallying call to the rest of the lads that we have the ability to do it.

I genuinely feel that self-belief and confidence is the key to success, especially at this level. What I'd give to be able to possess a squad of footballers who, regardless of whether they are two up or two down, have the same self-belief in their minds at all times.

Conceding a goal by misfortune, luck or shear class does not change one's ability within a twinkling of an eye. And nor should a goal in the Alliance Sunday League before the break. So as I tell the lads as much, they appear, one-by-one, to raise their own spirits and in turn those around them.

Here at CSKA, we don't always take the easy route however, so when we reach the 47th minute you'd be forgiven for thinking our minds and bodies would become deflated when Trinderbox pounce to make it 2-1 so early in the second half. A goal of brilliance it wasn't but they simply appeared to turn up for the second half a few minutes quicker than ourselves and for all the fight and spirit we showed during the team talk, we were now back to square one, or rather beyond it, with a goal to chase.

At this point, I guess most sides would fall away at the seams and simply roll over to the superior opponents who have finally broken the visitors resolve. Not today though. Not us.

Looking back, I'd go as far to say that the 11-2 cup defeat on this very ground was the making of us this season. It gave us the kick start for the run we've been on since. No one wants to leave the pitch feeling as low as we did after our cup exit whether it be once a season, once a month or every week. That defeat was like a wake-up call to our squad and so today, we'll ensure we don't leave the park with anything left in the engine.

In the middle of the park, Seany Ward and Paul run themselves into the ground, tackling left, right and centre and working up and down constantly. Warner continues to make saves that leave the game in the balance whilst Lee and Brice remain as inspirational as Sunday league players can be.

Despite Trinderbox getting the upper hand, we find ourselves still in the game on 70 minutes and I am ruing a missed chance when I hit a shot from the edge of the box and see their keeper tip the ball around the post.

Time is pressing and we know that if the game were to end now, we could be proud of the performance and the result. But it'd be just another statistic for the record books. Another addition for our 'games lost' column and another three points for the machine that is Trinderbox would be the way the league would record the encounter.

I cannot help but imagine how great it would have been to have taken points off the league leaders. I look across to Irish Chris and signal to him to take the corner as I walk into the box and try to distract their keeper. The box is crowded and there are bodies all over. My centre halves lurk on the edge of the box and with a sharp turn, both Seany Ward and I disperse from the danger area to free up space in front of goal.

Chris' corner kick, hit with power and precision, could not have been delivered any better as the ball is whipped in at pace and met with the firm and determined forehead of Jon Brice who glances it past the keeper and into the far corner of the net.

Celebrations are this time harder to mute and play down but Lee does a great job of rallying the troops at the back and now our minds are a little less than twenty minutes away from taking a point from Trinderbox.

Our opponents make two changes in a bid to catapult them to the three points they desire whilst I make one alteration to the side replacing Maggs, who's tireless running and work rate has seen him pick up a yellow card and one knock too many, with the lively and determined Danny boy.

Whilst Trinderbox are expected to press for a late winner, it is we who hold all the trump cards now. We break moments later and Jay agonises as his effort is just wide of the mark but his strike gives extra emphasis to our hopes and endeavours and now we believe more than ever.

No longer are we asking the referee for the remaining minutes on his watch. We want to continue and to press for that winner that now appears to be elusive to the league leaders. With the referee telling the home side there is a minute left on his watch, we break once more with urgency and desire. Jay spreads a sweetly timed ball to Chris on the flank who skips his man to leave it two on one. There is just one defender between Chris and me. Now we bear down on their goal.

Behind us, the referee is glancing at his watch whilst sprinting to keep up with play. Players further back stop and once more watch on whilst spectators on the side gasp at what could be about to happen. The defender refuses to make an impulsive decision and chooses to remain midway between my winger and I in the middle, forcing Chris into trying to either beat him or deliver a pinpoint cross.

Jay is now sprinting to support and their defenders are using every last bit of energy their legs allow but as Chris crosses he loses his footing and the balls sails onto the roof of their net and with it, the whistle is pulled to the mouth of the referee who brings proceedings to an end.

One by one, my men emotionally and physically look to collapse. We traipse off, disappointed and a little downbeat. Just like we did back in December, we look like a beaten side as we leave the pitch and shake hands with those opponents we pass. We are not the broken team we were last time around though and for the first time all season, Trinderbox have been denied from taking maximum points from a league match.

I pat my players on the back, shake their hands, tap their shoulders and give them a wink. Each and every one of them receives an acknowledgment and they all deserve it. We fought so hard and gave so much and the disappointment only goes to highlight how far we've come since the last time we played here.

"That is by far and away the toughest game anyone has given us" states their stereotypical Sunday league boss as he wanders over in his sports jacket, flat cap and cigarette in hand. *"Absolutely fantastic. If you boys don't finish second, I'll be amazed"* he concludes as he shakes my hand and returns to his own group of disappointed lads.

It's funny how this game can turn over the course of a few months.

Alliance League Division Five Table:

	Pld	+/-	Pts
1. Trinderbox	18	127	52
2. CSKA Carnabys	**18**	**23**	**37**
---			
3. FC Komrska	19	17	35
4. Harrow	19	21	30
5. Phoenix United	17	26	31

Scabs, Scabs, Scabs.

Notts County v Rotherham United
Meadow Lane / League Two / 27.03.10

It'd be easy to be mistaken for a broken record at present. Today, with Rotherham coming down to the Lane, it is a big one. A massive three points and a massive 90 minutes of football lie ahead. Then again, at this stage of a season, every game is massive. Every game carries extra weight and significance. Every game has the power to impact on the promotion push, a relegation battle or title hopes.

Today my spirits could not be any higher. The sun is shining down upon me as I make my way towards the train station, Hughes is set to return to the side after missing the last two games and the form book suggests that it'll be Notts coming out on top. I pray the form book is correct.

As I pull into Nottingham station (or rather as the train pulls in – I'm not the one driving it), members of the public are much more aware of a game being on than they normally are when Notts County are at home. There are policemen on each platform, lined up on the platforms and at the station front. For today they expect Rotherham United to bring a modest contingent not seen down here since Bradford on the opening day.

Back in 2009, when the season was much younger, fresher and open, I travelled to watch the reverse fixture at The Don Valley Stadium in Sheffield. What a shit day out that was for all involved. A lifeless ground, a soulless atmosphere and a poor game of football to boot.

Today promises much more however. Now unbeaten in ten league games, we sit second in the table with confidence in ourselves. If we can come out of the next two games with the unbeaten run intact and with a few more points on the board, it'd appear the likelihood of throwing promotion away would be...well very unlikely. The past two games, since we were held by Bournemouth, have seen us take four points on the road which looking back, was a fantastic return. Despite Davies missing a spot kick at Crewe before the break, a Mike Edwards goal gave us a 1-0 win prior to a 0-0 stalemate away at Bradford City.

After the game I was fortunate enough to interview Steve Cotterill down at the ground who talked at length about the unbeaten run:

> *"If you had offered me two draws from those games, I'd have taken it. I sat up thinking about this the other week. I'd have taken that over one win and one defeat. It keeps the momentum and the unbeaten run going".*

After the interview I spoke to some of the lads in my team about our clubs form and uttered similar words which some seemed to fail to grasp but the simplicity of it all was glaringly obvious for me. Either that or maybe I just got lost in the whole 'managers-who-talk-in-riddles' phenomena and adopted it as my own approach.

I arrive at The Navi and already the place is filling up. Earlier than usual, with both the weather and opposition apparent reasons for the early influx, the atmosphere is good whilst the crowd expectant.

I sit talking with my old man and my uncle Danny whilst some kids play on the table football in the corner and many a person passes through to the court yard at the back. It is starting to feel like the end of the season is upon us with a change-in-fortunes in the sky. Despite the forecast of possible snow for later in the week, today the weather is good.

As we discuss the run-in, and in turn move onto the World Cup, there is an overriding sense that these coming months could be very special in the memory of Notts fans all over. The beers flow quickly with numerous girls behind the bar trying to pour as quick as punters can drink. Small choruses of songs breakout, albeit half heartedly, in the courtyard and one or two red shirts mingle in with the black and white stripes.

"*Wheear are t' toilets?*" asks one chap in a broad, rich, Yorkshire accent as my old man points him in the right direction.

With kick-off approaching, we are eager but anxious whilst also being extremely excited and nervous for the game that lies ahead.

"*Three points today and the pressure would really be off next Saturday*" notes my uncle and he is spot on. However, regardless of today's outcome, the visit of Bury a week from now will be another massive game. One game at a time I think. One game at a time.

As we arrive at the ground, it is confirmed that the interest in today's game has reached the highs of the Bradford match back in August. The queues outside the Derek Pavis Stand are some twenty deep. Fans with cash are stood there at the ready, programmes are being flogged between the lines by more...well shall we say sensible looking sellers than before and fans are milling around, singing songs and meeting old friends.

Before me, my old man and his brother pass through the turnstiles whilst behind appears our Kieran with his mate Danny.

"*Sorry son, no tickets left. Just have to sit where you want*" says the guy behind the desk as we hand over our £20 notes. Some things may never change down at Notts.

"What's it like? What's it like? What's it like to be a scab?" sing the highly predictable and original Miller's fans. In fact, I am somewhat surprised I had not heard similar prior to getting to the ground. All the same, we'll let them enjoy their big day today as we give them the entire Jimmy Sirrel enclosure to themselves (what with them bringing enough to only fill two fifths of it).

"Say we are going up, we are going up" respond the Kop as we walk up the steps and back into the sunlight that is beating down on the Meadow Lane turf. The grass is being watered and the crowd seem to be in fantastic voice.

We arrive at our seats in good time, moments before the sides walk out and we remain on our feet.

"Come on you Pies, come on you Pies!" sing all three stands in unison. Today is the big one. We all know it. It's the culmination of a little rivalry we've had brewing with one another. They appear to dislike us and we have a similar opinion of them.

The players exchange handshakes, the Gaffer shakes hands with Ronnie Moore, his counterpart, and the sides switch ends as Thommo loses the toss. In just over an hour and a half, we'll know much more about our destiny and likely route up into what will hopefully be League One.

Rotherham get the game underway and with their main man Le Fondre in fine form, Notts are only too aware that they have to keep a close eye on him. On Thursday when I joined the guys from BBC East Midlands Today, BBC Radio and the Evening Post in the press room, the Gaffer was asked about the clubs turn in fortunes and, in particular, today's game and Le Fondre.

"Have the lads been made aware of the fact Le Fondre has scored and won many penalties this season" asked one journo.

"It has been addressed" smiled the Gaffer as he was placed on the spot. *"We know what to expect from Rotherham. I'm not privy to discussing what their players get up to in public though."*

Translated, I read this as *"Yes he is a diving little so and so. We'll be careful not to kick him when the ref is looking"* but that was only my translation.

In Le Fondre, Rotherham have a man as deadly and as vital as our very own Lee Hughes however but as long as the likes of Thommo, Edwards, Lee and Hunty are on their game, I have high hopes for today.

Rotherham attack down the right from the off and their wide man Marshall gets an early chance to run at Hunt. Hunty stands his man up and he continues to grow as a player, perhaps somewhat spurred on by the confidence that a certain Mr. Eriksson had in him during his time at the club.

Notts respond almost instantly and from nowhere, a direct ball over the Millers backline suddenly sees Lee Hughes bearing down on goal with little over a minute on the clock. If a tame effort could be described as lacklustre, this one is feeble as he seemingly had one eye on lofting the ball over the oncoming Andy Warrington as the veteran keeper left his line.

We look across at one another, bewildered, frustrated and a little annoyed at such a gift being spurned by such a player. We regroup and start again though and as the away enclosure torments our number nine, we simply sing his name to appreciate his awareness to get in behind in the first place.

"*Scabs, scabs, scabs, scabs*" shout the visiting fans with poison in their tongue. It is only the same as perhaps other clubs get for varying reasons all over the country though.

Ironic cheers are returned in the direction of the Rotherham section but pretty soon after, we are given reason to ignore them as Craig Westcarr is found in space on the right hand side. Undoubtedly in his finest form of the season to date, Westcarr bends in an incredibly dangerous ball into the famous corridor of uncertainty and as Rodgers connects with a right foot volley, seats clatter upon themselves as they fold upwards and we all come to our feet.

The noises are met by the thud of the ball to post though and as Warrington's goal shakes, so do our heads as two early chances pass without the ball finding the net. The momentum is ours already and the Kop is in a confident mood.

"*E-i-e-i-e-i-o, Up the Football League we go...*" and in turn, Rotherham reply with, well the exact same.

Westcarr again torments on five minutes when his ball is met by Rodgers in a similar position although this time, a less clinical connection sees the ball flail across the face of goal and out for a goal-kick.

The Notts boys back peddle but with the travelling Rotherham fans trying to encourage their lads, it appears obvious that our lads are in the mood to perform and we don't have to wait too long for further proof. Thompson is energetic and positive down the right, and still in the early stages of the game, he sells a dummy to the Millers left-back before pushing past him and delivering a fine cross into the box.

This time it is Hughes who generates the cries of despair from the stands as he connects with his head but sees the ball crash against the upright. Rotherham are let off again and now we begin to wonder what will become of this game. Already we should be out of sight and with a comfortable lead. But at 0-0, the game is still tight. Very much in the balance and with all to play for.

After twenty minutes, Rotherham threaten for what is the first time in the half and when Gunning finds himself with time and space for an effort, we'd be forgiven for expecting the worst. As he pulls his effort across Kasper's goal though, we feel relieved that those missed opportunities have not come back to haunt us already much like they nearly did for Bournemouth last time out at Meadow Lane.

Workman-like and resilient, Rotherham steady their ship now. They become more structured and more focused on keeping their shape as the half passes the midpoint. Hughes continues to search and twice nearly gets in behind their backline but despite the exciting start, the game changes pattern and we are watching a very different game of football come the half hour mark.

Bobbles and grassless patches aplenty, the ball fails to settle on the sandy surface. Notts struggle to get their feet on the game in much the same way Rotherham don't play the football their fans have become accustomed to. To our left, the Kop gradually decreases in volume. They are tense and more on edge now. Kasper's wayward kicks receive a moans and groans from the stands whilst Bishop and Ravenhill in the middle of the park work like Trojans to win and then retain possession only for others to lose it just as quick.

Come the break, it is no coincidence that the brightest buttons in each side have been the wide men. With Davies always the obvious outlet for Notts and Marshall in turn Rotherham's most dangerous option, the middle ground has become an area that the ball by-passes rather than goes through.

At the back, Lee and Edwards end the half heading everything that flies in their direction, game-by-game increasing their reputation and proving their worth. They won't be knocked back by some League Two forward intent on making life difficult that's for sure.

As half time arrives, our spirits remain positive. I call Mark to give him the lowdown as he's stuck coaching in Leicester whilst I also call Paul who is sat in the away end for Leicester's game with Derby County.

"This goal will be on every own-goals and gaffs DVD for years to come" he tells me as City trail their East Midland rivals by the solitary goal.

As we settle ourselves for the next 45 minutes, the whole atmosphere and mood begins to alter. Now, rather than two sides wanting three points, perhaps it is more two sides not wanting a defeat.

It is certainly how it feels as the play gets underway and both sets of fans are more reserved and focused on the game.

At the top of the Kop, the beat of the drum maintains momentum. A small group of the home faithful continue to bounce up and down. *"Black and white army"* they sing in a proud, boastful-like manner. In the away stand, we are treated to chants about being scabs and very little else. They give Hughes some stick too. In fact, their whole day out appears to be focused around being anti-Lee Hughes and anti-Nottingham miners. Whatever floats their boat I guess.

Notts' only early chance comes when Hunt hits a looping effort just over Warrington's goal. We stand and clap but we know we must create more if we are to take all the points today. At the other end, Rotherham show more endeavour than the first 45 minutes but given their performance so far, it's not hard for them to do.

Suddenly out of nowhere, Nicky Law is sent forwards down the left for the visitors. With our skipper Thompson approaching, Law delicately lifts the ball over his man before striking a superb effort towards the Notts goal. Kasper Schmeichel, ready and alert, stands strong and parries away from his goal as bodies press and arrive in the box at pace. The enigmatic Marcus Marshall arrives at the back post and reacts quickest however, hitting an effort back at goal as Kasper is stranded.

The ball flies through a crowd of players and we gaze on in agony. We see Kasper slam his fists into the ground and Le Fondre wheel away, arms aloft. The red shirts across the park rise and the Jimmy Sirrel stand erupts in celebration. For a few seconds, we are gutted, deflated and empty. We have been hit where it hurts and on the balance of the game, against the run of play.

Through a crowd of players and with the distraction of 2,000 Yorkshire men deliriously jumping around, I spot a lone, bright, yellow flag. It's held aloft and flaps gently in the breeze as Notts fans all around are in despair. Notts players, for those brief few seconds, look as though the wind has been well and truly taken from their sails but there waves that small little flag of hope. Le Fondre argues with the referee. He denies making contact and feels the goal should stand. The referee's assistant suggests otherwise and it remains all square. The score remains firmly at 0-0 and all still to play for.

With this, the Kop reignites. Looking to lift the boys and push the side forwards. Amongst them they celebrate Yorkshires misfortune as though it were a goal of our own.

"Sit down Ronnie you twat" shout some of the Notts fans with Cheshire grins etched upon their faces. Can't beat winding up the opposition bench when they begin to rant at fourth officials.

Now Notts must respond in kind. Rodgers motions forwards and cuts inside his man. With Davies calling for the ball at the back post, Rodgers floats a neat ball with the outside of his right boot towards the potential match-winner. As pressure from their defenders is forced upon him, we still expect good things when this boy is near the ball. As a result, we feel slightly disappointed when he meets the ball only to hit the side netting.

The game is now stretched and up for grabs. Cotterill is lively and vocal on the side line.

"Hunty, Hunty, Hunty, Hunty" but still the defender does not hear his calls. He becomes louder and rawer in his delivery. *"HUNTY, HUNTY, HUNTY!!!"* and finally said Hunt hears the cries and obeys the signals as hand gestures, finger pointing and other arm movements make him fully aware of what he is being asked.

The black and white shirts continue to stem forward and press the Rotherham backline into their own half. Cotterill appears to feel momentum swinging once again after what had been a tightly contested 30 minutes in the fifteen minutes before and after the break.

Hughes pops up, strong as an ox and determined to break the deadlock. He heads a well directed ball across the face of goal and I slam my fist down in a Kasper-esque way as it is cleared from the line by skipper Ian Sharps.

With the chance suddenly nothing more than a mere statistic, Rotherham return up the other end to strike fear into our hearts. A goal now? A defeat at this point in the game? After this unbeaten run? Not worth contemplating. Fortunately Kasper agrees and as Ian Sharps heads a goal-bound effort moments after a clearance in his own box, he is left to look on as our shot stopper clutches the balls tightly.

Matty Hamshaw comes on for Westcarr but it appears all too late in the day to make any alterations to change the destiny of the game. In front of our responsive Kop Stand, Kasper spins the ball out onto the deck. Rotherham's defence back peddle, awaiting the final onslaught. The final push we hope can bring all the points.

The ball is driven, flat and with pace, deep into the Millers half. Notts men press on for a final time, hoping to create one last chance. No time for short balls out or working from the back now. Hughes, tormented for 90 minutes by those who wish they had him in their side, holds off his man some twenty-yards from goal. The ball lands perfectly

246

in his vicinity and his flick-on asks questions of both the Rotherham defenders but more importantly, little Luke Rodgers.

He pounces as though his whole career had been waiting for this very second. He beats his man to the ball as it skids off Hughes' head before landing perfectly in front of him. One touch away from his man and a glance up at Warrington in the Millers goal and his chance has arrived. One split second in time where everything seems to pause.

There are not many moments in football that gives you this. That second in time at which everyone in the ground is solely focused on one object. When the outcome of a game of such importance is so finely balanced and one man's heartache is another man's pure joy. Or in this case, 2,000 away fans heartache is 7,000 home fans moment of extreme jubilation.

This is what makes football so magical. It could have equally been at the other end of the pitch. It could easily have been Le Fondre bearing down on goal in the dying seconds. But it isn't.

"GET   IIIIIIIIIINNNNNNNNNNNNNNNNNNNNNNNN!!!!!" we scream as I turn, jumping into my old man's arms. At 27 years of age, I am jumping up and down with both he and my uncle as our Kieran and Danny fall into the row in front such are their celebrations. Everyone around us appears just as delirious. Just as crazy. Just as ecstatic. The arms and bodies partly mask the view as Rodgers belts the ball against the underside of the bar and into the back of the net. Although it ricocheted back out again, the linesman is in no doubt it crossed the line.

Matty Hamshaw turns away, much like Roger Hunt back on July 30th 1966 when he saw no reason to follow up Geoff Hurst's effort. A different game of a different magnitude it may be but equally as satisfying today. I said pre-match that out of this week and next week against Bury, this was the one I wanted to win the most. This is the team I wanted to see us enjoy victory over more than any other.

We're bouncing up and down now and no one is stopping us.

"E-i-e-i-e-i-o, up the Football League we go, when we get promotion this is what we'll sing, we are County, we are County Cotterill is our King....E-i-e-i-e-i-o...." the home support rejoices. Rotherham fans sit down, slumped back into their seats. Distraught, drained of energy and gutted.

We don't sit now. Normally, here in the Pavis Stand, fans are somewhat reserved in their support but not now. The Wheelbarrow song reverberates around this famous stadium and with a mixture of the sun, the songs and the pure pleasure of sharing this moment with other generations of my family, I cannot be any happier than I am right now. For promotion now is surely a done deal.

The board is held up to signal there are three minutes remaining and at the same time, Rodgers is withdrawn and replaced by Hawley. The delight on the Gaffers face as he embraces Rodgers is picturesque. He has a smile from here-to-there and beyond. His eyes light up and his joy is as apparent as anyone else in the stands.

Rotherham punt a few balls forward but, with time now against them, they are panicking. Their fans try and show some pride in their club and start to sing songs for their team rather than ones to antagonise us but we no longer care for their part in this event.

As the whistle blows, the importance of the three points is so obvious, I cannot help but breath it all in. Some twenty-stone fool from the Millers section jumps over the barriers and makes a bee-line for Hughes. He cares not one jot. He waves at their fans, as though thanking them for spurring him on. Several stewards become seven as eventually one manages to cut across the big bloke's path and seethe him down with a sliding tackle.

"*Hughesy, Hughesy, Hughesy*" we chant. He turns, grinning even more than Cotterill. He has once again produced the goods even if it isn't his goal that has done the deed this afternoon.

Luke Rodgers returns to the pitch to receive the accolades whilst Davies, Thommo and Hunty ensure that the lads deliver their own applause to all sections of the fans.

From a distance, it appears a section of Millers fans are actually congratulating Notts. A respectful applause or so it appears. I hope it is the case as it'd be a gentle reminder of what this game is about.

In our end, we just continue to sing "*I had a Wheelbarrow, and the wheel fell off, I had a Wheelbarrow, and the wheel fell off...*"

Coca Cola League Two Table:

	Pld	+/-	Pts
1. Rochdale	37	45	78
2. Notts County	**36**	**43**	**68**
3. Bournemouth	38	9	67
----
4. Rotherham United	38	10	65
5. Chesterfield	38	2	61
6. Bury	38	1	61
7. Aldershot Town	38	10	60

Kissing The Badge

01.04.10

'I'm not a great fan of badge kissing.
We're mercenaries in football, there's no question of that."
(Roy Hodgson on those who falsely show love - 2008)

I would say I was certainly not the badge kissing type. I hate it when players do it, knowing full well that they are not local to the club for which they pucker up their lips for. It's fake, transparent and a little clichéd in an era where players can change clubs as often as you or I change shoes. That said, my mate Sam The Toffee has had the same pair for five years so I guess we cannot tarnish everyone with the same brush.

Off the top of my head, Liverpool have two lads who are entitled to kiss the badge, United have the likes of Ryan Giggs, Paul Scholes and Gary Neville whilst elsewhere, there are not too many worthy of such a photo-opportunity after netting a goal. Ironically it is players such as John Terry, who people seem to love to hate, that have the right to carry out such demonstrations of love and commitment.

At the start of the season, Harry Redknapp said *"badge kissing is just a load of old tosh really"* and was duly slaughtered for it. I presume this was because he once left Pompey for rivals Southampton only to return back to Pompey at a later date. Despite that, I think his comments were rather honest, blunt and warranted. At least he is not pretending to have undying love for the clubs that he takes charge of unlike some players who kiss different badges within months of each other (for this see Ronaldo for Real Madrid shortly after leaving Old Trafford. I have never have been keen on the winker).

Oddly enough, the reason I have been thinking about this whole sign of affection is because Jade struggled to understand how I could tell her I loved her last week (in fact just days ago) and now I'm telling her that I see no future for her and I and wish to end it.

It's been a strange week really for various reasons at home but I cannot help but realise now that it has all been building to this. I have held back from calling time on the relationship but deep down, I've simply not been able to work out a solution in my head whilst delaying the inevitable.

A few weeks ago I sort of met someone else. For the record, no I didn't, haven't and wouldn't do that to Jade and I already know what you are wondering. I spent an entire lunch break sat in my mum's car in town during the week in which the whole thing came out and I told her the full story and gave an explanation for where I am at in my mind at the moment. She had sensed there was something wrong and I agreed to tell her what was troubling me.

She wasn't impressed with it at all. I'd have been surprised if she was. Ultimately, she knew that I would have to do what made me happy. The past seven days that started so well with a win against Rotherham has become one of the worst weeks in not just this season but living memory for me.

After beating The Millers on the Saturday, I duly went out and drank too much before getting home too late and thus ruining the dinner Jade had made for us both. This being the meal she had cooked by way of an apology for the fact we'd both been too busy for one another the week previous made matters worse. From there, it went downhill quickly. On Sunday morning CSKA Carnabys lost for the first time in nine league games to a promotion rival which saw our own hopes of going up badly dented. That same evening, Jade returned home to a kitchen with masses of pots, a living room full of muddy footballs and a washing machine crammed full of damp, dirty shirts as her fiancé lay fast asleep in front of Spanish football following some lunch time drinking down The Boat with Paul and Sam The Toffee.

Shortly after I woke, she realised that I had forgotten to book off the start of the week as previously planned with me saying *"Can you iron my shirt and trousers for work?"* the worst way to have such news delivered and from there it did not get much better.

Unfortunately, Monday then saw me bump into the woman who I'd sort of met during March and from there, my mind was very much elsewhere for the rest of the week and not where it should have been; getting things between me and Jade back on track.

By Wednesday I had opened up to my mum, had talks with the other woman (without anything happening) and generally decided that I could not carry on with the pretence that I was happy with the hand I had in my current life.

So when Jade asked me *"Why did you tell me you loved me the other day?"* I could only be as honest as possible without making the situation worse. I explained that whenever I said it, I'd have meant it and I'd never say such a thing if it were not true. After all, I am no badge kissing mercenary who'll soon be smooching with another badge regardless of what she, her family, friends or even you think of me based on my explanations here so far.

However, my explanation was fairly feeble. I'd not fallen out of love with Jade but I'd stopped being happy and that was more a reflection of myself than it was of her. We had arguments and we had discussions. We had discussions that led to arguments and arguments that led to conversations but each time we returned to the same place and it was starting to feel like a slow painful death. It felt like watching your team slaughtered in the first half of a FA Cup Semi-Final knowing that the dream is over and the story has come to an end. Despite this, you are forced to sit through the closing stages just to find some sort of closure on the whole experience.

I feel somewhat cowardly now that she has left the house but I also feel like a weight has been lifted from my shoulders. I am not expecting this to be some quick fix or find that happiness will be cast upon me and I'll joyfully bounce along the pavement like the man in the Mr Soft advert but it's going to be one step at a time to try and make sure I am happy and content in what I do.

Had I have told Jade that I was ending it because I'd met someone else, that would have opened up a whole new can of worms which, at the time of talking, I no longer had the energy for. It would also have given her the wrong impression of the whole situation too. She'd initially assume that I'd been having some sort of affair and everyone we both know would have been made aware of it whilst she'd have probably gone for the jugular and smashed up my John Lennon Epiphone Acoustic.

I would not have blamed her for refusing to hear me out or allowing me a chance to explain that I had not met someone for who I was leaving her for. Even if she had listened, she'd not have accepted it. I know as much because I'd not have accepted it either. As I previously said, meeting someone else just sort of opened up my mind a little more and made me believe that there was something else out there for me that would eventually make me happier than I currently allow myself to be.

Much of this is true, partly because the other woman is not available, but also because I am a firm believer that you cannot be happy and content with someone until you are happy and content with yourself and at the minute, I am certainly not happy with me or my life. More concerning though is I am not totally sure where this has all come from. I remember being a bit fed up last summer and I have feelings now reminiscent of that time. I think because of how busy I have been, everything has just been delayed perhaps.

It's certainly all out in the open now though.

Relationship Status:
Abandoned.

Dead And Buried

Yesterday morning Jade left the house for what would be the last and final time (or so I thought). It was over pretty quickly. She came back for a talk and to ask me whether there was any chance what-so-ever of patching things up and within twenty minutes she was banging about downstairs taking whatever she felt was owed to her and causing a mess in every room possible. Ironic considering how much she tried to keep me on track with the tidiness.

I'm not exactly in great spirits right now. I'm not going to pretend I am. It certainly is not a case of being *"glad the bitch is gone"* as many people try and pretend is the case when a relationship breaks down. For me, this is not the ending I imagined. In fact I did not imagine any sort of ending. For all the arguments and disagreements I genuinely thought we'd always iron things out and get back on track but this time, it did not seem possible.

Various factors contributed towards the downwards spiral but eventually, it was one or two factors too many that caused us to part-company. It was not mutual consent in the way clubs agree with a boss that it is *"for the best"* but more a resignation from me that I could not continue the way things have been of late.

I'm not proud of the way I handled the whole situation at all. Not one bit. I just did what I had to do. Especially given the fact I had sort of met someone else. For once, it was not football that was occupying my mind and pulling at my heart strings but it was another girl. As I say, proud of it I am not.

However, I did not leave Jade for the other girl and that for me is a vital detail in this whole thing. I don't want Jade to hate me and nor do I want her to lose all contact with my family who have much time and love for her. The other girl was not the reason, more the catalyst. She opened my eyes into a different kind of person I could be. I could indeed become a person not stressed about this and that or concerned about my future. Had it been another day, it might not have been like this. I might have been with the other girl. But as I say, I have not left Jade for her. I have left Jade as I no longer want what it is we have or rather had. It sounds too clichéd to suggest I need to find myself though.

This morning I feel weird as I stroll downstairs. A half empty living room with bits and bobs she wanted to take with her upon departing left in a box.

"I'll fetch the rest when you are out" I heard as I left the house to go for a walk and leave her to it.

I slowly motivate myself to make a bacon cob (basically a bun or bread roll depending on where you are from) and a cup of tea. I open the morning papers and I sit in silence reading the news ahead of today's games. No nagging to do the pots from last night. No shit, Saturday morning TV to put up with as I read the back pages. Just silence. I eat my cob, sip my tea and sit back whilst I decide if I am really in the right frame of mind for football.

Then, without warning, a random phone call. Mark is definitely going to be down at Meadow Lane having been unsure earlier in the week due to work commitments and within seconds I am up and about and sorting myself for a day down at Notts. Is it just what I needed given the circumstances?

I pile up more pots on the side in the kitchen (let's face it, the urgency for such chores is null and void now) and I run upstairs to get my jacket and scarf. It's almost a case of not having enough time to think about whether or not I want to go. I either go now or not at all so before I know it I am on the train and buying a lager from the little bar in the middle coach.

A few beers later and I have forgotten about the more pressing parts of my life for the time being. Where next? What now? Where is my life going? All that sort of nonsense that all too often weighs us down and stops us from living is temporarily forgotten about with a drink or two and as I put it to the back of my mind, I meet Mark and his mates in The Globe.

I drink quicker today, especially considering by the third round of drinks I am usually playing catch up and opt out for the next one. Whether I am subconsciously drinking to forget or I am drinking because I fancy drinking, I am not entirely sure. Three points is what has come to matter today though. The target, promotion and daring to dream that we could still go up as Champions is what it is all about now.

It is on-form Notts against Play-Off chasing Bury and the mood around the pub is very positive.

"Come on you Pies!" are the rallying shouts as the room fills up and the taps keep pouring. My old man is not down today but one or two familiar faces who know him say hello and ask me how we'll do today.

"Three points - no problems" I respond each time. There is no doubt in my mind any more.

Mark on the other hand is edgy still. He is insistent that at some point we will slip up and it will cost us in the run-in. Even by his new found pessimism, surely we can't mess this up even if second spot is the best we can hope for.

As the atmosphere builds we move onwards and stop off at The Navi. Just as packed and louder out the back, the bars are raking it in this afternoon. With each passing pint that I sink, the game eases its way towards the back of my mind along with my troubles. I am drinking to the success of 2009/10. I am certain now of what will be and I have not a single doubt that next term will be spent in League One.

However, more than a reasoned opinion and observation of our fortunes, I think I am more of the viewpoint that it has to be the case because otherwise, what was the point in it all? What was the point in the endless hours of arguing and the late night discussions about Boxing Day games that never happened? Why did we disagree over small, insignificant things such as whether Rochdale away was worth the hours and the money? Now we have to seal promotion otherwise it will have been for what?

Eventually, as The Navi fails to live up to the demands of the punters, a few of us make our way to the Kop. Singing voices already warming up, Bury have brought a fair crowd from the indications outside the ground but they'll have a job to be heard today. Many fans are viewing this as the last of the real big tests prior to Rochdale in five games time.

We stand and sing and soak it all up. The summer sun shines through although the true warmth still escapes us somewhat and Bury fans gather in the away enclosure just a few feet away from us. They wave cash and sing clever songs about our club cheating our way to being promotion candidates. It matters not one bit though and as the sides walk out, we have eyes only for our side on our own turf. We look on at our history makers in black and white.

"County, County..." sings The Kop to the beat of the drum. Kasper runs over towards us and salutes us as one. The sides do their shuttle runs, their stretches and their pre-match rituals as Hughes looks laid back, full of life and he smiles to all stands making sure to give the Bury end a wave and a grin as he talks with the mascots and ensures they are enjoying their big day.

Thompson loses the toss (again) and pretty soon our boys are trotting off down the other end to ready themselves for another tough, vitally important 90 minutes of football.

"E-i-e-i-e-i-o...." and the whole stand rises to join in as the teams get things underway and we attempt to draw the Magpies towards us.

We bounce to the beat as Bury try and out sing us but we are not going to sit back today and have our atmosphere stolen. I am louder than normal and showing my passion as much as ever. I want this so bad. I need it.

We jump to attention as the ball is floated into Hughes just inside the box. Just yards away from Mark and me, Hughes controls and then dinks a tempting ball into the box for steady Eddie to fire home with just four minutes on the clock.

"Goal for the Magpies, number four, Mike Edwards" and we roar as we inch ever so closer to a route out of League Two.

Mark joins in with the songs now as do the three chaps with us. Bury fans are shocked and stunned by the early goal and the balance being shifted before they've even had time to find their bearings.

Now Rodgers attacks towards us. Waiting to ignite the game further still and cause problems for the Bury backline, he cuts inside his man, drifts past a second and fires just wide but we remain stood, loud and proud and urging our lads on towards victory.

Minute-by-minute the game passes by and as it does I see less of it through my own eyes. I react as the crowd reacts and I sing as the stand sings. Bury try and muster some support and twice begin to murmur as Kasper is tested at the other end but I am beyond fear now. I am watching the game but not taking it in or giving it much thought. With 39 minutes on the clock, up we jump and I am off under the stand to grab myself another drink.

"Come on Notts" I yell watching over my shoulder as I sprint up the concrete steps and away from the pitch.

I see an old mate under the stand, I buy us both a beer and we try to and catch up but I am not really having the conversation. I am involved in it but it's not registering. Mark joins me and we start to dissect the half.

"Need to be careful not to let them into the game" Mark tells me. I don't give it much thought.

I drink up and motion towards the stairwell as we hear the sides kick off for the second half. Bury's following sound much louder and more purposeful with their songs now. The atmosphere in the Kop is still fantastic though from what I can hear and as I return, spirits all around me appear to be high although I am not sure what level my own are at.

Rodgers is at it again breaking at the Bury defenders with directness and pace. He runs at their right back before knocking a timely ball into the box and as I return to my seat Westcarr cuts across the ball and smashes it into the back of the net for 2-0.

"Sealed!" I tell Mark and he now smiles with a look of relief.

Now we appear to have more confidence than ever before. The pitch is still cutting-up and still with its imperfections but Notts stroke the ball about like never before. A neat ball is played wide to Clapham who pops up on the right and ventures forward with grace. He shimmies and looks inside before sliding a ball into Davies who takes a neat touch to set himself up before volleying home number three of the afternoon.

There is no stopping the Kop now as each one of us to a man dances along to the celebratory music on the tannoy and we wave to departing Bury fans who've seen enough already.

"Cheerio, cheerio, cheerio..." echoes around the ground as a fair few fans depart with thirty minutes still on the clock.

Time now fades to insignificance. Davies whips in a dangerous free-kick and Hughes is on the mark to head home from close range as the Bury enclosure empties and the party atmosphere is all around me as the Magpies show yet another team at Meadow Lane that they are worthy of the automatic spots.

With the game nearing its conclusion and fans cheering each and every pass, we watch on as on 81 minutes, big Delroy Facey completes the finishing touches netting from close range after Edwards followed up a Ricky Ravenhill strike.

Dreamland it may be but it now feels all too easy. No euphoric, last minute, clincher this time around. This game was done and dusted long ago.

We sing and dance our way out of the ground. We cheer other results and we marvel in the performance as each and every one of us appears to be smiling more than ever now. It was a great way to forget about the real world and every day things.

A staggered walk off the train, down the platform and out of the exit and I am thanking my lucky stars that my house is so close to the Loughborough Station. I walk onwards with a thick head and a desire for food now as the drink starts to take its toll. Across the lights and some hundred yards or so later, I push my key in the door and I am home safe and sound.

I'm feeling shattered. Drained, tired and with mixed emotions, I am just grateful that Notts have given me reason to smile this Saturday evening. Before settling down and phoning for a Curry, I trot upstairs and grab a quick shower. Thinking back in my head of the goals I'd seen today. I re-live Eddie's opener along with goals from Westcarr, Super Ben, Hughes and big Delroy Facey. Get in!

What a game. Bury never stood a chance really.

I think to tomorrow. I need to bag a goal or two for myself as CSKA look to push on in our own hunt for promotion. Still with points to win and still aiming for success, it'll be a vital game. A relaxing evening lies ahead with a nice curry and football highlights on the box. It's my first ever Saturday on my own in this house. It will be strange one for sure but I have that to get used to now.

I walk down the hall way, towel wrapped around me. Feeling refreshed and no longer so tired and heavy headed. I walk into my bedroom and it hits me hard. No bed. No wardrobe. No bed side cabinets. All of them are gone and all without warning.

Shit!!! She knew I'd be down at Notts.

Coca Cola League Two Table:

	Pld	+/-	Pts
1. Rochdale	38	43	78
2. Notts County	**37**	**48**	**71**
3. Bournemouth	39	10	70
4. Rotherham United	39	9	65
5. Chesterfield	39	4	64
6. Northampton Town	39	12	62
7. Aldershot Town	39	10	61

Any Road Will Take Us There

Shrewsbury Town v Notts County
Gay Meadow / League Two / 05.04.10

Until last night, Bank Holiday Monday did not hold much for me after recent events at home. Mark called me up to offer me a ticket and a lift to Shrewsbury and just like that, I had an excuse to not stay at home alone, tidying up when everyone else would be enjoying the football calendar.

The 'other girl' that I met last month had suggested we meet up for lunch today and at one point I was looking forward to that. Just for a chat and a bit of a catch up really. However, she's had to cancel as she is visiting her in-laws with her partner which should be enough of a wake-up call for me to suggest lunch was not a good idea anyway.

I must have been strange company today though. I was surprisingly upbeat from the moment Mark arrived at my door to begin our journey to Play-Off hopefuls Shrewsbury Town. After obliterating Bury and then finding out that I no longer owned a bed, my Saturday could only be described as containing mixed fortunes. I was fortunate enough to have someone on hand to sort me out with a second hand divan however and after setting that up and trying to tidy away all my vinyl's that Jade had kindly left everywhere, I crashed out with a bottle of beer and watched Notts smash Bury once again on the Football League Show.

I then somehow managed to muster the energy yesterday morning to get to Leicester for another big promotion battle for CSKA. I scored the goal that gave us a 3-2 lead in what can only be described as the muddiest conditions since records began, and we eventually took all three points in a 4-2 victory which meant we remain in second place. I then postponed a big house tidy-up for a night out given the fact that I had remembered I have a new found status (single), so considering this, I should be shattered and out for the count this morning.

Mark, in true Mark fashion of late, was a little pessimistic ahead of the game. It's not so much the fact that he thinks we are set to lose but more that he believes we are due a defeat and would rather air on the side of caution.

By my reckoning however, the whole question mark surrounding promotion will be sorted by the next time we hear a full-time whistle down at Meadow Lane. Today Shrewsbury, on Saturday Northampton and then we host Lincoln at home. Take maximum points from those three games and it'd be a done deal surely?

Upon arriving near the ground, I could not help but notice the relative smallness of the whole place. It felt like we were a much bigger club invading a small lower league club despite the fact only ten Football League places separate us both. Shrewsbury fans appeared rather subdued despite the added bonus of Bank Holiday football.

At the end of February Shrewsbury were firmly planted in the Play-Off places and looked destined for a place in the top seven come May. However, four consecutive defeats in March as well as a loss away at a rejuvenated Torquay last week and their season has come to a standstill rather than a gradual grinding halt that is sometimes suffered by one of the chasing pack.

We sang about our blessed Wheelbarrow more than ever, we savoured our pre-match drinks and we approached the ground with an air of confidence that we no longer had concerns about our form on the road. After all, only Bournemouth had beaten us in the league in our last nine trips away from Meadow Lane and now, given the fact that Steve Cotterill has the side focused and intent on winning the division, very few of us could see it going wrong.

A classic it was not but a win it was once again. Rather fittingly, it was Ben Davies against his former club that gave us the only goal of the game which ensured that we'd maintain the pressure on table topping Rochdale and their boss Keith Hill who is as fond of Notts as we are of him.

More importantly, neither Rochdale nor Bournemouth managed to out-score the other as they drew 0-0 at Spotland whilst fourth placed Rotherham lost 3-0 at Aldershot. After all was said and done, it was a perfect Bank Holiday.

Coca Cola League Two Table:

	Pld	+/-	Pts
1. Rochdale	39	43	79
2. Notts County	**38**	**49**	**74**
3. Bournemouth	40	10	71
4. Rotherham United	40	6	65
5. Aldershot Town	40	13	64
6. Chesterfield	40	2	64
7. Bury	40	-1	64

Well Respected Man About Town
Beeston, Nottingham / 08.04.10

Articulated, polite, warm and endearing. I already knew as much about his character prior to my meeting with Colin Slater at The Priory in Nottingham as we approach the business end of the football season.

Memories from my childhood and also those from more recent times, always find their way back to Colin Slater and the hours of tension spent with my Dad and a transistor radio at the dinner table. These memories are as fond as those down at Meadow Lane.

Growing up, it was not financially viable to see Notts home and away, week-in, week-out. In fact it is not financially viable today, even with only me to support. But my love for Notts County and also away games was never an issue for me and my Dad.

If it was local, we used to try and catch the games when we, or rather my parents, could justify the outlay. However, on those occasions when the purse strings did not allow us, we'd sit around the oak dinner table in the kitchen of our semi-detached and tune into Uncle Colin and his coverage of the Magpies on the road.

He delivered, without failure, charismatic, exciting and insightful reports and reviews for our club, be it a cold Tuesday night in January or a warm day in May as the season drew to a close. Not many clubs, I am almost positive it can be said, can look back on what has now become over 50 years with one man at the forefront of the clubs media coverage in the local area.

Way back in 1959, Colin Slater moved to Nottingham from his home town of Bradford to take up a post with the local rags in Nottingham and to this day, he still reports on a club that has become his own and in turn, he has become one of us.

For the first hour or so, myself and Colin sit with a mutual friend Mark Beeby and the pair discuss Mark's latest project in the East Midlands which involves him trying to raise funds to deliver better quality sports sessions to youngsters with physical and learning disabilities.

It is a responsibility that Mark has been dedicated to ever since I first knew him through coaching and his passion and ambition to always improve and give more to community is a clear common denominator between himself and Colin.

Colin, you see, is trying to help Mark with contacts and links within the Nottingham area of who may be able to help Mark in fulfilling his latest goals so understandably, the pair are encompassed in the subject and show enthusiasm on something that in fairness, I know little about.

Mark and Colin's friendship, one might think, is not the most obvious of friendships but once again, it is one that was born out of a common love and that love was and still is Notts. When Mark took his old man, and former Notts County player Oliver Beeby, to a game a few years back at Meadow Lane, Mark went up to Colin to reintroduce his Dad some 45 years or so after they'd have first met.

Oliver was one of the first Notts signings after Colin joined the Nottingham papers and due to this, both would share similar memories of a time long forgotten by most.

"Don't tell me" Colin said looking towards Oliver as Mark first introduced himself. *"Oliver Beeby? Signed from Leicester City in 1959"* as Mark was about to enquire as to whether Colin remembered his Dad.

Of course he remembered. For Colin is a gentleman and also someone who appears interested in those around him more than what you'd imagine from someone who is in such a busy, demanding role meeting new names and faces all of the time.

From that day, Mark gradually got to know Colin as more than just the man on the microphone and from it, a friendship was formed upon which Mark and Colin would be able to share some good memories and swap interesting stories.

As we sit down to eat, the discussion soon turns to Shrewsbury and Northampton away in the next week or so. These are two massive games against two sides that are clearly in the shake-up at the time of the season when it matters most so understandably they are a hot topic.

In the week building up to my meeting with Colin and Mark, all three of us exchanged e-mails on Notts County's fortunes and the demands that would be placed on the side in the coming weeks. As we tuck into a carvery, Notts sit seven points behind leaders Rochdale with one game in hand and 37 of our 46 games played. More importantly, we now sit six points ahead of the non-automatic spot of fourth where Rotherham have also played two games more.

"It's nail biting stuff" Colin points out between sips of his lime soda. *"The boardroom and the dressing room want to go up as Champions though. To do that, I think they will need eight wins from the last ten games"*.

My gut feeling is we no longer have anything to be concerned by. A run of seven wins and two draws since Steve Cotterill took charge of first team affairs means we have halved the gap between us and the top and have become much closer to having a guaranteed promotion come

May whilst we have let in just two goals in the process, both against a good Bournemouth side.

However, Colin and Mark have been here before on numerous occasions and both are older and wiser than me. So their reluctance to accept that we've virtually done enough is understandable.

"I think we'll slip up in one of the next two" says Mark. *"We have to lose at some point?"*

For me however, we don't. We look solid and, given the current form of both ourselves and others, there is nothing to suggest we are going to fall flat on our face on our travels just yet. Colin? He sits on the fence and in true 'football talk', maintains that Notts need to take it a game at a time. He's been in this job for some time after all.

After the meal, Mark departs and makes his way back to his Hinckley home whilst Colin and I go to a quieter area of the pub to talk more about his time with the club and his tales of the past.

"When I go back to the beginning, I arrived in Nottingham when the City had two evening papers and the morning paper. I came onto the Nottingham evening news and the football news which was a big pink paper" remembers Colin.

For Colin, we currently sit in a position that is not dissimilar to where it all began for him.

My first season was 1959/60 and Notts County had suffered two successive relegations and found themselves, for the first time ever, in the bottom tier of English Football in the Fourth Division. But it was a successful season. Notts County gained promotion finishing second behind Walsall and it was a very good time and start for me.

For anyone who has ever had the pleasure of listening to Colin talk, whether it be on the radio, television or in his company, you would know that the manner in which he delivers his thoughts and views is nigh on perfect. He has what I'd consider the perfect radio voice. Concise and well pronounced, he adds a little extra to vital words which gives those listening to him a perfect picture of what he is talking about.

No man can describe a *"goal for Notts County"* in the way that Uncle Colin does and for this, it is clear as to why Notts love him.

So in his 50 years reporting on the club, I could not but ask what his major highlights had been?

The promotions in the Jimmy Sirrel era. The promotions in the Neil Warnock era. The promotion under Sam Allardyce. They're the outstanding seasons and they are the ones you remember with pleasure. Partly because in order to achieve those promotions, we had the team that had the best players and without them, there is nothing.

Albeit it obvious, he is right of course. I remember fondly the sides that played under Warnock, mainly because I was watching the best players in the division week after week during those campaigns. It was a pleasure to see the likes of Tommy Johnson and Mark Draper in action and in turn, others around them improved their game and excelled.

So it is no coincidence that the current crop of Notts players are managing to make me feel like a kid again. Perhaps it is down to the fact that they are sparking memories of when I was a kid or perhaps it is just the fact that good sides bring out the eternal hope and optimism of youth. Colin expanded on this explaining:

There are similarities with all successful sides and I would say the start of those similarities begins with a good goalkeeper. First and foremost, clubs don't win anything without a good goalkeeper. I'd say Notts, this season, have earned around eight or ten extra points because of the goalkeeping of one Kasper Schmeichel. He has been worth those extra points alone.

When Notts County were heading to the old First Division under Jimmy Sirrel for example, we had Raddy Avramovic and the two of them have been the best keepers I have ever seen. Of course under Neil, we had Steve Cherry who was also very good.

The team also has, when successful, a good spine. So you need a really effective central defensive partnership. Neil Warnock again had this with Craig Short and Dean Yates. Dean was at the club when he arrived, and Craig? He [Neil] more-or-less brought along with him from Scarborough for £100,000. And today, just the same. A spine down the middle, we have Graeme Lee and Mike Edwards. It is vital.

Of course, there is more. You also need someone upfront who will deliver goals. And Notts County have one in Lee Hughes. I remember the day he signed, a Scout from the Premier League rang me up and said to me Lee Hughes will get you 30 goals and promotion. There was no doubt in his mind of this and by word has he been shown to be correct.

Other things in the side matter of course. But that spine. Goalkeeper, Central defence, a finisher. If you have not got those...?

You also need some real ability to create something from midfield. Notts County have been lacking for years and years and years in that department. But that has been put right this season as we have three players of above average quality in Ben Davies, Neal Bishop and Ricky Ravenhill.

They are players who are full of creativity but they also work very hard as well. They seem to complement one another. Neal and Ricky are not too different but they work. Then you look at the Sirrel era and you had, for me, the best player I have seen in the black and white in Don Masson. But Don Masson was a genius. No question a real genius. He was the fulcrum. Of course, Neil Warnock also had such players bringing in Mark Draper to the side and he gave him his chance and he had others, such as Dean Thomas and Phil Robinson, who acted as the hard-cop to Draper's good-cop if you like.

Suddenly Colin is alive and talking at free-will about players I remember only too well. Time passes us by and before we know it, we have talked at length about those players of yesteryear and the pleasure they brought us during those seasons.

Colin sits, almost still but for his facial expressions. Hands clasped together except for occasional gestures to highlight his emotions, he is oblivious to the numerous people walking by us and noticing him, or perhaps just his voice as we sit at the far end of the pub near the exit for the smokers. Continually referring to me on first name terms, he makes me feel at ease and comfortable and I am no longer asking a set of questions but having a mere conversation. One football fan to another.

At Notts, we have hit some real lows and again, Colin will have witnessed more than most.

Teams think success is theirs by right and it isn't. Not even Manchester United. And I think that most Notts County fans know better than this. They know it is transient, it is hard earned and that the good times can disappear as quickly as they come, if not quicker. But you can have hope and like with now, there is hope and earlier in the year the hope was more that we'd achieve some sustained progress. But let us hope that this is still right.

In football, hope is sometimes all you can have. We know that during the summer of 2009, much was promised to us and much was made of the new era and the bright future. Now? Well I am just glad the club is still here and still in existence and again Colin echoes these sentiments whilst citing past experiences as being a warning sign for not just Notts but other clubs in the future.

I've had to contemplate the thought of there being no Notts County several times over the years so this [winding up orders] was no different. It is well documented that I played a key role in helping save the club from going out of business in 1965 when I managed to persuade two great figures in the World of Football in the form of Andy Beattie (former Scotland Manager) and Peter Docherty (former Northern Ireland Manager), to come in as unpaid advisors to the club. They agreed to come along and further down the line we managed to secure the funds to save the club on that occasion.

Then there was numerous threats of going out of business during the period of administration between June 2002 and December 2003 and I think there is similarities to when Haydn Green saved the club with a round figure of £3,000,000 and with what Ray Trew is doing now.

Notts County has lived on the wire for quite a few of the 50 years I have been here. It'd be nice if it was to not happen again.

As we sit, very much with the club on the wire once more, we cannot help but think that we had been promised so much more than what we now have though. Colin remembers all too well the euphoria that came with the takeover back at the start of the season.

First of all I was taken by surprise. Two people, the Notts chairman at the time John Armstrong-Holmes and the vice-chairman Roy Parker. They'd been overseas repeatedly to Dubai. They had met, and in principle agreed to sell the club onto Munto Finance. Then they saw it as needing, and whether it was needed I have some doubts, but they saw it as needing the support of the Supporter's Trust who had acquired the shares of the late Haydn Green.

I think why I was a taken back by it though was that previously there had been other stories, other rumours, others indications and other straws in the wind that other people were interested in taking over Notts County Football Club. And it did not seem, and this may not be the case but it is how it appeared at the time, it did not seem that those other parties were given much encouragement to pursue their interest. Suddenly Munto were being given all the encouragement in the World.

265

It was feelings such as this that concerned a small selection of Notts County fans back in 2009 when the story was first leaked that a possible takeover was on the cards.

Now someone such as John Armstrong-Holmes, who was of course in a very powerful and influential position must have had his own reasons had he not encouraged other potential investors and he had his own reasons for believing at the time in Munto Finance. He has obviously since said that he wished he had never heard of them however. But I was taken by surprise because suddenly, it was clear that the supporters trust were prepared to sell the club onto new owners.

There was a special meeting at Wheelers. It was a feverish atmosphere in which fairly short shrift was given to people who asked critical questions. There was such a ground swell that this was it and Notts County were going to become, almost in the twinkling of an eye, the premier club in Nottingham. People were carried by the euphoria that evening.

I tried to make sense of things but could not always do so. There were straws in the wind that everything was not perhaps what it seemed. The Sol Campbell business, being well documented, was one of them. Then there was another. Matthew Lorenzo came into the club as a Public Relations Officer. I have known Matthew's father Peter Lorenzo, a big writer from Fleet Street for many years. A lovely family. But Matthew disappeared very quickly as well. You could try to make sense of this. But there was none.

However, there was one person who was the glue if you like. And that was Sven. As long as Sven was there and seemed to be working, head down, showing loyalty and commitment, it seemed to almost contradict all other vibes we were getting.

And it was a contradiction that, given his status and standing within the game, managed to keep the support of the fans well and truly behind the cause despite doubts and inklings that all was not well under good-ship-Munto.

On a weekly basis I had conversations during those hectic months that almost always led back to the statement "*as long as Sven is here*". We read the bad press. We were engulfed by it almost daily. We had rival fans, fellow fans, neutral fans and jealous fans all reminding us of the bad things that were happening and eventually, they were starting to outweigh the positives.

Colin continues:

People up and down the country would always ask about him. Did we expect him there? Was he coming to games? And of course, yes he did. And I said yes he attends every match. He watches the juniors and the youth team games. He goes to functions. He is an ambassador around the City.

As a fan, I felt it was a credit to the Swede to the very last. He didn't just take the job and do it for the ride. Had he done so, he'd have soon sat back when the Munto fiasco erupted. Some fans say he was waiting for his big pay day. Holding out for the matters within the club to be resolved so that he could get what was owed to him. As the facts now show, it was simply not the case.

Talking after the most recent takeover, which as a result saw Sven-Goran Eriksson step down from his role as Director of Football, Notts' new Chief Executive Jim Rodwell could not praise Sven enough for his selflessness during the final few weeks.

Sven has been a gentleman throughout this and his only concern was for the future of the football club. He had a five-year contract but he graciously agreed to forfeit nearly everything. He understands the situation we have inherited and he told us that the most important thing to him was to see the football club survive. I cannot tell you the exact figure but we could not have gone close to meeting the sum involved.

And the glowing reference from Rodwell was further enhanced as Colin and I talked about the former England Manager.

"What he did, when you'd expect to be talking about him, he talked to you about you. Tell me about yourself he would say. Tell me about the city, the history."

Colin explains how Sven made people feel special and important. Ironically, and without Colin perhaps even realising it, I can safely say that my company for this evening was cut from the exact same cloth as Sven.

"What matters looking back is he was as highly regarded in the dressing room by the players as by any of us who were on the periphery. He had a bond with the players and they trusted him" Colin continues as we discuss the Swede at length.

At this point we pause however, catch breath and I grab us both another drink. A coke for myself, ensuring I keep a very clear head, and a lime and soda for Colin. Upon my return to the table, Colin cannot wait to start asking questions himself however. Where I am from? Where I grew up? My background and my hopes as well as my dreams and ambitions? It suddenly becomes Colin Slater interviewing Luke Williamson and it is the ease at which he makes one feel comfortable that is responsible for the time we have escaping before we realise it.

Whilst I am fascinated by his background and his memories, I cannot help but ask him about the last few months and what it has meant to him to report on it all as it unfolded.

> *Peter Trembling was very helpful in giving briefings to me, so the things I said [on BBC Radio Nottingham] were based on leads and conversations we'd had together. Sometimes I may have picked things up from elsewhere too. But if I had done so, and if I ever challenged them to him, he would speak reasonably and rationally. Very full and in-depth. There was a long public debate for instance about whether Munto Finance would be approved for the 'Fit and Proper Persons Test'. I was given sight of correspondents at the time and from those correspondents, I was not in any doubt that they would be approved by the Football League. I did not say I expected them to be approved and I did not say I believed they would be approved to calm down the fears of supporters. I said what I said because I had seen the documentation that told me they would be approved.*

As time passed and stories began to unfold about Munto and the clubs finances, some fans suggested that there were not enough questions asked of Trembling and Munto earlier on in the whole episode. Colin explains his approach to what is deemed necessary to ask however, stating:

> *As a professional you ask the questions that you think need asking at the time. You think about it a lot. Myself and Robin [Chipperfield of BBC Nottingham] would sometimes get together before a show and discuss questions and angles so to speak about. The things we asked were not off the cuff. They were not thought up on the spot. We were careful about the questions we posed."*

In fact I get the impression that Colin was not so much insulted but upset that some fans felt the relevant questions were not asked.

> *All of us take seriously the responsibility that we have to do our level best to get to the truth. Not to convey falsehoods to our listeners but to be a critical friend to the club at all times and not to be taken in. There are many off-the-record briefings in all walks of life in media but, should you be a reliable*

individual, then the off-the-record briefings can be more frequent as the source knows you will use the information reliably.

Speaking of when Sven-Goran Eriksson was set to be announced onto the scene, Colin's face lights up as he recalls the days very well.

I got a 24 hour lead before anyone else that he was coming to Notts as a Director of Football. It was announced on the Tuesday officially but I had it on Radio Nottingham at 11am on the Monday. I was interviewed that same afternoon by Sky Sports as they had caught on that perhaps I knew more than anybody else.

Of course, I know who had told me. They told me making it clear I was free to use the information freely and publicly but they also told me, I think, in the knowledge that I would use the information in the right way and so I am on Sky and Five Live and so on that day.

If anyone could perhaps understand everything that was happening at the club, it was Colin. After all, this was the man who had been at close quarters with all the big names that were involved down at Meadow Lane in the months that followed.

"When people asked me down the line could I believe it, I'd always say, well yes. I see him, I talk to him, I've had meals with him. Of course I believe it. They were so bewildered that they assumed so was everyone else."

Despite the fairytale winding-down somewhat at the turn of the year, Colin still shows the passion and excitement in discussing the club as he did in the news features from last summer. He conveys a sense of feeling privileged to have been so close to all the action as it happened and smiles with each little story or memory that he unveils to me as we sit and talk.

It has been the busiest six or seven months I have ever known. Never before have I been so busy. I was on various stations all over the world. I have a studio facility at home so I did not need to be out and about. It was quite an adrenaline rush.

The very day Sven arrived I saw the biggest, most dramatic and extraordinary press conference I have ever seen. I sat on the front row. I was told I could have one of the first two questions put towards him. And then I had to get across to another part of the 1862 suite to do a piece from a view point from which we

269

could best view Sven. I had to somehow navigate my way through the busiest of rooms, full of camera crews, photographers, reporters and such.

He was the first man since Tommy Lawton, I suspect, who would be considered as the one man who brought real stardust to Meadow Lane.

With that said, Colin has a satisfied smile on his face which reminds me of a joyful child, content with the life the world has dealt him. Colin never appears to boast or name drop. He does not possess the characteristics of someone who acts as a show off. He simply enjoys sharing his experiences with me in a manner that he hopes I too will try and put to good use.

As we begin to wind-down our conversation, I ask him about his own highlights of the last 50-plus years in Nottingham and what memories he will always cherish.

The thing I value more than anything is that through all the up's and down's I have made some real and lasting friendships. I believe for instance that Jimmy Sirrel and I were good friends. I saw him last of all in hospital the week he died and I valued him as a real friend.

I am also enormously flattered, and I mean this because I have not played the game since I was at high school and never played the game at what you might call a high level, but I am greatly honoured to have been offered, and to have accepted, the role of President of the Former Players Association. So I feel deeply humble that the former players have placed me in that role. It has been a job and a place of work but it has brought some rich and lasting friendships.

And for Colin Slater MBE, what does he still have left to achieve?

I no longer think in career terms anymore. I have hopes. The experience of working at the New Wembley would be nice and I long to work at the Emirates Stadium. I think it is something different and better and I would love to work there. There is nothing like going to these places like Manchester United, Arsenal, Chelsea, Liverpool and Everton. And I hope as Notts County progress and reach the bigger stage, I will reach more listeners and that when Notts County hit new levels, I will still be at the microphone.

It's a nice way to end our chat which, although intended to be formal, pretty quickly became a general conversation between two people sharing a passion. As we leave The Priory, Colin offers to drop me off at Beeston Train Station to which I gratefully accept and we set off on the short journey by car.

We talk a little more en route about myself and the book and he also asks of mine and Mark's friendship and as we arrive at Beeston Station, I am wishing our meeting did not have to end. He refuses to simply drop me off at the entrance, instead driving in and offering to let me wait in the car for the next train to arrive but I insist that I will be ok to stand on the platform and he graciously accepts and thanks me for taking the time to come and speak to him.

I cannot help but realise it should be me thanking Colin, of which I do several times and in turn he wishes me luck with the book and says that he hopes we will meet again in the future. Before leaving, he reminds me with a glint in his eye that *"In 2012 the club will be 150 years old and the first club to reach such a milestone. I hope and trust that with this big date coming up, Notts County are in a place that merits the history of Notts."*

I cannot better his words and I do not try to as we shake hands and wish each other a safe journey home.

Sealing The Deal

Notts County v Lincoln City
Meadow Lane / League Two / 13.04.10

As I walk across Trent Bridge towards Meadow Lane I know that technically we still need points. Danny (the mate, not the uncle) and I speculated very little as to who would be starting on the way over as the side has changed very little since Steve Cotterill arrived at Meadow Lane. We listened to Match Talk on BBC Radio Nottingham and queued for far too long on the A6 behind a tractor but now, at last we are here and we are heading to meet my old man in The Navi.

On Saturday we won at Northampton following another 1-0 win at Shrewsbury. Both games won by slender margins and both thanks to Ben Davies goals, we now have three consecutive home games from which we should seal the deal and confirm our destination for next season.

Tonight though, I am somewhat frustrated. Press Officer Ralph Shepherd had kindly arranged for me to sit up at the top of the Pavis Stand tonight with the likes of BBC's Colin Slater, Colin Hazeldeine, Robin Chipperfield and former Notts legend Dean Yates. Until a few days ago, I was set to sit amongst them, watch the game from their vantage point and talk to them about the season and how it had been reporting on this dramatic campaign.

However, with Lincoln City here for league game number forty, I am all too aware that a win tonight should theoretically confirm promotion for Notts and because of it; I feel I should be watching the game with my old man.

With two games in hand on our chasing pack, three points tonight would see Notts rise to the 80 point margin. Meanwhile, Aldershot, Rotherham and Chesterfield all sit on 65 points with only five games remaining meaning the best total they can hit is...80 points. Given the fact we have a far superior goal difference to everyone else in the country, let alone League Two, and given the fact that we still have seven games left, you can see why confidence is sky high at present.

Coca Cola League Two Table:

	Pld	+/-	Pts
1. Rochdale	40	38	79
2. Notts County	**39**	**50**	**77**
3. Bournemouth	41	9	71
4. Rotherham	41	4	65
5. Aldershot	41	13	65
6. Chesterfield	41	2	66
7. Morecambe	41	11	64

Added to the our three points gained over at Northampton, Rochdale amazingly crashed 5-0 away at Torquay, Aldershot only managed a draw with Port Vale and Bournemouth and Rotherham lost to Lincoln and Morecambe respectively. Whereas at one stage everyone was on form, suddenly it appears we are the only ones intent on achieving promotion.

So as we arrive at The Navi, instead of giving him the truth, I just pass off the invite to the press area.

"How come you aren't up in the press room then?" asks my dad.

"Turns out there wasn't space" I tell him as he passes me a beer and we take a seat near the bar.

You see, to this day, I can still remember the exact moments that Neil Warnock and Sam Allardyce won us promotion and each occasion is remembered fondly with me by my dad's side. To sit up in the press room this evening, above the fans and looking down from a great height, I'd feel as though I am cheating a little bit and it just would not feel right like the right way to enjoy it. Especially given the circumstances.

I e-mailed Ralph yesterday, thanked him for the invite but explained my situation. As a true Notts fan, he fully understood.

After the winter that was (or rather wasn't for football), we are set to play our tenth evening game since the turn of the year tonight. It is rather ironic that it is Ray Trew's former club Lincoln City that will be the side hoping to temporarily dent our dreams ahead of the title decider next Tuesday against Rochdale but their modest following appear to be in fairly good spirits considering they sit nineteenth at present in League Two. I cannot help but think their spirits are high because the season is nearly over though. We've been there after all and sometimes you feel ready to draw a line under it all and regroup.

As we find our seats prior to kick-off, the sides are already out on the park and warming up as Thompson loses the toss and the players switch ends. Nights such as this are often in danger of becoming too relaxed at times. With one side seeing the season out after relatively little success and the other needing just three points from seven games, the result almost seems irrelevant as fans talk about the game ahead.

More common subjects appear to be who Notts will try and replace Kasper Schmeichel with in the summer rather than can we see off the locals tonight but either way, the fans have turned out in force with an extra three thousand on the gate compared to a Tuesday night game two months back against Macclesfield.

Fortunately, for anyone still intrigued as to the result of such a seemingly inevitable games, we don't have to wait long for Notts to signal their intent for the evening. Within the first 60 seconds, that man Lee Hughes rises above all others inside the penalty box to glance home past Lincoln keeper Rob Burch and into the empty net from a superbly delivered Ben Davies cross. Already we are joyous in the stands.

"E-i-e-i-e-i-o, Up the Football League we go...." sing the Kop faithful as the music blares out over the crackly tannoy speakers and the Notts dugout celebrate the early lead.

Hughes trots back, smiling at the bench and giving the Gaffer the thumbs up, as the fans all around me sing his name and replicate his dance.

"Not a bad start?" questions my old man with an equally broad smile.

However, Lincoln are not here to make up the numbers and no sooner had we sat down and joked about how many goals we could rack up tonight, a long ball is launched forward towards the Notts penalty area. Rising slightly to better my view over those already standing, Graeme Lee hesitates as he expects Schmeichel to come and clear and before we know it we are all square at 1-1 as Steven Lennon nips in and pokes home past our Danish keeper. How it happened or whether it was in the script, none of appear too sure as Kasper gives a glaring look in the direction of Lee and Notts look to restart the game for the third time in four minutes.

The lively start does not end there though. Moments later we are putting our heads in our hands as Davies sees a free-kick shift inches wide of the upright and if we were betting men, we'd all be wagering the big money on further goals now.

As the Kop Stand sings, we sit and watch the game intently from here in the Pavis. The game is open and both keepers are on their toes and off their lines when called upon. Then suddenly Lincoln's backline wish to offer Craig Westcarr a similar opening to that which Lennon netted the equaliser and as Westcarr gets in behind the indecisive defence, Rob Burch appears to bring down the pacey Notts man and the home support erupts with appeals.

At first sight, the decision seems obvious as Westcarr rounds the keeper before falling to ground. We watch on with amazement however as Lincoln clear their lines and play continues. Although we are all bewildered, we have the upper hand now. Surely a goal will come soon enough if we continue to plug away.

Then on sixteen minutes, with Notts still pushing on and Lincoln seemingly stretched at the back, we are outraged as Moses Swaibu cuts across Westcarr with a late and high tackle leaving our man sprawled out on the turf and referee Mr Quinn sprinting across to take action.

We all jump and demand to see justice and no sooner had the Lincoln man found his feet, a red card is pushed in his direction. The ironic cheers and various fingered salutes are directed in Swaibu's direction as the big man trudges off, baffled and confused.

Now we have the best part of 75 minutes against ten men. Three quarters of a game in which to see them off and seal our route to League One. However, if we think the visitors going down to ten will make the outcome inevitable, we may be disappointed as straight away Lincoln start to spread the ball about and play with a freedom that appeared lacking last time we met them at their place with a 3-0 rout.

Shortly after the dismissal, Kasper is called into action twice in as many minutes and now the whole ground is apparently urging the Notts side to find their touch, form and stride and begin to take control as Kasper claps his hands together and motivates from the back.

A quick throw on the left from Westcarr and now Lee Hughes is alive. He turns inside and with a good sight at goal, he fires an effort only to be thwarted by Burch not once but twice as the keeper makes two match-saving stops to keep his side in the running.

"Come on you Pies, come on you Pies!" we sing to push the side on further. More chances like that for Hughes and we know that come full time we'll be in a party mood.

As half time finally arrives, we dissect a frantic and action-packed half of football underneath the stand as we listen out for other scores around the league.

"Rochdale 0, Darlington 1" comes the announcement and we all raise a plastic beer cup to the news that as things stand, we've gained a point in the push for the title despite being held by this Lincoln outfit. Elsewhere, Rotherham are being held at the The Don Valley Stadium to

Northampton but to all intents and purposes, this game matters very little now as our destiny is steering us firmly away from The Millers.

"I had a wheelbarrow..." sings the full-to-the-brim Kop stands as we jog up the steps for the second half. This quick half-time drinking is doing me no favours of late. I'm eager to get back up top and as the game gets underway, we take to our seats and hope that we can make tonight an evening to remember.

Instantly we put Lincoln on the back foot and we're discussing what positive pearls of wisdom Cotterill has used on the lads.

"They look much brighter" says Danny and at that point we jump to our feet as Thommo puts a fine cross onto the head of Hughes who is denied, once again, by Rob Burch in the visitor's goal. Despite his increasing involvement, Hughes is being held back by a resilient and determined Lincoln side so we look towards the likes of Davies or Westcarr to step up to the plate.

Then on 65 minutes, and with a Westcarr corner seemingly cleared out of harm's way, we watch and hold our breath. Hughes, with a split second decision, plays a fine first time ball from the left wing to Ricky Ravenhill. A neat take on the bounce, Ravenhill then spreads the ball back out to Westcarr before the Notts side push into the Lincoln area. Westcarr, with time and space to look up and pick out a ball, delivers a fine, low cross towards the back post where Graeme Lee makes amends for his earlier error powering home a header into the roof of Lincoln's net and celebrating in front of the Family Stand.

"Get in!!!!" my dad says clenching his fists and ruffling my hair. I cannot help but check my phone now. Rochdale still trail to Darlington. Still 1-0 and still very much on the balance, we're currently making up ground on them fast.

"I had a wheelbarrow, and the wheel fell off, I had a wheelbarrow, and the wheel feel off, County, County, County, County" and a roar goes up as the goal scorer is announced and Notts win back possession.

Steve Cotterill passes on information to Neal Bishop from the side line whilst Kasper applauds his back line from the edge of the box. We look in full control now knowing that Lincoln have to do what only Northampton, Torquay, Accrington and Bournemouth have managed all season. Score twice at Meadow Lane in the league. Even Northampton only managed it when they already trailed 5-1. The omens, we believe, are looking good.

Now we appear even more alive than before. In the stands we all sing, in the dugout we look confident but focused whilst on the pitch we roam and probe, searching for the killer goal to end any hope of a

Lincoln comeback. Hughes creates another chance for himself, this time from distance. He cuts inside his man and we anticipate a run on goal only to see the main man fire at goal early and hit the foot of the post. He shows little frustration though, smiling as the ball spins out for a goal kick and the clock continues to tick towards victory.

With just minutes left, my old man is readying himself to leave early once more.

"Still a few minutes left" I tell him placing my hand on his shoulder. He remains seated and Notts win the ball back once more with Bishop. Now Westcarr picks up the loose ball and with a deft pass, up pops Delroy Facey on the edge of the box to turn his man instinctively and run onto a fine pass before hitting a thunderous effort past Burch and against the underside of the crossbar and in. What a strike and what a way to cap off a good nights work for the big man.

The song is balled-out out for County's number 22 as he turns away from goal, arms aloft and accepts his teammate's congratulations as he is mobbed.

"Rochdale still trailing" I tell my dad and Danny. *"Still 1-0."*

The goal is a perfect way to seal the points and from the sideline Cotterill looks as delighted as anyone as the boys skip back to their own half to see the game out.

For sentimental reasons, as the clock hits 90 minutes, Cotterill withdraws three of the biggest match winners we possess as Lee Hughes, Ben Davies and the born-again-Craig Westcarr are replaced by Jamie Clapham, Johnnie Jackson (back from his loan spell with Charlton) and little Luke Rodgers who if reports are to believed, is set for a move to join Hans Backe in the MLS this week with the New York Redbulls.

"Only one Luke Rodgers, one Luke Rodgers" sing the Notts faithful as within seconds he goes charging down a ball in the corner and nearly manages to poleaxe the Lincoln defender by the corner flag. *"...walking along, singing a song, walking in a Rodgers wonderland."*

The whole place is buzzing and even my old man is remaining put now. On the touchline there is a crowd gathering around Cotterill with Lee Hughes and Tommy Johnson stood alongside him, joking away and sharing the moment.

With that said the whistle is blown and we let out the biggest celebration in recent memory.

"E-i-e-i-e-i-o, up the Football League we go" rings around the ground loud and clear. The Lincoln bench and their players exit sharply but on the pitch, Notts players are not going anywhere just yet.

We applaud and sing and watch on as Rodgers runs over to the Kop for what looks like the most obvious farewell in Meadow Lane's recent history. He throws a shirt into the crowd and they sing a song as all his team mates join him and shake his hand and pat him on the back.

He may not be as prolific as Hughes but makes no bones about it; Luke Rodgers has made some big contributions over the course of the season. With ten goals to his name, it's just a shame he could not add to his total in the dying minutes tonight. Next month, he could be partnering Thierry Henry on the other side of the pond in New York. But tonight, by the banks of the River Trent, he celebrates what is now promotion and another step to a possible title. Rochdale have lost and we have continued our march. It may not be mathematically confirmed or technically assured but we know deep down *"the Notts are going up, the Notts are going up"* and it feels great. More importantly, for the first time since the start of the season, Notts County sit top of the Coca Cola League Two table.

Coca Cola League Two Table:

	Pld	+/-	Pts
1. Notts County	**40**	**52**	**80**
2. Rochdale	41	37	79
3. Bournemouth	42	10	74
----------------------------------			
4. Rotherham United	42	5	68
5. Bury	42	-1	67
6. Chesterfield	42	2	66
7. Aldershot Town	42	11	65
----------------------------------			
8. Morecambe	42	9	64

The Title Decided

Notts County v Rochdale
Meadow Lane / League Two / 20.04.10

Forgive me if you have read the next few words before....but this is the biggest game of the season.

Ok we now know that in terms of League Two, we've done enough. Next season we will be plying our trade in League One. Who knows? I may be writing an extension to these little memoires about life in a bigger division, against somewhat bigger clubs. The division above promises to be just as exciting too. As things stand, there is a chance that Leeds United, Millwall and Charlton could all still be playing their football in League One come 2010/11 whilst both Sheffield Wednesday and Crystal Palace could be joining them and us as they battle for survival in the Championship.

On Saturday just gone though, our fate as well as that of title rivals Rochdale, was sealed with wins at our respective footballing homes. As Notts blistered into an early 3-0 lead after eighteen minutes, we were jubilantly bouncing about, enjoying the sunshine, the goals and the company of fans all around us. Shortly after we accelerated into an early, winning position, Chris O'Grady put Rochdale 1-0 up at home to Northampton and for them that is how it remained for them.

Two sides, who were vying for promotion and all the prizes that come with it, both led. They are also two sides with very different outlooks and perspectives. For at Meadow Lane, at full-time, we rose to our feet, applauded the lads 4-1 win and sung with joy at our impending promotion. It was nothing more than a modest celebration. The job was not over though and we knew there were still five games to go, including Rochdale at home. We were fully aware that there were five games in which we could seal the big prize.

Promotion is great but it is the top spot we want. We don't want to finish second to anyone and all the fans around me felt the same. The words were uttered all around me.

"It'll be a massive game on Tuesday."

Massive doesn't cover it though.

Miles away, up North at Rochdale's Spotland home, they celebrated too. They burst out from the stands like a river pushing open its banks, flooding the field, jumping up and down and showing their delight. Make no bones about it, The Dale fans were celebrating a job well done. The fans were not looking towards Tuesday nights clash. They were not thinking of the title. They were just glad to have sealed promotion and in turn, their first campaign since the early seventies outside of the bottom tier of the professional game.

For me, the difference in mentality and aspirations was all too clear to see but at the same time, can you blame them? One Dale fan I spoke with pre-match down at The Navi said how he had waited all his adult life for this season. A supporter since the age of eight, and only now, well into his 40's, could he really enjoy his clubs success. Despite the problems and issues that Notts County have encountered over the decades, at least there has been some movement and some highs and lows.

For Rochdale, many years of mediocrity must have felt like a long term sentence.

"I'm just happy to be here, looking at that league table" he tells me glancing up at Sky Sports News on the TV screen above us.

As I walk around to the Kop with Mark, the queues are huge. Not like the modest scores of fans you would normally get down here on a Tuesday night that is for sure. Danny and another of my brother's mates, Simon, are over in the Pavis Stand tonight and already I am told the atmosphere is immense.

"Are you in The Kop? It sounds amazing" reads my text from Danny.

With the anticipation of a great game and something of a celebration now on the cards, the local support is clearly showing up in force.

As we enter the ground, the Dale fans are clearly present and correct, singing and shouting and adding to the whole atmosphere and occasion. As things stand, we sit just one point ahead of our northern rivals and with a game in hand. Even defeat today but a win from our game in hand would mean we stay above them so when you weigh up what a victory would do? Well it would more-or-less guarantee us the title. Talk about a change in fortunes.

The Kop is in full motion and packed to the rafters for which I am sure the local council will find some problems with given the health and safety issues of the stand in recent years. As the Wheelbarrow is sung around the stadium, Rochdale begin with their ever-so original and extremely witty songs about taxmen and financial irregularities. It cannot take anything away from the achievements here though at Meadow Lane because frankly, we don't care.

"Stand up, if you pay your bills" comes the first cry and we give an ironic cheer.

Bless them for trying to wind us up. Do they not realise every set of fans before them have reeled off attempts to antagonise. We've had plenty of clubs, as well as creditors, try and wind us up this season. One more won't hurt.

"Where were you when you were shit?" or *"Scab, scab, scab"* becomes a little tiresome after a while so we can laugh it off.

Today there is an immense confidence about this place even if Mark besides me is telling me today could be the game we slip up on. If truth be told, Mark has been saying this for some time now. Game on game he has raised some doubts. I think Notts fans must be programmed to expect something to go wrong.

Mark suggested as much prior to the Rotherham and Bury games at home as well as the Shrewsbury and Northampton one's on the road. Yet we won all four encounters with an aggregate score of 9-0. Me? I have nothing other than total confidence tonight and as I have said before, this means so much to me now, I cannot imagine it not working out well.

The season has carried so much drama. So many twists and turns have been experienced along the way that I find myself so enthralled and taken in by it all that I need the success as much as anyone. Oddly enough, I received a text off Jade after the win against Morecambe saying *"Congratulations."*

There was little more to it than that but, given how much she knew it had meant to me, she clearly realised the importance of the victory when she saw it on the news that evening. Other than that, I've heard very little from her though so I think she is past being angry now. Fortunately for her, she has moved on but after everything that has happened I still feel that I am owed a title winning season. I genuinely need it.

As the sides walk out, the atmosphere is electric. I may have uttered these same words before but tonight? Well it has just gone up another notch and it is a feeling I cannot remember since way back in the early nineties when the likes of United, Arsenal and Chelsea visited the Lane. Over in the Pavis Stand, there is more noise and emotion coming from those seats than I ever remember and even from here you can see the tension and hope in their faces.

"Keith Hill, what a wanker, what a wanker!" sings one or two in the Kop. By the third rendition, the whole stand is singing it to show exactly what we think of his press spouting's about Notts and the way we conducted ourselves this season.

Say what you want about Munto-fucking-Finance and the mess that they left here but it is not of our own doing. You cannot lay blame at the fans who were sold up the river and nor was it Ray Trew's fault as he is having to fork out cash left, right and centre to keep the money men at arm's length and ensure Notts have a future.

"Stand up, if you pay your bills" and again we yawn.

The game is underway at 100mph and the fans are baying for an early advantage as Notts kick towards the Kop end. Dale's enclosure is pretty much full and vocal but every word that is uttered from their fans seems to be anti-Notts (much like Rotherham) rather than anything positive about their own boys until they break out into *"Dale, Dale, Dale, Dale, Dale."*

As they do, Delroy Facey works his way out wide into a dangerous area before crossing a ball which is slightly over-hit. Craig Westcarr chases, no longer the lazy one that infuriates the fans, this lad has earned his respect surely? He crosses low and hard towards the near post and the alert and vibrant Hughes meets it on the half-volley but fails to keep it down. An early chance though none-the-less.

"Come on you Pies, come on you Pies!"

With the summer approaching, these end-of-season Tuesday nights are fantastic for the soul. Notts continue to press but Rochdale see enough of the ball. O'Grady fails to connect when Kennedy plays a neat ball into his path and Kasper berates his backline, showing anger and demanding perfection as we realise we have just been let off.

Next, Graeme Lee finds himself with a chance when a goal mouth scramble in front of the Kop sees him poke an effort low and across the face of goal but Fielding is equal to it and reacts well to keep the score at 0-0. From here, Dale gain confidence and for the remainder of the first half hour, they certainly are the better side.

Their passing and interchanging and bright movements off the ball means they are seemingly first to everything. Mark looks nervous as though his doubts are finally going to come home to roost and Dale's following becomes louder and more prominent with each passing move. At the back, Lee and Edwards keep things tight and Kasper, whilst being on his toes and awaiting a hard night's work, remains relatively un-worked and at ease as his back four presses tirelessly and close down the opposition well; a common trait since Cotterill arrived at the club. Sol who?

Rochdale's brightest spark, Chris O'Grady, becomes somewhat agitated however. Dropping deeper to pick up the ball becomes a common practise for the forward as the game continues at a frantic pace. Dropping further to try and create and ignite the visitors play, he continues to search. It was he who netted at the Spotland when Dale beat us 2-1 on a windy and rainy night back in November and I remember it all too well. It was a time when the whole world and his dog appeared to be against us. Now, however, it appears O'Grady is about to become very popular down at Meadow Lane. Out in the middle of the park he dwells on the ball for a split second. He looks around and plays a hospital ball towards a team mate which is so far off the mark it is hard to see the intention of the pass in the first place.

Bishop pounces, anticipating the moment well. Lively and switched-on, he picks the ball up and instantly slots it into the path of the one man you'd want to see awaiting the ball, Lee Hughes. Hughes bears down on goal, two defenders in his wake. We stand, seats clattering against their backs once more and we raise our eyebrows, arms and hopes as we have on many occasion during the campaign so far.

"Yeaahhhhhhhhhhh" as me and Mark jump up and down and hug one another amongst those around us. We turn in opposite ways and embrace others. The away end is silent!

Hughes, on the half hour mark, has taken the ball perfectly in his stride, weighed up his options and then lobbed Fielding from the best part of 25-yards to give Notts the lead against the run of play.

"That's why we're Champions, that's why we're Champions" we sing, pre-empting our fate as Dale trail 1-0 on our patch.

Hughes makes a beeline for the Kop to give us his trademark dance with flailing arms and bouncing legs. It is the type of goal which has been bread and butter for him this season but, for most forwards at this level, is not a chance that is often converted. To his credit, Fielding appeared to get a hand to what was a fine shot but all eyes and fingers should be focused on O'Grady in the middle of the park as it was his error that left Bishop with the time and space to open up the Dale backline.

Now we have to hear their fans sing about Lee Hughes being a murderer. From memory, I can only recall two or three sets of fans not singing such songs during the campaign. A lesser man would buckle or not be able to perform under such abuse from the stands but Hughes continues to do his job, find the net and give Notts County fans the pleasure of his ability on the pitch.

Notts now looks like an altogether different proposition. A ball is swept forward and Ben Davies latches onto the loose pass before cutting inside. He jigs his way past the defender, feints away from the second and then strikes a good effort towards goal only to see it fizz just past the far post. We applaud and admire the lad's ability and then show our appreciation in song.

"Super, super Ben, Super, super Ben..."

283

As half time approaches, it is now Notts that do not wish to hear the whistle after much of the half was dominated by second placed Rochdale. O'Grady has not only being kept at bay but has also gifted us the opener. It could not get much better. As referee Mark Halsey draws the half to a close, we stand and clap the lads off knowing we are halfway there to a job well done.

"Fourteen points and you fucked it up, fourteen points and you fucked it up" we sing at Rochdale as they trudge off. No doubt Keith Hill will give them a rousing talk at the break but for us, we believe we can cope with whatever they throw at us now.

A quick beer at the break is sunk to settle the nerves of those around us but for me, the nerves are no longer an issue. Not only do we have the meanest defence in the division, but also the sharpest attack. With it looking as though Luke Rodgers may have been off to the States a few weeks back, good old Delroy Facey has stepped up so much so that Rodgers (still with us) and Hawley cannot break into the side.

In the stands, all the talk is about Torquay away now. Who has and who hasn't got tickets? Who is and who isn't going? For me, it will be an exciting weekend away on the coast. It'll be a case of beer, atmosphere, fun and celebrations. For now there are other tasks at hand though and as we finish our drinks, we hear the Dale fans try and raise the money issues again much to the delight of the Notts faithful who throw it back at them.

"Fourteen points and you fucked it up, fourteen points and you fucked it up."

As the second half begins we'd be fools for expecting no Rochdale onslaught. The fools may not have been far wrong though. As proceedings get underway, they certainly have the better of the possession but, in pure chances, very little comes their way. Early in the half O'Grady receives a ball with his back to goal and the Kop. Graeme Lee remains on his shoulder holding him off and holding up play as defensive support works back but by the time O'Grady turns and shoots, we rise to our feet with arms aloft to welcome the ball into the hands of the all-encompassing Kop Stand.

As the floodlights begin to become poignant, the night sky darkens and the Dale fans pray even more for an elusive equaliser, Notts look as comfortable as ever.

"This is in the bag" is the message from Danny over in the Pavis Stand.

The game is stretched from end-to-end however. Neither Fielding or Schmeichel have to make a clear cut save for a period of time but we are happy when Notts finally get the ball down and show some promise.

Hunty picks up possession midway in the Dale half, bides himself a little time and then hits a venomous shot at goal which clatters against the woodwork and over. To our right, the whole of the Pavis Stand jumps to their feet, hoping, wishing and expecting. But the chance has passed.

Minutes later, Hughes pulls out wide and receives the ball from Ben Davies. The talismanic striker turns provider, this time drilling a fine cross towards Facey at the back post who finds himself with space and time but executes a header poorly and we look at one another knowing that it was a chance to finish Rochdale off. Had that been Hughes?

The game is far from over although much of it is now spent with the Kop on their toes wishing for the clock to speed up. There is a 50-50 in the middle of the park and the ball breaks to Howarth for Rochdale. Rather like Davies in the first half, he skips his man well before hitting a rocket of a strike towards Kasper who seems to get a finger to it and pushes it on to the bar which shakes and shudders as though pounded from close range. It's a let off for Notts and how we know it.

"Keith Hill, what a wanker, what a wanker..." resonates as the manager stands in his dug out ordering his players to up their game. Steve Cotterill on the other hand gives us a glance and a wave upon request as we inch ever closer to victory.

Notts are not finished just yet though. Facey and Westcarr combine as we attack the Family Stand and we are still showing desire for more goals. Westcarr finds Hughes in space who pulls his man outside before cutting back inside. Again our seats flick back as we rise but again we have heads in hands as Hughes' left foot, curling effort is well saved by Fielding from close range.

The game is now on tenterhooks. At our end, Westcarr dwells on a ball on the edge of his own box before playing Graeme Lee into trouble just yards from goal. Dale press and close down and when they win the ball on the edge of the box we look around, annoyed and amazed as our own complacency nearly costs us dearly. Fortunately, Howarth's effort flies wide and with it, Dale's hopes begin to fade even more.

A few Dale fans begin to vacate the ground but if they were honest in their own assessment, hopes for a Dale title winning season began to fade much earlier than this evening. As Halsey holds the whistle to his lips and raises his right hand, the Notts technical area is already swamped with backroom staff such as Tommy Johnson, Dave Kevan, Carl Muggleton and many more who await the moment they can firmly say that the title will be ours.

As the fans rise to their feet, the Dale fans clap and applaud their boys and empty the away end instantly. For Notts and for the Kop, we stand and wait as our boys wander over. Hunty jumps on the shoulders of Delroy Facey as Hughes leads the celebrations and acknowledgments for the fans. One by one, each of the players comes over to show their thanks to the fans. The importance is clear for all to see.

"Champions!" is the message from Danny as I check my phone upon leaving the ground. As I meet Danny and Simon by the old tree near the entrance to the Pavis Stand, we are greeted by an old boy, eccentric and buzzing.

"We've done it boys. We've done it. I won't shave until we are in the Premier League now" he says with a youthful laugh as he darts off and tells some other stranger the exact same thing.

Notts will go to bed tonight four points clear and still with a game in hand. Destiny is now our own chapter to write and Keith Hill has more moaning to ponder upon.

Coca Cola League Two Table:

	Pld	+/-	Pts
1. Notts County	**42**	**56**	**86**
2. Rochdale	43	37	82
3. Bournemouth	43	12	77
4. Rotherham United	43	5	69
5. Bury	43	-1	68
6. Aldershot Town	43	11	66
7. Dagenham & Redbridge	43	9	66
8. Chesterfield	43	0	66

"E-I-E-I-E-I-0"

Darlington v Notts County
Front Room / League Two / 27.04.10

I was weighing up my options until really late last night but I just could not justify the trip this evening. So with my feet up, a beer in my hand and BBC Radio Nottingham on the wireless, I have settled down to listen to Notts away at Darlington.

Sat on 86 points and with three games left to play I am a little disappointed that our title looks likely to be confirmed on the road, miles away from home, in one of the most northerly parts of England. Our rivals Rochdale, with just two games left, sit in second place with 82 points so a win this evening will make the league title ours mathematically rather than technically as it currently stands.

Having made the trip down the road to Port Vale at the weekend, I was as surprised as anyone when, for the first time since his tenure began, Steve Cotterill saw his Notts side lose. Despite going behind early on, Graeme Lee was on hand to pull things level on 25 minutes but as the game remained open and stretched, Vale re-took the lead on the half hour mark and it remained that way for the rest of the encounter.

Given the fact the previous fourteen games under the Gaffer had seen us turn our season around I guess we can't really complain. There were over a thousand of us that had made the short trip to the Potteries for a game that we expected would produce three points. When we heard on the hour mark that Rochdale were trailing 2-0 away at Hereford, we suddenly realised that this was our chance to see the side secure the title.

Port Vale acquitted themselves well however and to be fair, they looked like one of the better sides we'd been matched against since the turn of the year.

A tiny little part of me now hopes that we don't seal the deal this evening though. I cannot help but think it would be nice to do it at home, in front of a sold-out Meadow Lane crowd. Given our tremendous form on home turf, it'd be rather fitting for it to end that way given the manner in which it all started with that 5-0 hammering of Bradford City back in August.

However, tonight may see us crowned as Champions on the road so I settle down as Colin Slater introduces the teams and Notts begin the brighter of the two teams, understandably so given Darlington woes at the foot of the League Two table. I'm relaxed, despite wishing I could see the title wrapped up in person and when, on 33 minutes, Johnnie

Jackson coverts a cross from Delroy Facey for 1-0, I cannot but smile and accept that tonight will be the night.

"Looks like they'll do it this evening" I say to my old man at half-time when he calls up. For him, it is confirmation that he'll probably give Cheltenham at home a miss this coming Saturday now as he has the opportunity to play golf down at his local course and the title should be confirmed.

I potter around the house during the interval as we talk football but eventually my dad wants to change the subject to *"how are you in yourself?"* and at this point my enthusiasm wavers a little. It's not that I don't like people caring but the repetition is as draining as the feeling of being on your own at times.

As the sides emerge for the second half and I hear uncle Colin and Dean Yates come back on the Radio, there is a knock at the back door. It's not Jade, for she has rinsed the house of all she wished to take with her a few weeks back. It's Emma. For the record, Emma was the 'someone else' I'd met and the 'someone else' for who I guess I had my head turned by. She's due to move away in a few months with her partner of four years so I'd be forgiven for wondering why she was at my back door at gone 8.30pm on a Tuesday night.

As I welcome her in and we take a seat in the living room, I turn the radio down and we begin to talk over a cup of tea. It appears my decision to leave Jade has left her with own conundrums to deal with and suddenly her life is becoming very complicated because of it.

I feel guilty in some ways but pleased that we can both sit and be honest with one another. She tells me that part of her wants to be with me and she cannot imagine the alternative of not having me around and I admit that, given the option, I'd love the opportunity to be with her too.

It's an honest sort of chat that I neither expected nor envisaged us having though. Mainly because she is settled already in her life and because I was never totally sure I had the same affect on her to that which she had on me. If I had any doubts prior to this evening, they all but evaporate as the conversation continues and she tells me that she's considering telling him (her fella) it is over.

Suddenly an apology:

"You did not mind me turning up unannounced did you? I was not interrupting anything I hope."

After politely explaining I had Notts on the radio, she insists I finish listening to it as we boil the kettle once more. Less surprising than her sudden appearance at the back door, I now learn that I've missed Notts in blistering form as Mike Edwards, Craig Westcarr and Luke Rodgers have all added their names to the score sheet in the space of the last eight minutes.

"Bloody typical" I say angrily forgetting that company is right by my side.

"Sorry. I should not have made you miss it" she says but I tell her not to be so soft and that I am glad she came over.

To be perfectly honest, this is the moment more than any other in the past few months that has made me feel an unnerving amount of guilt. Had Jade made me miss three Notts goal, albeit on the radio, I'd not have been best pleased. That would not be fair though. I had neglected the fact that she existed between 3pm and 5pm each Saturday and had put my own passion top of my list of priorities. That said, I'd become so bored with my normal, every-day life, I needed to reignite my love for something. The intensity for which I enjoyed football was always the primary candidate for such a void.

As I pop the mugs of tea down on the coffee table, uncle Colin joyously describes another Luke Rodgers goal and with it Notts County lead Darlington by five goals to nil.

"Get in!!!!" I say making Emma jump and some tea spill on the table.

As we drink our tea, we skate around our impending problem and talk about every day things that carry little importance. She enquires about the book, I vaguely explain what it is about and before we know it a few hours pass as we talk the night away.

Despite her appearance at my place this evening, I still hold doubts over how serious she is about making a life-changing decision herself. I explain that becoming single, for me, was something I had to do and not a direct result of meeting her. Her problem lies in that she wants to be with one of us. She just isn't sure which one. Deep down I know the real answer to all of this though and throwing away all that she has for me would not be a sound decision by any stretch of the imagination.

Coca Cola League Two Table:

	Pld	+/-	Pts
C 1. Notts County	44	60	89
P 2. Rochdale	44	36	82
P 3. Bournemouth	44	14	80
4. Rotherham United	44	6	72
5. Aldershot Town	44	12	69
6. Bury	44	8	68
7. Port Vale	44	15	67
8. Morecambe	44	7	67

A Day In The Sun

So consumed within the furore of all that has been, gone and remains, today is the day we had all dreamt of for, not just the last nine or so months but the seasons that had preceded this one. To all intents and purposes, rain could have fell from the heavens today in a normal, disheartening sort of way and still we would not have seen or felt it. Today there is no rain however. There is just glorious sunshine which is descending on this part of Nottingham for the home finale.

The season began with hopes and ambitions within these stands at Meadow Lane. Fans, both young and old, drew on varying experiences from which to gauge their own dreams but to a person, we all dreamt of a similar outcome.

If I were to say that there were not occasions that I started to worry I'd be a deceitful but transparent liar. When we lost at Chesterfield in mid-August, for the first time I accepted the reality that this was not to be a fairytale in which we'd win every game and slaughter opponents home and away. It was not to be like one of the football fiction novels I read as a youngster. Ten days later we draw at Barnet and then followed that with a draw at home to Burton Albion. Suddenly hopes began to alter and become more realistic.

Games on the pitch from which we lost points were far from the biggest fear for me and my fellow Magpies as the season progressed. Unless you have thumbed your way to the very end of the book to see how the story ends, you know already that on so many occasions, so much was at stake for this club.

Had it not been for the original takeover with Munto Finance, we would have undoubtedly not been where we are today, already promoted and with a party atmosphere down at Meadow Lane. We would not have had the pleasure of the likes of Kasper Schmeichel and Lee Hughes within our ranks and we certainly would not have seen some fantastic victories and a cup run to whet our appetites for bigger things.

Whilst Munto were eventually exposed as bad news, it was a step on a ladder which led us initially to Peter Trembling (the jury appears to still be out) and then, and more thankfully, Ray Trew. Had each incident not preceded the next, surely the likelihood of Trew leading us to promotion would have been pretty slim.

It is all about the butterfly effect I guess. Somewhere, in a parallel world with just one minor alteration in history, today Notts County are set to play in front of just a few thousand fans after merely managing to survive another dull and lifeless campaign in League Two. Like I say...somewhere. Not here though.

When I arrived at the ground today with Danny, such was the excitement around the game we were unable to get in to the usual spot in the Pavis Stand to watch the game. So, for the first time all season, we are sat up in the higher parts of the Jimmy Sirrel Stand ready to watch the newly crowned Champions of League Two meet a Cheltenham side who are theoretically safe if not mathematically. Should they lose their last two games and Grimsby win both of their games, and if Grimsby can turn around a goal difference which currently sees them worse off than Cheltenham by thirteen goals (breathe), and if Barnet can win one of their final two games, then and only then, Cheltenham would go down.

With the sun gleaming in our eyes and the sight of scarves and flags being waved all around us, we quickly head back down underneath the stand for a much needed beer upon arrival inside the stadium. Although today is a day for celebration, it is also something of an anti-climax to a campaign which has seen many nervous afternoons and evenings at Meadow Lane.

Thinking back to games against Bournemouth, Chesterfield, Rotherham and Rochdale, all I can remember was the tension and the anxious feeling in my gut. I'd tap my toes as I gently bobbed up and down waiting for the sides to emerge. The nail-biting stages of the games where we were under pressure and the sighs we let out when opportunities of our own came and went were all part of the drama, and in turn, the overall enjoyment of those games.

Despite having many comprehensive victories, I can't remember seeing so many games that kept me on the edge of my seat with the match firmly in the balance too. Those games when the clock seemed to move at a speed that irritates dependent on the score line. Only in the stands of football grounds have I ever heard of twenty minutes being "*a long twenty minutes*". This must be as opposed to the fifteen minute versions of twenty minutes that occasionally come along when your team is trailing on the road.

As we reminisce on the season that has passed and the five star performance we had away at Darlington, we also look towards an exciting summer and the World Cup. Talk about daring to dream. League success followed by being crowned World Champions in South Africa. If this were to happen, I'd have to retire from the game on emotional grounds. It'd never be beaten surely?

As we hear the announcer welcoming stars of the past on to the field of play and a warm reception is given to them and other guests up above, we sup up our second pint and make the short journey back up to the stands to join Danny's old man.

It is warmer now and certainly fuller with most seats visibly taken in each direction except those marked off with big black sheets. I have no doubt that the ground would have been close to 18,000 had health and safety decisions made by the council permitted it. We are the lucky ones and although it feels as though we are sat in a foreign part of the ground, I do not care today.

"I had a Wheelbarrow..." reverberates from the Kop as the area around the tunnel becomes compact and chaotic with camera crews, press, stewards and back room staff. We rise to our feet to welcome out Cheltenham and their small following are acknowledged by their players as the visitors part to form a guard of honour for the Champions who are set to emerge from the tunnel.

The fans all around me are in great voice and not a soul is sat down in his or her seat now. Heroes of the day and soon-to-be club legends, we await their arrival at the head of the tunnel as both the Sirrel and Pavis Stand's join The Kop in song.

"Champione, Champione, ole, ole, ole..."

The atmosphere reaches fever pitch now and as we come close to some sort of crescendo, out strolls our skipper John Thompson in the prominent and defined black and white stripes of Notts. Following him is Kasper Schmeichel in bright, exuberant yellow, gloves aloft and applauding the fans for what we expect to be the final time at Meadow Lane and then, one by one, each player follows suit.

The players in red applaud Notts as they make their way onto the pitch and between the two rows of playing staff from Cheltenham. Now the whole stadium is rocking.

Schmeichel, Thompson, Hunty, Lee and Edwards. Bishop and Ricky Ravenhill with Westcarr and the inspirational Davies. Up front, Hughesy and Facey.

Each one a Champion and each one welcomed out to the appreciative Meadow Lane support. Steve Cotterill takes to his seat in the dugout against one of his former clubs whilst man-by-man, the Kop sings a song for the starting eleven in black and white.

As the skippers are called over by the referee and the mascots trot off towards the Pavis Stand, we stand once more with a rallying cry and a call for one last performance in front of the home fans to send us on our way.

"Come on you Pies, come on you Pies!" we all sing in tandem and with it the game is underway.

The sun beats down and straight away Notts settle down into a short passing game, making our struggling opponents chase and harass like headless chickens who are secondary characters in a masterful script. All eyes, cameras and judgements are placed on the eleven Notts men today and immediately they soak up the challenge to play like champions.

Kasper with his range of kicking, Davies with his trickery and Hughes with his work rate all look for the ball. Bishop, viewed by many fans as the non-obvious player of the season, tackles, wins and distributes accordingly as his partner in crime, Ricky Ravenhill backs him up and helps hunt down the play whenever the visitors take it into their possession.

The game is still young but with each minute that passes us by, the atmosphere becomes more relaxed. For today there is no pressure. It is just a shining spotlight with no real consequence to the result. Up and down the country there are games with little or no meaning. A chance to play for pride in a mid-table battle or an opportunity to shine with a Play-Off place already booked or safety guaranteed.

Even the most pessimistic of Cheltenham fans would not see relegation being their fate following the next 180 minutes of football for their club. The fans give out an *"olé"* as the ball switches from Thompson to Hunt and back again via Lee and Edwards.

Notts are weighing the visitors up. Waiting for their opportunity to pounce and then bang. They'll go for the jugular.

The Kop continues to sing and encourage and on twenty minutes they turn up the volume as they welcome Ben Davies to the far corner from where I am sat to take a corner kick. A short clap for the fans and he spins the ball in his hands trying to find the sweet spot he wants to strike. With the big men forwards and the poacher Hughes on hand, we rise as the ball is whipped in with venom and the net ripples from a distance as the ball lands firmly in the back of the goal.

We jump up and down and we smile, laugh and rejoice. If anything, we are surprised we had to wait this long and we congratulate one another as players appear to jump on Graeme Lee at the back post.

The whole ground is bouncing about to the beat of the big bass drum at the top of the Kop as we sing and cheer the opening goal showing little acknowledgment for the opposition restarting the game. In the middle of the park big Delroy Facey wins possession back almost instantly though and we give a rapturous cheer as his quick foot work finds Davies.

Suddenly we are focused once more and all eyes are on Hughes breaking through the middle as Davies plays a sweet, right footed ball, over the top into the path of our marksman who controls with a killer touch before firing past the oncoming Scott Brown in The Robins goal. Two goals in two minutes and we are clearly too good for this lot.

Once more bouncing and once again we sing, we are well and truly in the party mood now as Notts appear to outnumber the League Two strugglers. Seconds later Craig Westcarr latches onto a ball in the box after a Hughes flick-on and as he drives his effort across goal, we are somewhat disappointed to see the ball hacked off the line. We have the momentum now and Brown is surely set for a torrid time between the sticks?

Only four minutes since the opener and with the fans demanding more, Davies once more places the ball down to deliver a set-piece for the big men coming forward. This time he curls the free-kick into the danger area and as bodies collide in the area, one man above all others breaks free from the pack with an out stretched head. That man Lee Hughes looks back at the referee as the ball nestles neatly in the back of the net and Brown comes surging out to contest the goal claiming Hughes used a hand. But we aren't bothered how it came about are we? All four corners celebrate in unison as three goals in four minutes means the game has already been put to bed.

"*Champione, Champoione...*" we sing once more and Hughes trots back to the halfway line with the Cheltenham ranks angered and infuriated.

"*Goal for the Magpies scored by number 11, Ben Davies*" and we cheer even if somewhat confused.

"*Must have gone straight in*" we suggest as we extend our smiles wider than the River Trent.

Sometimes three goals in such quick succession can see a game die in front of your very eyes. There is no need to take any more risks or to try any over ambitious attacks after all. There is often no need to give any more once the game is within your control.

Today is an entirely different day. It's the last home game of the season and the last chance to entertain the public that adore you and appreciate your efforts. The punters who basically pay your wages are out in force and in the mood for a goal fest in which to end the campaign at Meadow Lane.

Cheltenham start to launch balls forward, if only to have a momentary break from defending. Just six minutes after number three and with contrasting spirits in both camps so apparent, they cannot do anything but watch on as we are given more to shout about.

A high and aimless ball is hit forward by the visitors and left back Stephen Hunt gives the Cheltenham lads a taste of their own medicine hitting it directly back at them with pace and height. Somehow, with the ball travelling awkwardly, Westcarr manages to nick the ball into a corridor just behind The Robins back line and who should be there when we rise once more to our feet but that man Hughes.

He takes the ball in his stride, pulls away from the desperate attempts of the defenders and then neatly cuts inside his man before regaining his feet, composure and touch and curling the ball into the bottom corner to make it four goals in just ten minutes.

Call it a rout, a goal glut or a supreme show of clinical finishing and ruthlessness. Either way Notts have torn Cheltenham open as though matched against a park team from the Victoria Embankment playing fields down the road.

Hughes wheels away towards the Kop to do his dance and this time there is no doubt about the name on the score sheet as he records his 30th league goal of the season with a trade mark finish that has been reciprocated on numerous occasions at Meadow Lane over the past nine months.

"*Hughesy, Hughesy, Hughesy...*" we chant as the main man continues to smile as much as anyone who's ever plied his trade down these parts.

"*I had a Wheelbarrow, and the wheel fell off...*" we sing as the whole ground stands, arms aloft and showing pride in their club. The small Cheltenham following to our right sit, deafly silent and already starting the motors to their cars in their minds, as we enjoy the day. A torrid final trip for them this season and maybe, just maybe, one or two are starting to have concerns about that goal difference of theirs.

With the game in the bag and the celebrations in full swing, the Gaffer Steve Cotterill withdraws Lee Hughes, a doubt before kick-off, and introduces Luke Rodgers with time still to go before the break.

Standing ovations were made for moments like this and with 30 goals to his name for the campaign and accolades put in his direction every week, no one deserves such a show of appreciation more than Lee Hughes for his part in the season's success story.

On a weekly basis he has put in selfless shifts often running himself into the ground for the side and both his team mates and the fans know just how vital his contribution has been. Understandably, there have been fans from opposition followers each week that have attempted to single him out for preferential treatment due to his chequered history.

If he'd been playing for another club in this division I have no doubt that our own fans would have given him exactly the same treatment, such is football. Fans love a target and for them, Hughes has been an easy one at times. But he has done the most he possibly can do for his reputation as a player and for the club he represents by simply giving his all and doing what he does best with minimal fuss on the pitch.

As he leaves to join the bench, we have a rare occurrence as Cheltenham see an effort at Kasper smothered rather easily. An ironic cheer from our own support and a quick release from our number one (technically our number 23 but it doesn't quite sound right) and away we go once more on the attack.

To say the game is insignificant is not fair. Not fair to those performing on the park, to those grabbing the goals and to those visiting players fighting for their League Two survival. But once the game became a non-contest, it began to feel like we were waiting for the final whistle so that we could soak up the atmosphere a little more and see our lads lift the League Two trophy.

We break, as do the players, and run down beneath the stand for another beer and the afternoon begins to pass us by. There are no disgruntled voices in earshot today. No moans or groans or dissatisfied fans who sometimes still manage to find fault when all appears fine and dandy.

For much of the second half we continue to control the game but, as with any game poised at 4-0 at the break, the spectacle and drama has been killed off somewhat for the second 45 minutes worth of action.

On 81 minutes we are given an opportunity, after 35 minutes of pretty much nondescript football, to have one final cheer at Meadow Lane this season before the lights go out. A long, penetrating ball from Kasper lands precisely on the head of Westcarr who's resulting flick falls equally as perfect for little Luke Rodgers.

In one neat motion he turns, spins his man and then delicately lofts the ball past the on-rushing Brown to make it 5-0.

"There's only one, Luke Rodgers, one Luke Rodgers, walking along, singing a song, walking in a Rodgers wonderland..."

We'd waved the boy goodbye a few weeks previous as he was all set for the MLS and a move to Hans Backe's New York Red Bulls. Quite fitting it is that today he signs off the season at Meadow Lane with a neat finish given the job he has done during the campaign, albeit sometimes in a cameo role.

We respectfully stand just seconds later to give a standing ovation to Kasper Schmeichel, who we expect to see signed by a Championship or Premier League club during the coming months, as the keeper is replaced by Russell Hoult. As Colin Slater had said to me a month or so ago, Kasper was worth numerous points alone with his contribution. Despite the fact he'll have spent just one season here, Schmeichel will be considered a true fans favourite and club legend for years to come.

At 5-0, today is a resounding and comfortable victory which means that come the close of play, we have survived the entire home campaign with just one defeat at home in the league back in December when Accrington came to town on the day the club ownership was passed to Peter Trembling.

Once more the stands are alive and jubilant faces are everywhere to be seen. Friends embrace and jump up and down on each other's shoulders as fathers lift young kids to give them a better view of the celebrations whilst over on the touchline it appears that every member of Notts' back room staff is on hand to spill onto the pitch to join the action when the full time whistle goes.

The only anticipation now is for the final whistle and then, with all due respect to Torquay next week, it is over. Once again the Wheelbarrow song rings around the stadium with a small section of Cheltenham fans still sat down and looking on. They are quiet, solemn and feeling very similar to the Bradford, Northampton, Hereford and Bury fans of whom all saw their sides hit for five here at Meadow Lane during the course of the season.

It's a shame my old man was not down today but in all honesty, this campaign was wrapped up much before this afternoon so today was, as previously mentioned, an anti-climax of sorts.

As referee Mr Pawson looks to his watch and pulls the whistle to his lips, we are all, to a person, already stood and waiting for the moment. It's not the ecstatic cheers you hear when you clinch a 1-0 win over your rivals but it is more one of confirmation. Done and dusted. Job complete.

For the next ten minutes, I don't speak. I stand, smile and watch on. I, watch as the lads clap the fans and trot off down the tunnel to ready themselves for the presentation. I like many others have waited a fair while for this. We have had to take in some awful games, weeks, months and seasons in order to enjoy this bit of success so regardless of whether other clubs begrudge us the moment in the spotlight, we're going to take it. Cheltenham fans must feel like a gooseberry of sorts. How disheartening it must be to be away from home when the hosts lift the coveted award for their hard work.

The Kop maintains the volume. Songs are sung and fans stand waving flags, scarves, shirts and any item of Notts merchandise they can get their hands on. Then, one by one, we are given the names over the loud speaker of the men that have made this day happen. The stars of the show and the heroes of the campaign that mean we leave League Two behind. The fans favourites, seasoned pros, promising youngsters and big name players alike all share the limelight and glory. For today, each one is crowned a Champion as are we all according to Ray Trew in the programme notes.

"Champione, Champione...." we sing as the players gather on the purpose built podium put together hurriedly on the centre circle by Coca Cola League officials. Still I stand quiet. I am soaking up the sun and breathing in the success. I don't know if I'll ever feel this good again about football so I will make the most of it.

Coca Cola League Two Table:

	Pld	+/-	Pts
C 1. Notts County	45	65	92
P 2. Bournemouth	45	18	83
P 3. Rochdale	45	35	82
Pl 4. Rotherham United	45	6	73
Pl 5. Aldershot Town	45	14	72
6. Morecambe	45	8	70
7. Dagenham & Redbridge	45	9	69
8. Bury	45	-5	68
9. Port Vale	45	11	67
10. Chesterfield	45	-2	67

You Can't Always Get What You Want

CSKA Carnabys v Trinderbox - III
Mossdale Meadows / Alliance League Division Five / 02.05.10

Today I am hit with the stark reality that one of my three major footballing hopes for 2009/10 has failed to become a reality.

If I am honest, it was not so much today that the penny dropped but more a week or so ago. Either way you look at it, today is the day that hopes are diminished however.

Eleven days ago I netted my first ever hat-trick for CSKA Carnabys as we played away at FC Kibworth on a cool, calm Wednesday evening. The frozen pitches of December and January now just a distant memory, some sides in our division have had to contest with playing Wednesday-Friday-Sunday- Wednesday-Friday-Sunday in the final two weeks of the league season to ensure that come May 2nd, all their fixtures have been completed and the table has a finished look to it.

Despite becoming a master at scoring braces (scoring six competitive braces already prior to last week) I finally netted an elusive hat-trick as we romped to a 4-0 win on the road leaving us in second place, on 47 points, with two games remaining.

Unfortunately, our final two games would see us travel to an in-form, mid-table Hat & Beaver side before hosting champions Trinderbox on the final day.

Last Sunday we surrendered our second place in the table as we lost 5-2 at Hat & Beaver and, given the fact it was only our third defeat in fifteen league games, it was quite hard to take given the importance of the match. But when all was said and done, it meant that we had to beat Trinderbox on the final day whilst hoping that two other sides both lost at home, in order for us to win promotion in second place.

The omens for this morning were never good however. We had several big players missing through injury whilst first choice keeper Warner was away (yes, away for the biggest game of the season) resulting in a centre-back-come-left-back playing in goal in the form of Maggs. In addition, Trinderbox were still on a roll having registered 23 wins and two draws in the last 25 league games and with the Division Five trophy set to be presented after the game, they appeared to be in no mood for spoiling their close-to-perfect season.

Despite this, for much of the game we matched them once again. We battled, worked, pressed and created whilst Trinderbox struggled to

300

raise their game and give themselves a fitting send-off for end of season party that was set to start after the encounter.

With twenty minutes left on the clock, somehow we led the league leaders 2-1 despite Trinderbox having the lion's share of the possession after the break. But as the minutes passed our resolve became weaker and the make-shift side we had out looked stretched and desperate to hang on.

Had our season ended just twenty minutes earlier we'd have still had a chance to see ourselves win promotion dependent on other results. However, with the final minutes of our season apparently crumbling around us, we conceded three goals in quick succession and left the field with a second consecutive 5-2 defeat. At just the wrong time, in a long, hard-fought season, we'd fell by the wayside and lost our grip on promotion.

It's hard to be too critical of the lads. If anything, this season has been an over-achievement. But after throwing points away last week we knew the likelihood of going the same way as Trinderbox was slim so when we have it confirmed that Phoenix United and FC Komrska had both won, we knew that we'd dropped to fourth place in a season that saw us second for much of the campaign.

Alliance League Division Five Table:

	Pld	+/-	Pts
1. Trinderbox	26	126	74
2. Phoenix United	26	21	52
3. FC Komrska	26	41	50
4. CSKA Carnabys	**26**	**21**	**47**
5. Harrow	26	26	46

Oh I Won't Go And Be Beside The Seaside

Torquay United v Notts County
Nowhere in particular / League Two / 08.05.10

So this weekend, around a thousand Notts County fans are making their way to Torquay for what is to be the clubs final game in League Two for, well let's say the foreseeable future.

At long last, Notts have got out of the doldrums and are heading to what is considered dizzy heights for us; League One.

For me however, I have opted out of the trip despite having managed to get a ticket when demand seemed to spiral a few weeks back when they went on sale. I guess back then, there was a chance that it could have been the title decider. The be all and end all for seeing who'd become Champions. It isn't though. The league title is well and truly tied up. In the locker. Done and dusted.

We sit nine points clear of anyone and as newly crowned Champions of League Two. It makes you wonder why anyone was ever worried really. So as I sit down in The Boat down the road from mine, having a beer, I don't mind that I am missing today's trip. I have passed my ticket on to someone who couldn't get one with his mates and instead, I am reflecting on the year that has been.

I appear to have much to reflect on too as Sam The Toffee comes down for a beverage or two. We discuss women, my ex, his ex and Emma. We briefly talk about football and then get back onto the subject of women and in particular Emma. It's no hidden fact that a week today will see her leave the area and with it, another chapter in my life will firmly shut.

Further talking in the week did little to resolve where she was at in her own mind but given the fact that she is due to move in just a few days, I have very little to go on that suggests she is about to turn her whole world upside down.

If truth be told, I don't blame her either. I'm about as sound an investment as Notts County would have been for Ray Trew had he realised the full extent of the clubs debts when he first got involved. But if I think my personal life has been something of a rollercoaster story, then the football club that has encompassed my life so intensely of late is clearly on another level.

From the takeover to Sven. From Sol Campbell coming and then Sol Campbell going. To Charlie being sacked, us being off the pace, Hans coming in and then parting ways. And finally (and it seemed like the final part) Steve Cotterill coming in and Notts suddenly steamrolling their way to the title under the ownership of Trew.

It was as simple and easy as that. It doesn't matter that today we will draw 0-0 away at Torquay. It does not matter that we have not sealed promotion with a win on the road. We are Champions. We are the elite of our division. We are super Notts. Sam and I are drinking to that if nothing else.

Coca-Cola League Two Table:

	Pld	+/-	Pts
C1. Notts County	**46**	**65**	**93**
P 2. Bournemouth	46	17	83
P 3. Rochdale	46	34	82
4. Morecambe	46	9	73
5. Rotherham United	46	3	73
6. Aldershot Town	46	13	72
P* 7. Dagenham & Redbridge	46	11	72
8. Chesterfield	46	-1	70
9. Bury	46	-5	69
10. Port Vale	46	11	68

Promoted via the Play-offs

For Club and Country

I don't get the nonsense that surrounds 'Club v Country'. I never have and I never will. Do you ever get asked *"Who do you love most? Your Mum or Dad?"*

Of course not, mainly because it is not, and should not, be an issue or a question that needs to be answered. They are not in direct competition, unless your family is really messed up and your folks wish to battle for your love in order to make themselves feel more complete as a person. But that should be in a whole different book about mind games and feuding families.

For football, your club will never play your country (unless you are from Hong Kong and you support a Premier League club at which point it appears the rules change and clubs can go out and play against a Hong Kong XI). Anyhow, I am drifting away from my point here.

Supporting your country should not have any consequence or direct intrusion on your love for your club. Fans that feel the need to tell you that they would always pick club over country perhaps have some insane insecurity in which they feel the need to highlight their support in every way imaginable. They do so by wearing their shirts at every given opportunity, changing their online profile names to include the club initials as a middle name (I am friends with a few on Facebook who, to be fair, are thoroughly nice people. I just don't get why they add NCFC as a middle name) and in some cases, demand you listen when they tell you how much they love their club over their nation.

From my experience, Manchester United fans are the worst for it. Mainly because a huge slice are from the other side of the Irish sea perhaps but they take great pride in supporting 'brand United' first, foremost and only. I'd go as far to say as that hearing United fans sing anti-England songs is the most disrespectful, verbal diarrhoea, I've ever heard from a terrace.

Watching England during the World Cup has been an all somewhat different experience to watching Notts. I loved the night at Wembley when I saw us beat the Croats during qualification and that win was as memorable as Notts County's wins against Rochdale at home or thumping Burton away.

I cheered Frank Lampard as much as Neal Bishop and willed the likes of Rooney and Crouch to score goals as much as Hughes and

Rodgers, because for me there is no difference. I am a Notts County fan and I am English.

That is why today hurts so much. That is why my summer has ended prematurely. Like hitting a brick wall at 100mph, the 2009/10 season ended this evening without a hint of it being prolonged further and I am hurt.

I am gutted because I put so much effort into it. Physically and emotionally, I built myself up for the World Cup so much and perhaps my old man was right when he voiced his concerns about my expectations and efforts.

For the duration of the tournament, my house became a World Cup House. We featured on the local news, we had well wishers on Facebook and Twitter and it became an occasion that the group of us (including myself, my skipper Lee and some twelve or so mates) will still remember for years to come despite the way it all came crashing down around us.

Had the States not scored against Algeria in the dying moments of the final set of group games we'd have met Ghana instead of Germany in the Second Round. Had we done so, we may have seen off the Africans, gained more confidence and began to fulfil our potential. However, there is no greater burden than potential and nothing more pointless than if's and buts'. As my old man always says *"if your Auntie had a dick she'd be your Uncle."*

He is a wise man is my dad.

So I lay down in my World Cup House with hundreds of shirts, scarves, pendants, framed pictures, inflatable footballs, flags, iconic posters and an actual replica World Cup sat on my fire place. I lay and ponder with another bottle of beer; the umpteenth one today (I started early).

I had some ten or so days off work during the tournament. I consumed far too much beer and laid down far too many little bets for fun. I became the all consuming punter on so many levels. Now I am left with nothing.

I flick on re-runs of Fantasy Football with Baddiel and Skinner from the mid nineties. I am tired but not ready to pass out. I am sleepy but not quite prepared to shut my eyes. I am torturing myself with the reality for a little while longer as those around me, one by one, depart the house, smile, thank me for my hospitality, and leave.

At the start of 2009/10 I had several hopes. In no particular order of importance, they included:

- Notts County to get promoted.
- England to win the World Cup.

- CSKA Carnabys to get promoted.
- Jade to say yes upon my proposal.

The OptaIndex of my life would indicate that two of these became reality. The index would also show that the last of the four was reversed by my own doing. That reality will now have time to kick in.

Football, to all intents and purposes, is over. The World Cup could stop tomorrow for me. Yes it'd be great to see an underdog knock out a big gun. Or it'd be great to see some high scoring, end-to-end encounters. In truth, I couldn't give a fuck now and when I think to World Cup's of bygone years, I remember little beyond England's exit.

I am now left with a house I cannot afford that needs serious cleaning. A house that needs to be de-World-Cup-erised and will have a void where Jade once was. I knew some time ago that my decision making was perhaps not the sharpest of my attributes. In the cold light of day, it feels terrible to know you have done something that deep down you know you should not have done so abruptly though.

Did I end it with Jade because I needed to give more to Notts County and football in general or did I give more to Notts because I ended it with Jade? Was it ever because someone else made me question my life or was that an excuse so I did not blame the whole thing on a game of football?

I am not saying I wish I had Jade back in my life or that I regret everything I have done. But I am also not saying I stand by my decision either. I just wish I'd perhaps been a little less hasty it coming to the decision as then, and perhaps only then, I'd now be able to know whether I made the right one.

Oh, and had Lampard's goal been allowed, I still stand by some insane logic and belief that we may have done the Germans.

FIFA World Cup 2010 – Second Round:

England   1-4 Germany

Reflection

It's a new dawn at Notts County and I am back at Meadow Lane for the first time since May 1st. Nearly three whole months have passed and my word how I have missed it. After the season that was, I could only see the summer months getting better and better.

England in South Africa was supposed to be a special occasion. Perhaps I was spoilt with success last season but I genuinely felt we had a chance. For whatever reason we choose to highlight England's downfall, it cannot mask the disappointment though and so in the aftermath, I did not bother trying to explain it or make sense of it.

I spent the four weeks of the World Cup in my very own World Cup House which had the BBC down on behalf of East Midlands Today and I spent a morning with Jeremy Nicholas and his crew filming a piece about what exactly had been the catalyst for this obsessive, compulsive problem of mine.

Then, unfortunately, everything started to go a bit wrong because we had to start watching the games. There were drab group openers with very few goals followed by equally drab group games in the second set of matches. Tight groups eventually became finalised by slender margins but in turn we then saw further tight games in the Second Round whilst mixed in with all these games, we had to watch a poor, weak England side.

Since then, I am the first to admit, I've lost the plot. My intensive season of football had come to an abrupt end when England crashed out to the Germans. I had taken in over 60 live games since last July varying from park football to friendly games and from League Two to a World Cup Qualifier.

I watched the best part of 500 games on the box, I penned detailed accounts of each game I attended at Meadow Lane, I planned training sessions twice a week, I watched classic football moments in the late hours most Friday nights with a bottle of lager and on the whole, I felt like a young kid that had discovered the game again for the first time.

Come the end of the season, I had a 1990 Subbuteo set laid out on my dining room table, I had wall charts in each and every room of my house ready for the World Cup and my Irish friends had pasted pictures of Thierry Henry on the inside of both my downstairs and upstairs toilets (previous landlords; if you are reading, which you won't be, it won't come off).

I was also collecting football stickers, football cards and small Corinthian figures whilst old programmes from the seventies and eighties were readily being purchased via eBay just for nostalgia purposes.

Then, just like that, it ended. Life went back to what most would call normal. I began opening my mail again and checking what I did not have in the fridge (which appeared to be everything). I stopped fretting about who may or may not be injured in the coming weeks and I no longer needed to check my bank balance to ensure I had enough cash to get to Rotherham away or even Shrewsbury at home.

It felt like the lights had gone out on my hectic year. A year that had seen me meet so many new people up and down the country from different walks of life. I looked around and everyone else was carrying on as normal. The football lads of whom had spent most of the World Cup camped in my front room had returned back home with their wives, fiancés or girlfriends and I was now alone and feeling quite down.

People I had met and interviewed or shared pints with were on their summer holidays with their families and young kids. Eastenders and Coronation Street replaced the football coverage and Sky Sports News concentrated on the golf and cricket (golf and cricket???). I no longer knew what to do with myself and I actually realised that whilst everyone shared my vision during the season, the minute it ended they were off and doing their own thing without a thought for the mess that they'd be leaving behind....me!

Days merged into one another and I reverted back into my own little world, away from everyone else. I suddenly realised that I had got so involved and so intense were my passions, I had lost a sense of what normal was. I was no longer planning my days around football and the penny dropped that now I was alone. Alone and sat with my own thoughts and memories.

It was a very long fortnight.

When my relationship ended with Jade around Easter time, I guess the consequences of my actions and decisions were never really all that clear to me. An outsider looking in may have predicted what the outcome would be to the choices I was making. I did not.

When I brought the relationship to an abrupt end, I thought I knew best. I thought I was going to move on and better my life. She'd long to still be with me. She'd miss me and want me. I'd live my life doing the very things that had frustrated her and made me become, at times, intolerable.

None of the above happened however. She gave me space for some three or four days, returned, gave me a final choice and with it drew a line under the whole thing. She had already been *"getting over it"* long before I gave her that final answer that it was over so when she left for the last time, she made a choice of her own that she was to move on and make a clean start.

The grass is not always greener on the other side and I think only a fool would think it was. Despite this prophecy never ringing true, everyone ponders and searches for something that they perceive to be that little bit better. That little extra if you may.

This, of course, is not just a reference that can be used towards describing a relationship though. It's the same with everyday life and everyday occurrences and situations. Jobs, social lives, homes, health and finances. We all want to improve areas of our life and we all make choices that can affect such parts of our life but my problem on this occasion was that I made a judgement based on a gut feeling. When my gut settled and my mind was more stable, I realised that maybe the choice I made was a wrong one.

Regret is a horrible thing to live with but even worse when you are not 100% sure about the routes you have chosen. One massive thing about regret though is that often, you have a chance to right the wrongs. Receive a second chance or have an opportunity to make amends. For me, I did not get any of this.

She told me she was not angry with me. She did not hate me even. She no longer missed me and now just looked back on me and her as a period in her life. It was something that did not work out despite the intentions of us both heading into it. And she had certainly moved on.

She had a new house, was happy in her job and doing a secondary job on the side with a new bloke too. The new bloke happened to be also linked with the big circle of friends that I used to be very reluctant to get involved with and therefore, I had a lot to contend with on reflection.

She wished me well when we last spoke and from that moment onwards, she became history. Just a period in my life like I was in hers I guess.

For all of this though, I cannot pretend I handled any of it well. You know your life is in need of a severe wake-up call when you folks drop shopping off at your back door as they know you'll have no milk in. After drinking the day away on the closing Saturday of the club season, pints with Sam The Toffee, and in turn Paul, turned into a far too regular occurrence down The Boat.

My health went downhill mainly because I no longer cared about when or if I ate. I would grab something as and when my body demanded and this meant my routine, sleep and sense of real-life began to deteriorate.

It's hard to put it all down in writing when you know the words you choose will be readily available for anyone to study, analyse or pass judgement. But I genuinely lost my way with everything that mattered during the summer. England v Germany was a trigger for speeding up my whole downward spiral. When my friend and assistant manager Matt became the last person to leave my house that night of Germany defeat, I can honestly say I have never felt so alone.

Some people reading this will maybe view it as a separate issue from the football that you've read about in previous chapters but rather than separating the two parts of one's life, I suggest that maybe we should all be aware of how closely linked they can be. I let my football addiction, and obsession, destroy something I had that was once a very special thing. I can never get that back. My worry is that despite this, I may still make the same mistake again down the line. Although I can see the lessons here, I don't know if I will ever fully learn them.

Thankfully though, for now, all that has ended and I have only myself to worry about...and football is back. This may only be a pre-season game but I am grateful for it.

As I sit in The Wheelers Suite at Meadow Lane with Mark, I notice Ray Trew and Jason Brewer the clubs finance director, making their way over towards me.

"Evening Luke, nice to see you again. How is the book coming along?" asks Ray and with that, it all starts again.

Ray buys myself and Mark a drink and then politely goes over to his wife and kids leaving us to the pleasure of Jim Rodwell.

We discuss Austria (where the side have just returned from a pre-season tour), the squad and the new arrivals and get onto the subject of a young lad called Krystian Pearce who is on trial having spent time on loan at Notts previously.

Mark remembers the youngster playing alongside Guy Branston in a Notts back four that was ripped apart, mainly due to an inept Branston performance back in 2008.

"He tried to lay all the blame on Pearce" Mark tells us both before Jim nips in.

"Oh he would. I am good mates with Guy and I can believe that. I love the fact he was voted the clubs worst ever player" he laughs. *"I'll tell you something funny"* says Jim as he nods his head and sips his beer with us.

"Guy has been staying at my gaff. Only for a night or two. It's turned into a month. Seeing him stark bollock naked in your kitchen drinking tea in the early hours is not what you want I tell you. He moved out today. I've had the cleaners in to fumigate the place."

We laugh, drink and go through the team sheet and we learn of another youngster, Matt Marshall, being spotted playing in Spain who's been named on the bench which also sees veteran winger Keith Gillespie included.

"Keith is one of them" Jim tells us. *"Not on trial as such. He called up Craig [Short], said he'd like to come down and pay his own way and so he is here."*

It is the cycle of football I guess. A favour for a favour. An old mate calling an old mate. What is clear is that Notts County's new boss Craig Short has a small, but solid looking squad for the coming season in League One and Jim thinks they look in fine form after the hard work in Austria.

We drink up and five minutes prior to kick-off make our way to our seats. The grass is greener than it was back in May and the fans are revitalised and hungry for football. The ground has had a lick of paint and the players come out, tanned, toned and hopefully fresher than ever.

What now? Well now it all starts again I guess. I am glad to be back in the real world.

Epilogue

For those who have read the book in its entirety, I hope you enjoyed it. You completion alone should be some sort of testament but I thank you for your persistence and hope that you have had an ounce of the pleasure from reading as I had from writing.

Writing this book is easily one of the most difficult and challenging things I have ever done. The length of the book itself is a reminder of how much happened in little under a year whilst the task of selecting what was and what was not relevant was extremely difficult.

Some people who I spoke with or interviewed may have read the book waiting to see what I made of their quotes and conversations but, ultimately, I had to leave some things out.

The biggest dilemma for me was whether or not to address the story of those fans who had opposed the Munto takeover in the first place. I was fortunate to meet with David Peck during the season who told me at length of those that he knew who had suggested that the deal may not have been in the best interests of the club at a time when most fans were willing the deal to go through as quickly as possible.

Admittedly, I was one of those fans fooled by the promises of millions of pounds and Premier League football but for that, I am not alone. Having considered at length whether or not to discuss these people who had spoke out, been involved with the supporters trust and believed the club were in trouble from the moment the new owners arrived, I decided that it had no place in my own story.

The main reason for this was that it was something I heard very little about until much later in the season, after Munto had arrived, Sven was on board and Hughes was scoring goals. To include such objections would have been a false impression of how I saw things because quite honestly, I did not take any of that it at the time it happened.

My honest opinion is that somewhere in all this is another book, written by someone who knows much more about takeovers than the average fan and has a passion for exposing those that exploited our club and gained from our loss. It was never my intention however to write an expose. My aim was to write an account of a League Two season from the eyes of a fan. Yes, my own story became entwined within the story of Notts' season but behind each fan is a tale of their own and as such, I felt it was right to open up the book to part of my world as well as the one Notts fans would be familiar with.

Since I finished working on the book, much has changed for both Notts County and I.

I eventually gave up my house which I had previously rented with Jade. Since I've been on my own money has certainly been somewhat tighter and I simply could not keep it going any longer as I was paying far too much for a place that was far too big for just me. I had the option to temporarily move to my old man's in Nottingham or my Mum's in Loughborough whilst I get myself back on my feet or alternatively, a nasty little terraced house just yards from my old house. They were the only affordable options.

It's no joy having to ask to go back to live with your folks after the best part of a decade or so away. I opted for my Mum's place as it was ideal for work and close to everything I know such as the CSKA and my band.

Long term, I think Nottingham is where I want to be again though. It is part of who I am and how I grew up and I think now feels like the right time to consider returning there and have a fresh start. That will be dependent on my future career path too I guess but I can honestly say that an office job never was my dream. For now, Loughborough is my short term option and one that is working out just Ok.

Moving back home and seeing my little sister on a daily basis has been fantastic (my mum remarried and my sister Eloise arrived back in January 2000 as a result) so I am now on hand to help her with homework or encourage her to be as much of a nuisance as I was at the age of eleven.

I am still single and I have not heard from Jade for well over six months. She cut all contact from me and even deleted me off Facebook (I believe this is the modern day version of being blanked in the street) and for now, I am getting accustomed to the single life where I don't infuriate someone on a daily basis.

Notts County on the other hand has been less stable than my own personal life.

Despite hopes being high that Steve Cotterill would remain in charge at Notts, the Gaffer left in the summer for pastures new with Portsmouth his chosen destination following their relegation from the Premier League. It's hard to not wish the Gaffer all the best as he left the club during the summer though. Without his guidance, who knows how the season may have ended. We were a massive fourteen points adrift of Rochdale when he arrived at the club. His record of fourteen victories in eighteen games and only one loss meant the point's deficit was not only closed but obliterated in those final few months with Rochdale finishing the season ten points behind us. A 24 point turn around by anyone's standards was just remarkable.

With the Gaffer gone, it was always going to be a tough dug out to fill.

In Craig Short, not only did the fans have a club legend in charge but it was also a young, fresh manager who appeared to have a very sound, sensible approach to the modern game. His signings appeared astute and the progress over the close season seemed to be positive.

Understandably we lost Kasper Schmeichel to Leeds United and Johnnie Jackson to Charlton but in came former Chelsea man Jon Harley, Blackpool forward Ben Burgess, Krystian Pearce from Birmingham, Doncaster's John Spicer, Preston's Liam Chilvers and goalkeepers Rob Burch and Stuart Nelson. In addition, we appeared to looking to make the most of the loan market with a host of players coming in on short term deals from top flight clubs.

Just as importantly, the main nucleus of the side that were Champions remained with the Danish keeper the only exception so in Lee Hughes, Craig Westcarr and Ben Davies, we still possessed our main match winners.

Having lost on the opening day to Huddersfield, and then the subsequent game away to Oldham, Notts failed to adapt to League One in the opening few months of the season however and we had to cling on to wins over Dagenham and Yeovil to give us hope for the season ahead.

An intense night at London Road saw us beat the only locals of League One, Peterborough, by three goals to two in a dramatic night's entertainment but further defeats followed and the side did not appear to be able to find their feet. As Notts went on to lose three from their next four after the battle of London Road, Craig Short was relieved of first team duties along with assistant Dave Kevan and fans were starting to panic.

Lee Hughes spent far too much of the opening months on the treatment table rather than knocking in goals whilst the players did not help Short out with a shocking four consecutive games where we went down to ten men due to a sending off (watch them back and some appear harsh perhaps but four games on the bounce cannot be construed as constant misfortune).

Since Short's departure, much more has happened with the arrival of Paul Ince and Alex Rae as the new management duo and departures of back room staff such as Mark Draper and Tommy Johnson. There are no two ways about it. Things are changing at Meadow Lane but the board appear to appointed someone who has high ambitions to develop as a Manager and I only hope that Ince can improve his reputation whilst establishing us as a League One club.

The club appears to be on a much more stable, financial footing, morale is good and most of the fans are satisfied at the time I am writing this which, coming from Notts fans, means things must be ok. I assure you we like to moan much more than most and down the years, we've had many opportunities.

CSKA Carnabys are still ticking along nicely too and I have seventeen goals in nineteen games so far myself as we bid for promotion in a restructured division which ultimately meant last season was a back door promotion despite finishing outside the automatic spots.

Having said all this, football is football and in turn, I am all too aware that you are only a game or two away from a crisis so for now, I'll keep everything crossed for Notts and CSKA and come May I will be waiting for it to all start again.

As for England, well I think a massive part of me lost patience for the last time after the World Cup. I felt the time was right for the FA to act, make a fresh start and bring in some new ideas. Instead we continue with Fabio in charge of a side that has some bright new sparks in the likes of Wilshere but not enough of an overhaul to suggest anything will change anytime soon. That said, I still love my country and hope I can be proven wrong by our Italian boss and out-going 'golden generation'.

Writing these thoughts down, it dawns on me that Football is a never ending drama. And I mean never ending. There will always be a 'next game' or a 'next season'. Players will always eventually depart under a cloud of disappointment or resentment, except the rare few that retire having given their best years to your club. In turn, there will always be a new saviour or fans favourite arriving at the gates of your club with expectation or potential.

Perhaps it is this continuing pattern of inevitability that keeps us coming back. For year on year, we can hope once more and dare to dream the impossible dream.

After all, you just never know when a Middle Eastern Consortium and former England Manager may end up on your door step. Here's to hoping.

Notts County 2009/10

Playing Staff	Apps.	Gls.	After?
1. Russell Hoult	6	0	*released and then signed for Hereford as Coach*
2. Brendan Moloney *	19	1	*returned to Nott'm Forest after loan spell*
3. Matt Ricthie *	19	3	*returned to Portsmouth after loan spell*
4. Mike Edwards	46	5	-
5. Graeme Lee	36	4	-
6. John Thompson (c)	47	0	-
7. Matthew Hamshaw	24	0	*released and then signed for Macclesfield Town*
8. Ricky Ravenhill	48	3	-
9. Lee Hughes	45	33	-
10. Neal Bishop	51	1	-
11. Ben Davies	51	15	*signed for Derby for undisclosed fee January 2011*
12. Kevin Pilkington	0	0	*released and then signed for Luton Town*
14. Sean Canham	1	0	*released and then signed for Hereford United*
15. Karl Hawley	37	4	-
16. Ben Fairclough	0	0	*released and then signed for Hinckley United*
17. Jamie Clapham	39	1	*released and then signed for Lincoln City*
18. Stephen Hunt	38	3	*joined Lincoln City on loan January 2011*
19. Luke Rodgers	48	13	*signed for New York Red Bulls on a free transfer*
20. Craig Westcarr	50	11	-
21. Johnnie Jackson	30	3	*signed for Charlton Athletic on a free transfer*
22. Delroy Facey	20	3	*released and then signed for Lincoln City*
23. Kasper Schmeichel	47	0	*signed for Leeds United on a free transfer*
24. Daniel Jones *	8	0	*returned to Wolves after loan spell.*
30. Ade Akinbiyi	11	0	*released*
32. Sol Campbell *	1	0	*left by mutual consent before signing for Arsenal*
45. Nathan Fox	1	0	-

* denotes leaving part way during 2009/10 season.

2009/10 Managers	Pld	W	D	L	After?
Ian McParland	14	6	4	4	*sacked Oct. 09 & went onto coach Ipswich*
Kevan & Johnson^	2	1	1	0	*made way for Hans Backe*
Hans Backe	9	4	3	2	*resigned Dec. 09 & now manages New York Red Bulls*
Dave Kevan ^	11	6	3	2	*made way for Steve Cotterill*
Steve Cotterill	18	14	3	1	*left to manage Portsmouth, summer 2010*

^ denotes caretaker role

Backroom	Role	After?
Sven-Goran Eriksson	Director of Football	*left Feb.10 & now manager of Leicester City*
Dave Kevan	Assistant Manager	*left club Oct.10 with Craig Short*
Tommy Johnson	Coach	*left club Oct.10 with Craig Short*
Carl Muggleton	Goalkeeping Coach	-
Paul Godfrey	Physio	-
Marcus Svensson	Fitness Coach	*left club Sep.10 to join Arsenal*
Mark Draper	Kit Man	*left club Feb.11*
Mick Leonard	Head of Youth	-
Michael Johnson	Youth Team Manager	-

Results 2009/10

Date	Fixture		F-A	Att'.	Notts Scorers

AUGUST

Date	Fixture		F-A	Att'.	Notts Scorers
8	Bradford City	H	5-0	9,396	Davies, Hughes x2, Moloney
11	Doncaster Rovers (CC-1)	H	0-1	4,893	-
15	Macclesfield Town	A	4-0	2,785	Ravenhill, Hunt, Wright OG, Westcarr
19	Chesterfield	A	1-2	6,196	Edwards
22	Dagenham & Redbridge	H	3-0	6,562	Hughes, Hawley, Jackson
29	Barnet	A	0-1	2,858	-

SEPTEMBER

Date	Fixture		F-A	Att'.	Notts Scorers
5	Burton Albion	H	1-1	8,891	Hawley
12	Northampton Town	H	5-2	7,154	Ritchie x2, Hughes x3
19	Morecambe	A	1-2	3,335	Davies
26	Port Vale	H	3-1	7,561	Hughes x2, Collins OG
29	Lincoln City	A	3-0	5,527	Rodgers x3

OCTOBER

Date	Fixture		F-A	Att'.	Notts Scorers
3	Cheltenham Town	A	1-1	4,134	Rodgers
6	Bradford City (JPT-2)	A	2-2*	3,701	Westcarr, Facey
11	Torquay United	H	2-2	8,812	Westcarr, Davies
17	Rotherham United	A	0-0	5,738	-
24	Crewe Alexandra	H	2-0	6,545	Rodgers, Westcarr
31	Shrewsbury Town	H	1-1	7,562	Lee

NOVEMBER

Date	Fixture		F-A	Att'.	Notts Scorers
6	Bradford City (FAC-1)	H	2-1	4,213	Hawley, Jackson
14	Bury	A	3-3	3,602	Hughes x2, Ritchie
21	Aldershot Town	H	0-0	6,500	-
24	Rochdale	A	1-2	2,770	Davies
28	Bournemouth (FAC-2)	A	2-1	6,082	Hughes, Westcarr

DECEMBER

Date	Fixture		F-A	Att'.	Notts Scorers
1	Darlington	H	4-0	4,606	Rodgers, Hughes x2, Davies
5	Hereford United	A	2-0	2,727	Westcarr, Edwards
12	Accrington Stanley	H	1-2	5,855	Hughes
28	Burton Albion	A	4-1	5,801	Ravenhill, Hughes x3

JANUARY

19	Forest Green Rovers (FAC-3)	H	2-1	4,389	Hunt, Hughes
23	Wigan Athletic (FAC-4)	H	2-2	9,073	Hughes, Davies
26	Dagenham & Redbridge	A	3-0	1,196	Davies, Hughes, Ogogo OG
30	Barnet	H	2-0	6,444	Hawley, Davies

FEBRUARY

2	Wigan Athletic (FAC-4 replay)	A	2-0	5,519	Hunt, Caldwell OG
6	Grimsby Town	A	1-0	4,4,52	Hughes
9	Bournemouth	A	1-2	5,472	Bishop
13	Fulham (FAC-5)	A	0-4	16,132	-
17	Grimsby Town	H	1-1	5,163	Hughes
20	Aldershot Town	A	1-1	4,016	Davies
27	Hereford United	H	5-0	6,036	Westcarr x3, Rodgers x2

MARCH

2	Macclesfield Town	H	1-0	4,672	Clapham
6	Accrington Stanley	A	3-0	2,123	Davies, Hughes, Rodgers
9	Chesterfield	H	1-0	7,341	Davies
15	Bournemouth	H	2-2	6,120	Hughes x2
20	Crewe Alexandra	A	1-0	5,003	Edwards
23	Bradford City	A	0-0	11,630	-
27	Rotherham United	H	1-0	9,015	Rodgers

APRIL

3	Bury	H	5-0	7,005	Edwards, Westcarr, Davies, Hughes, Facey
5	Shrewsbury Town	A	1-0	6,287	Davies
10	Northampton Town	A	1-0	5,647	Davies
13	Lincoln City	H	3-1	7,501	Hughes, Lee, Facey
17	Morecambe	H	4-1	8,500	Hughes x2, Ravenhill, Davies
20	Rochdale	H	1-0	10,536	Hughes
24	Port Vale	A	1-2	7,459	Lee
27	Darlington	A	5-0	2,112	Jackson, Edwards, Westcarr, Rodgers x2

MAY

1	Cheltenham Town	H	5-0	11,331	Lee, Hughes x2, Davies, Rogers
8	Torquay United	A	0-0	5,124	-

319

League Two Table 2009/10

			Pld	W	D	L	F	A	+/-	Pts
1	C	NOTTS COUNTY	46	27	12	7	96	31	65	93
2	P	Bournemouth	46	25	8	13	61	44	17	83
3	P	Rochdale	46	25	7	14	82	48	34	82
4		Morecambe	46	20	13	13	73	64	9	73
5		Rotherham United	46	21	10	15	55	52	3	73
6		Aldershot Town	46	20	12	14	69	56	13	72
7	Pl	Dagenham & Redbridge	46	20	12	14	69	58	11	72
8		Chesterfield	46	21	7	18	61	62	-1	70
9		Bury	46	19	12	15	54	59	-5	69
10		Port Vale	46	17	17	12	61	50	11	68
11		Northampton Town	46	18	13	15	62	53	9	67
12		Shrewsbury Town	46	17	12	17	55	54	1	63
13		Burton Albion	46	17	11	18	71	71	0	62
14		Bradford City	46	16	14	18	59	62	-3	62
15		Accrington Stanley	46	18	7	21	62	74	-12	61
16		Hereford United	46	17	8	21	54	65	-11	59
17		Torquay United	46	14	15	17	64	55	9	57
18		Crewe Alexandra	46	15	10	21	68	73	-5	55
19		Macclesfield Town	46	12	18	16	49	58	-9	54
20		Lincoln City	46	13	11	22	42	65	-23	50
21		Barnet	46	12	12	22	47	63	-16	48
22		Cheltenham Town	46	10	18	18	54	71	-17	48
23	R	Grimsby Town	46	9	17	20	45	71	-26	44
24	R	Darlington	46	8	6	32	33	87	-54	30

C = Champions, P = Promoted, Pl = Promoted via Play-Off's, R = Relegated to The Football Conference.

*Dagenham Redbridge beat Morecambe in their play-off Semi-Final before beating Rotherham 3-2 at Wembley to earn promotion to League One.

The Who's Who (*in order of numerical appearances...or importance? I'm not quite sure actually. Just in some sort of order that seems correct.*)

Dad (my old man).

The very reason I support Notts, my old man brought me down Meadow Lane from a very young age and has been to blame ever since. We've enjoyed some great years and some truly awful years but my old man was always dedicated to my own game as much as Notts'. My fondest memories of watching Notts, and indeed football in general, are with my old man. I think this should be the same for everyone to be honest but that is because I assume my football upbringing and education was the 'normal' way it was done.

Seany Ward.

He's a huge Aston Villa fan but is exiled in Leicester. We met some time back in 2003 and have been good mates ever since. He has also played for two football sides that I have managed (including CSKA Carnabys at present), often bears the brunt of my anger in team talks but in general will always give me 100%. At the start of the season he was only too happy to come down Notts with me and enjoyed it so much so that it became his local team (if Villa is not local enough).

Mark Beeby.

Son of former Notts player Oliver, Mark and I first worked together coaching with Charnwood Borough Council back in 2003. A regular in The Kop, Marks passion for the club runs deep but shares hatred for Leicester (perhaps due to growing up in the area as a Notts fan). A true gent and great company for Notts games, Mark and I were introduced as fellow Notts fans on my first day working with him and we hit it off straight away.

Paul.

Also a member of CSKA Carnabys, Paul and I met when he joined my band back in 2006. A big Leicester City fan, Paul generally knows the game to an extent that I can sit down and talk for hours with him about the most random players, facts and memories and we always know what the other is talking about. We both now also share common love for Sven-Goran Eriksson to add to the common love that is Mark Draper.

Jade.

The girl I believed I'd marry and the girl I no longer speak to, see or hear from. I can't help but think my obsession with football went someway to destroying what we had. A Scot my birth, she was technically a Rangers fan although she hated football (it would be too easy to insert Scottish jokes here). She also had an ex who was Leeds fan fuelling my hatred for them even more than your average Leeds hater. Last known to be happy and doing ok for herself in Leicester somewhere.

My uncle Danny.

Uncle Danny is my old man's brother and another common feature in my favourite Notts County memories of yesteryear. Back in the late eighties and early nineties, he was as regular as my Dad and I. In more recent years, a love for golf and a passion for not sitting in the cold watching crap football limited his visits but he still loves the club. Looking back, he was my gold pass to getting into the warm VIP area's in The Pavis Stand many years ago, and he always had a spare loo roll for FA Cup games.

Danny (our Kieran's mate)

There are not many of 'us'. Danny and I both live in Loughborough (although he's been here all his life) and we both follow Notts. We first watched Notts together by accident rather than design but we have many mutual friends never knowing each other well enough to realise we had more in common than we did with the 'mutual' lot. A fan who shares many views with me, we chose to get season tickets together for 2010/11. Danny is also the main reason I actually get to Nottingham each fortnight too thanks to his lifts.

Our Kieran.

Not a frequent visitor but a visitor all the same, he's a big Chelsea fan but loves Notts too. We won't talk for months when Notts eventually draw Chelsea out of the hat in the Cup.

Sam The Toffee.

Evertonian drinking buddy and long time sufferer of being as pessimistic as a Notts fan.

Emma

Head turner who opened my eyes. Now just a memory of what could have been.